Socio-economic Democracy and the World Government

Collective Capitalism, Depovertization, Human Rights, Template for Sustainable Peace

Socio-economic Democracy and the World Government

Collective Capitalism, Depovertization, Human Rights, Template for Sustainable Peace

Dhanjoo N Ghista

Nanyang Technological University, Singapore

World Scientific

NEW JERSEY • LONDON • SINGAPORE • BEIJING • SHANGHAI • HONG KONG • TAIPEI • CHENNAI

Published by

World Scientific Publishing Co. Pte. Ltd.
5 Toh Tuck Link, Singapore 596224
USA office: Suite 202, 1060 Main Street, River Edge, NJ 07661
UK office: 57 Shelton Street, Covent Garden, London WC2H 9HE

British Library Cataloguing-in-Publication Data
A catalogue record for this book is available from the British Library.

SOCIO-ECONOMIC DEMOCRACY AND WORLD GOVERNMENT

ISBN 981-238-509-6

Printed by Fulsland Offset Printing (S) Pte Ltd, Singapore

In ever-lasting memory of the totally destitute
people — the street beggars, constituting the ignored "Fourth-World";
Who I knew in my childhood, and
from whom I derived so much love,
Who, through their dignified lives (amidst intense suffering),
enlightened me about life;
Wishing them eternal peace in the Effulgent World!

Contents

Preface

A milleniums-old Sanskrit shloka (verse), entitled *Samgacchadhvam* from Rigveda, reads as follows:

Sam'gacchadhvam' sam'vadadhvam
Let us move together, let us sing together;

Sam'vomanna'msi ja'nata'm
let us come to know our minds together.

Deva'bha'gam' yatha'purve
Let us share, like sages of the past,

Sam'ja'na'na' upa'sate
so that all people together may enjoy the universe.

Sama'nii va a'kuti
Let us unite our intentions,

Sama'na mastu vomano
our minds are as one mind,

Yatha'vah susaha'sati
as we, to truly know one another, become one.

This lofty spiritual concept of living is verily the civilized way to live. Its inner meaning is: "Let everyone move ahead together, speak clearly, conclusively and decisively; let our minds be understood by one another in the proper way. We all come from the Supreme Creator. Hence, as the sages and the saints in the past had enjoyed the collective wealth of the universe, let us, too, understand each other in the same way. Let our aspirations be the same, our hearts identical, and our thoughts emerge as one mind, so that we may live in harmony with all."

What a big contrast, to this above concept of enlightened way of living, has been our world scenario (at both socio-political and socio-economic levels), even in recent times over the past six decades. We will first briefly wander down this ignominious lane, in order to survey the gross abuse meted out to humanity, and then conceptually outline the means and social structure for restoring human dignity.

The current socio-economic political setting

In the developing (previously colonized) countries, the socio-political order has been characterized by (1) abject poverty, with the people lacking even the basic amenities of living; (2) gross discrimination and social outcasting of groups of people due to their race, descent, caste, color, culture and poverty; (3) abrogation of human rights, the right to enlightened governance, and the right to expect and demand competent and transparent governance on the part of the governing politicians; (4) de-culturization, marginalization and de-empowerment of entire communities by the intolerant regimes of big nations, along with ruthless stifling and crushing of dissident voices and movements for cultural rights and autonomic governance; (5) state terrorism perpetrated by communist countries against their own people; (6) terrorism by some freedom-demanding zealous groups against governments and regimes, considered by them to be inconsiderate and unsympathetic to their socio-economic predicaments; (7) terrorist attacks on civilians by religious groups, opposed to the situation of hegemony of world nations and positioning of foreign military bases on their lands.

The corresponding socio-economic order in the (previously colonized) developing countries has been characterized by (1) the developed countries of the world taking advantage of cheap natural resources and labor of under-developed countries; (2) professionals from under-developed and developing countries migrating to developed countries for better prospects of living standards; (3) multinationals operating in developing countries, by pretending to foster local industrial development while being unwilling to support local and indigenous technological incubation and training, thereby perpetrating dependency on them; (4) fictitious market book creation and over-investment along with currency manipulation, leading to industrial and economic capsizing of emerging nations; (5) corruption and bleeding of wealth by the politicians of these countries; (6) the widening gap between the developed and developing as well as under-developed countries.

Herein, we refer to the "Third World" as comprising of under-developed and poverty-stricken countries as well as developing countries and regions of the world. There is another and even more "deprived world," comprising of all the discriminated peoples of the world (based on dogmas and prejudices related to race and color, descent and caste, religion and poverty). We will term all of these discriminated people as the "Fourth World." Their plight is even more pathetic than the Third World people (many of whom are even responsible for this Fourth World discrimination), because they are totally outcast from the mainstream society, not allowed to mix freely, to use public means of education and medical care, transport and worship. If they dare to ignore these dogmas and taboos, they are physically assaulted, killed, lynched and burnt. In fact, even after the dismantling of (one of the Fourth World orders, namely) the apartheid order, the Fourth World continues in the form of casticism and racism, religious and ethnic intolerance and persecution. It constitutes an utter disgrace on the civilization of our times.

Third World under-development: Following the end of the colonial era started a prolonged cold war era between the proponents of capitalism and communism. Trapped in the communist colonization net were Eastern European nations, as well as many South East Asian nations and African nations (liberated from the colonial yoke), under an illusionary hope of developing themselves into classless social welfare societies. However, the formal wars against communist expansion were fought on East Asian soils, because the major powers did not dare to directly confront each other.

When most of the once colonized nations got their freedom, they were poverty-stricken. These Third World nations were uncertain as to which economic-political system to adopt. While capitalism was associated with the colonial countries, communism seemed to be an ideal system for the benefit of the majority population, namely the "employee class" people. The irony was that the capitalism route involved re-inviting the foreigners in the form of multinational companies, while the communist route resulted in living in a regimented and terror-stricken society. The tragic end-result is that, even today, most of these former colonies are under-developed. Would it not be ethical for these former capitalist and communist colonial nations (professing to be the civilized world) to substantially compensate these under-developed countries, for reducing them to the ignominious Third World state!

Neo socio-economic political system for dignified human living

Many new concepts concerning socio-economic system and electoral and governance system as well as global political order have been outposted along the contents of this book. It is deemed to auger for better appreciation of the book's subject matter and exposition, for some of these concepts to be introduced here (albeit even briefly), so as to serve as identifiable milestones as one starts reading the book.

The first concept is that of autonomous functionally-sustainable communities or FSCs (within the provinces or states of a developing nation), so as to enable economically backward areas to constitute economically viable units. It would also be helpful to the marginalized and segregated segments of the society to be provided their own FSCs, in which they could live with dignity and contribute to (and in turn benefit from) their own economic development and destiny. The second concept is that within the FSCs, medium and large scale corporations be organized as cooperatives, so that all the people in these corporations would be involved in sharing the wealth created by them, and thereby feel motivated to contribute to the performance of the corporations. The concept of all the cooperatives' members involvement in creating revenue for their cooperatives and in sharing the assets (albeit, in production to their contributions) constitutes the third concept of collective capitalism. Hitherto, business enterprises have been owned by few capitalists, for whom the relative low-salaried employees worked dedicatedly. While the company owners depended on these low-paid employees for their revenue generation, they never considered sharing revenue with them. In this new concept of collective capitalism, everyone involved in capital generation will also share the capital. In this socio-economic setup, there would be optimal utilization of human potentialities, so as to foster development of all aspects of the economy (for instance knowledge-based economy, and not just capital and production-based economy).

In the framework of this socio-economic system of collective capitalism, we can now proceed to develop the next concept of a people-centric economic-political system. Hitherto, we have had a kind of democracy in which the political parties operate as business corporations, by striving for public votes to get four- to five-year contracts to manage the governance of the community. These political parties bring their own preferences and prejudices into the governance policies, which are not necessarily in the best interests of the people. Hence, we are proposing that this pseudo democracy (or governance operated as a business) be replaced by a truly people-centric democracy. In this system, the associations representing the various sectors of the community would elect their most competent representatives to the local community government.

For this purpose, the FSC(s) would be organized into associations (as, for example, teachers association, farmers cooperatives' association, legal practice association, medical practice association, industrial cooperatives' association, and so on), agencies (such as for municipal, postal and police services) and councils (such as all the FSC township citizens' councils for environmental development and citizens' safety and sports councils). Each of these associations/agencies/ councils (representing all of the sections of the community) will nominate two candidates for the general public, who will then elect one of them to the FSC governance or legislature. By means of this electoral mechanism, in turn based on cooperative economic development, we are introducing the fourth concept of socio-economic democracy (SED), based on collective capitalism (CCP) and an electoral system by which only the most capable and qualified persons (in all the functional sectors of the community) would be elected to administer the various governance portfolios. This will be termed as the civilian Professional Governance System (PGS).

The next concept would be that, for all FSCs, the constitution be designed to foster enlightened living for the FSC inhabitants. In this fifth concept, the constitution will involve human rights in the broadest terms, to even include the right to employment (as well as to ensure that the minimal wage has adequate purchasing capacity for dignified living), the right to freedom-of-expression of views concerning societal policies, the right to civilian democratic governance oriented to people's welfare, as well as religious freedom and women's rights to dignified living, education and employment. Equally important would be the constitutional ruling debarring terrorist acts, while also precluding an FSC government to persecute inhabitants suspected of being critical of the government and to detain them without proper cause and immediate trial.

A number of mutually compatible FSCs would constitute a self-reliant socio-economic bloc or SEB, depending on how they can interact in a mutually compatible fashion. These SEBs would be equivalent to the provinces or states of nations. However, any two or more nations (of the world) or SEBs would be free and able to form mutually-benefiting self-reliant socio-economic zones (SEZs). The SEZs of a continent or sub-continent would be beneficially constituted into a regional (continental or sub-continental) federation or union (similar to the European Union), towards evolving the concept of cooperative living. This political grouping, to provide socio-economic benefits to the people and foster enlightened living, constitutes the sixth concept.

The governance executives of the SEB government (and thereafter of the SEZ and Regional Federation (RFD) governments) would be elected by the FSC legislative members, portfolio-wise. That is to say, all the FSCs' legislators in charge, for instance, of the law portfolio would elect one of them to be the SEB law minister. The vacancy, thereby created at the FSC level, would be filled by the second law-association candidate who was not elected to governance by the general public. Likewise, the SEB governance members would elect the SEZ governance members, and so on. Finally, we arrive at the momentous sixth concept of a global welfare-catering World government and parliament (with its elected ministers representing all the functionally-sustainable communities, socio-economic blocs, self-reliant economic zones and regional federations). The prime role of the world government parliament would be to ensure local, regional and global socio-economic political stability and physical security as well as the implementation of constitutional guarantees, so as to foster enlightened living for the people of all FSCs throughout the world.

The prime cause of neglect and suffering of people has long been due to the poor caliber of politicians, because of their incompetency and self-serving attitude. This is because we have had a politicians-centered political order, whereas we should have had a people-centric political order. Our civilian socio-economic democratic (SED) system would nullify the need and role of political parties and politicians. Hence by means of this (above delineated) global political structure, we would develop such a neo-humanistic and people-centric global order (devoid of hegemonism), wherein the government and their governance members are dedicated to the welfare of all the FSCs and their people.

There is one common thread woven through all these concepts, to in fact integrate them under one neo-humanistic philosophy. If we are to serve and bring up the abused and down-trodden segments of humanity, we have to first respect them. In order to respect them, we need to be modest and humble like a tree (that provides shelter and so many resources to human beings, as part of its unrecognized role). All the prevalent socio-economic as well as electoral and governance systems are not conducive to bring such modest, competent and noble persons into governance. This is why we have developed and formulated the above delineated progressive socio-economic, electoral and governance systems.

In a neo-humanistic society, the persons empowered by the people to serve in government will not hold center-stage. The media will also not be focusing on them, but instead relate to what the common people feel and do. However, neo-humanism is more than just economic and psychic concerns and development. It is concerning every human being's quest for continuing and lasting happiness, by journeying on the avenue leading to enlightenment as a desideratum. Hence, the persons elected to work in governance (at all levels) must themselves be neo-humanists or at least neo-humanism aspirants. Hence, the final and most important concept is that of neo-humanism, as the principle and mission of the universal society. Having introduced these concepts, we can now traverse through the contents, and describe the formatting of these concepts in a social sciences vein, while placing them in the appropriate context of the economic-political need.

This book is concerned with (1) terminating exploitation of deprived and lagging Third World nations as well as the socially discriminated and outcast Fourth World communities, and solutions for their self-reliance; (2) enabling discriminated marginalized and suppressed communities as well as socio-economically lagging communities to progress, to develop their full potential, and to shape their own destinies; and (3) creating a neo-humanistic socio-economic political order. The book systematically addresses the psychology, economic system, governance system and the global political order for a neo-humanistic global society.

It is to be noted that the neo socio-economic political reorganization and guidelines have relevance to both developing and developed regions of the world, as well as to both socially discriminated people and people enjoying social standing, because (as we have seen) their fates and economies are interlinked. So far, the First World could develop at the expense of the Third World, but now the unfair treatment of Third World nations can also pull down the First World economies. Similarly, the socially well-placed people (of developing countries) have hitherto disregarded with impunity the miserable lot of their socially outcast Fourth World people, while making them operate the lowly-regarded community services (such as garbage and sewage collection). However, from hereon, these discriminated people can have a unified coalition base to stand on, a constitutional safeguard to prevent atrocities meted out to them for centuries, as well as a legal appeal mechanism through a network of People's Courts (working independently of the political structure). If they decided to no longer carry out the menial chores, the socially well-placed group would be functionally paralyzed. Once they could develop the psychic (mental) strength and means to organize themselves socio-politically (and even into sustainable micro-communities), their social oppressors would have to deal with them on equal terms.

Hence our progressive concept of collective capitalism (CCP), instituted at the grassroots levels of FSCs, is relevant and applicable to both the South and North regions of the world as well as to well-placed and discriminated social groups. Likewise, our socio-economic democratic system will help to rescue societies from the clutches of the pseudo-ideology of communism and capitalistic democracy as well as from inhuman racial and caste prejudices. The combination of collective capitalism, socio-economic democracy and professional civilian governance (without involvement of political parties) will provide a conducive setup for all people to realize the full potential of human development.

Today, we are globally beset with humongous human sufferings (of starvation and AIDS, for instance), social turmoil, economic instabilities, political mayhem, inter-ethnic and inter-religious riots, all unbecoming of a civilized society. Yet, we are unable to invoke fresh and original approaches to alleviate these calamities. An indepth and introspective analysis and contemplation would help to appreciate the more noble and civilized way of living in cooperatives of communities, within a pluralistic universal society. Traveling down the historical memory lane, one can note that powerful empires had arisen, only to collapse in time. Multi-polar and uni-polar orders have never endured, besides being conceptually primitive. It is now high time for all of us to come together, and channel our ambitions for personal gains to the higher ideals of living by sharing, helping and moving together.

About the book

This is a book on socio-economic political restructuring for progression to an enlightened society. It offers guidelines for Third World development, as well as solutions to global and regional socio-economic inequalities and subjugation, in terms of:

- neo socio-economic democratic electoral governance systems;
- economic development, combining knowledge-based approach, social and financial capital with neo-humanistic values; and
- neo-global order, comprising of SEZs, RFDs, and the world government.

These new concepts are developed in a coherent and systematic fashion. The book provides a rational psychological approach to solutions for the socio-economic political turmoil in which we are living today. It is however acknowledged that in this initial template of a neo-global order, many aspects may not be conceived or covered. It is also possible that these concepts of a neo socio-economic democratic governance system as well as the global neo-political reorganization under a world government may appear to be too idealistic, and require considerable research. This role is left to the future architects of this neo-humanistic global society at both its micro and macro levels. Indeed, it would be such a fulfilling task for us to collectively work on detailing the micro and macro economic, political, governance and judicial aspects of this global order.

Many people these days are talking about having (1) a new format of locally empowering economic system which can provide local and regional stability, as well as (2) a new global order for political equilibrium (devoid of hegemonism) and based on parity among nations. People around the world also feel the necessity for an independent UN, that is not pressurized by the militarily powerful nations to either act or to not intervene in global and regional disputes, according to the interests of these influential nations. The people of developing countries also do not want to be beholden to the G-8 nations for continuing aid to rescue them from poverty, nor do they want the G-8 to enforce on them unfair trade modalities in the guise of globalization. Rather, they should constitute an economically self-reliant bloc to effectively deal with the G-8 economic-politics.

Moralistic people of the world are also looking for some sort of a world government that can provide a compassionate guiding hand to struggling nations, while serving the individual and collective interests of all nations. In this regard, the book addresses their needs by providing the charter and constitution role of FSCs for grass-roots democracy, within the benevolent political framework of a human rights implementing world government.

The book also introduces many other concepts of people empowerment that are now only being echoed. This is because the "World Summit on Sustainable Development," held in Johannesburg, brought together at least some representatives of the grass-roots folks, whose resources and assets have been harnessed and traded without their reckoning, let alone their being included in the economic loop. Some of these concepts are:

- natural resources to be harnessed primarily by the people-of-the-soil;
- non-privatization of natural resources of the land;
- cooperative economic development, with the generators of capital and revenue being also its recipients;
- economic democracy, to constitute the basis of political democracy;
- the issues and needs of the community can be best addressed by elected competent representatives of the various sectors of the community (such as the educational, healthcare, judicial, manufacturing, energy, community services and media sectors), and not by political parties having self-serving interests and agendas;
- since governments based on political party systems can be bought off, hence a civilian (non-party) based governance executive council would better look after the people's interests;
- based on the above principles, functionally-sustainable communities (of a self-reliant economic bloc) offer the best mechanism for addressing local needs, poverty eradication, collective generation and distribution of capital, with dignified living; and
- world trade and globalization can be globally beneficial, based on (1) recognition of the empowerment of local people in natural resources development, technologization, and export, (2) imports to be for items unavailable or better-performing items, (3) parity in renumeration for equivalent works across the globe.

The book also addresses concepts and principles in many other domains. On the vexing issue of terrorism, religiosity and movements protesting against cultural and ideological domination, we are proposing a neo-humanistic forum for dialogue and socialization, education and economic upliftment coupled with addressing of grievances, for "dismantling" terrorism carried out by people who feel marginalized. Eventually, the objective would be to integrate these angered people into the society by redressing their grievances and even (in the case of big communities) giving them the responsibility to manage their habitats according to neo-humanistic principles. In this format, they would have no choice but to cooperate (in a civilized manner) with the neighbors for survival. Indeed all local, regional and global rivalries and power struggles can be diffused by the promotion and glorification of the noble concept of cooperative living at the local as well as regional and global levels, under the aegis of the world government. This would indeed nullify the need for armamentariums and counter-intelligence agencies, which constitute a disgrace to the character and civilization of human beings.

The book offers a template for a neo-humanistic, non-hegemonial, local-to-global order, involving grassroots and sustainable economic development and political governance by community representatives working for the welfare of the community people. In catalyzing a new economic and political system, this book can conceivably serve as a very valuable teaching and resource source, as well as a multi-stage road map:

- involving the setting-up of functionally-sustainable communities (within Third World countries) to constitute self-reliant economic blocs (SEBs), as Stage 1; within each functionally-sustainable community (FSC), the governance would be managed by elected representatives of all the community sectors (such as the education, healthcare, manufacturing, electrical power, energy, water supply, sanitation, judicial and residential housing sectors), thereby dispensing with the unwieldy and corrupt system of political parties (that only serve their own agendas);
- to provide the mechanism and means for socio-economic political stability of the under-served regions of the world, as Stage 2;
- to help to bring together the so-called Second and Third Worlds socio-economic political countries into a stable socio-economic political block, to then serve as an economic political parity and balance to the present eight-nation global hegemony, as Stage 3; and
- to lead to the eventual and inevitable formation of world government, that will serve the individual and collective interests of all the communities of the world, without being dominated by a few economically and militarily powerful self-serving nations, as Stage 4.

The socio-economic system as well as the political and governance system of a society impacts and influences all phases of human living. In this most important arena of human thought and endeavor, this book charters a pioneering course for:

- Fourth World liberation and Third World development;
- providing a comprehensive charter of human rights for the benefit of the poor and backward, exploited and depressed communities of the world;

- the emergence of a progressive universal society; and
- addressing the unfulfilled needs of the marginalized and voiceless, humiliated and silenced people of the world as well as of the affluent and idealistic, influential and social activities dedicated to the progress of human civilization.

The world situation is deteriorating socially, economically and politically. This book delineates a neo-humanistic global order, for promoting local and global socio-economic justice, progressive civilian governance and a neo-concept of human rights, to serve as a beacon of ideological torchlight for an enlightened society, and (through it all) for sustainable peace. Echoing the concerns and wishes of the supreme neo-humanist Prabhat R. Sarkar (the propounder of "Progressive Utilization Theory" and Economic democracy), let:

- every human being be guaranteed the minimum physical requirements of life;
- all human beings get scope for full utilization of all their potentialities;
- all human beings get equal opportunity to attain the fulfillment of enlightened living; and
- in through this movement, let humanity be made conscious of the purpose and meaning of life.

Dhanjoo N. Ghista
(mdnghista@ntu.edu.sg)
completed at Osmania University (Hyderabad),
and revised at Nanyang Technological University (Singapore)

Acknowledgments

Herein, I would like to thank colleagues who reviewed the book and were supportive of it. In particular, I would like to thank Professor Johan Galtung (TRANCEND, A peace & development organization for conflict transformation by peaceful means), Professor Richard Falk (Princeton University), Edward Allbless, Solicitor (England & Wales) and Mrs. Eirwin Harbottle (Centre for international Peacebuilding) for their inspirational support and idealism. I am grateful to Professor Pauline Vaillancount Rosenau (University of Texas, Houston) for her painstaking review and many valuable suggestions.

My colleague Wai Mun Chia (at Nanyang Technological University) read the revised manuscript, and I very much appreciate her professional editing. Finally I would like to profusely thank Siva Kumar Kovvuri (Osmania University) for his tremendous work on word-processing and graphics of the book manuscript, Ian Seldrup (World Scientific Publishing Co) for processing the book manuscript for publication, and most of all Joy Quek (World Scientific Publishing Co) for making the book preparation process so enjoyable.

I gratefully acknowledge and thank

Ramakrishna Kotlanka	for the top picture on page 22 of chapter 1
Ruba Rajab (PRCS, Bireh, Palestine)	for the picture on page 248 of chapter 16
Niti Roy and Carol Li (AFP, Singapore)	for the bottom picture on page 22 of chapter 1, and the pictures on page 35 of chapter 2, page 126 of chapter 8, and pages 201 and 202 of chapter 13
David Carlson (Canadian Carlson)	for the picture on page 50 of chapter 3
Divesh Rana (Nepal News)	for the top picture on page 62 of chapter 4

Hiro Miyazawa	for the bottom picture on page 62 of chapter 4, and the pictures on page 92 of chapter 6, page 108 of chapter 7, and page 174 of chapter 11
Mirza Ateeq (Hilal Welfare Trust)	for the three pictures on page 75 of chapter 5
Angus Gardon (United Christian Interior ministries)	for the picture on page 188 of chapter 12
www.cultural-heritage-india.com	for the picture on page 233 of chapter 15
Noshir M. Lam	for the picture on page 262 of chapter 17 (from his book Parsi Zoroastrians on stamps)
www.crystallinks.com/shambala.html	for the picture on page 276 of chapter 18

Dhanjoo N. Ghista

Section I

From Under-Development to Self-Reliance

1

Introduction: A Kaleidoscopic Survey of Under-Development and Its Solution

1.1 Third World predicament

The indicators of under-developed economy are: a high proportion of population engaged in agriculture and low-level technology, an unsophisticated manufacturing sector, low level of education and literacy, poverty represented by a lack of basic living amenities, and meager per capita income. The etiology of Third World under-development can be attributed to: (1) political colonization, followed by the suffocating communist regimentation or exploitative economic colonization, (2) mock democracy and bleeding of wealth by incompetent and corrupt politicians, (3) destabilization of developing economies by currency manipulation and exploitation of cheap labor, through globalization, and (4) deculturalization and marginalization of entire communities by the intolerant regimes of some developing nations.

Under-development, in the context of the 20th century politico-economic systems, can be traced to the influence of political and economic colonization of the Third World, and thereafter to the traditional development options of capitalism* and communism for Third World development. In both these systems, work relationships are based on subordinated cooperation. Additionally in communism, the society is reduced to a production-distribution mechanism under a regimented system of control. Also, because the workers are not participants in the management structure and/or have shares in the company, the production efficiency has always been poor. It is no wonder that both capitalism and communism have failed to solve the problems of the Third World, and kept these nations under-developed.

*The capitalism, herein referred to, implies a socio-economic-political set-up in which the capital is concentrated with a few people and owners of corporations. This is distinct from what is advocated and can be termed as "collective-capitalism" (or social capitalism), wherein the corporational assets are shared with the employees and thereby the capital is collectively owned by its joint developers.

The 1980s and 1990s witnessed a deceptive economic boom of Southeast Asian countries, that were targeted to serve as producers of cheaper consumer items (from cars to televisions to computers) for the consumption of Western capitalist countries, through their multinational corporations (MNCs). The over-production of consumer items later resulted in decreased demand proportional to the supply. This was followed, in the late 1990s, by manipulation and destabilization of the currencies of some East Asian countries (in particular, assaults on the Thai baht by currency speculators, forcing its central bank to float its currency in July 1997), which made their cheapened industries vulnerable to being bought off at throwaway prices. In the wake of this crisis (and imbalanced supply-versus-demand of consumer items flooding the markets), the United States economy held its own, perhaps due to the investments and bank deposits of other capitalist and resource-rich countries. To make matters worse for these Southeast Asian countries, the MNCs moved northwards, to take advantage of even more cheaper (and larger) labor force.

The North-East Asian economy continued to rally behind fictitious over-sized markets for consumer items and fictitiously over-inflated real estate. But when it was recognized that these virtual markets and real estates could not be realistically justified, it triggered a mini economic collapse and massive layoffs. The MNCs and the capitalists must take a lot of the blame for this economic debacle, for over-production and over-expansion, and undermining public faith by fictitious profit displays for attracting public investments. The cheaper consumer imports into the US coupled with the current outsourcing and relocation of knowledge and service industry can eventually put US consumer, finance and IT industry out of business, and result in layoffs. The resulting decreased consumer spending and investment (due to the exposure of corporate-capitalistic corruption), now coupled with the panic of terrorism acts and unjustified unsustainable military engagements, are serious signals for the US economy going into a prolonged recession, triggering global depression and collapse of capitalism.

Not all of the capitalistic rhetoric may then be able to restore economic stability, because of the capitalistic-corporate economic system (and the associated democratic-governance system) not being people-oriented and hence unsustainable. In the wake of transplantation of major segments of the US industry coupled with the erosion of its revenue-generating industry (along with the increasing US import-export imbalance and the spiralling debt), it would be difficult for the US to sustain a global economy based on public investments in capitalist corporations and stock-exchange dynamics (even with out-of-proportion consumer spending), without ameliorating fiscal policies. We need an alternative people-centered and people-participatory transparent and cooperative economic system (involving both social and financial capital), associated socio-economic democracy representing the multi-sectorial needs of the community, and a governance system administered by executives elected by various sectors of the community (in place of the self-serving political-party system of democracy). Finally, it is in the interest of developing countries (and for all countries) to delink their economies from the US-centered unipolar economic system and form their own regional self-reliant economic unions, so as to continue to have markets for their exports and sustain their economy.

1.2 Asian economic scene

Since the 1980s, as the American MNCs ventured out into cheap-labor countries in East Asia, the American consumers have kept on buying cheap consumer items sold to them by these East Asian countries. This over-consumption and over-production contributed to the economic growth miracles witnessed in East Asia. As the US has kept buying more goods from the rest of the world than it sold to them, it has incurred ever-increasing current account deficit. In order to finance this deficit, the US has been selling corporate bonds and Treasury bills to the rest of the world. In turn, the big exporter-to-US countries have deposited their profits in these bonds and bills, in order to keep currencies competitive against the dollar.

However, this may not be a wise futuristic policy, why? The Americans work arena is being fast depleted, as its services industry is moving out of the US to the more educated developing countries. Hence, it is unlikely that the US economy can recover, because (as happened with its manufacturing industry) its knowledge capital industry is also being positioned abroad where human resource is more cheaply salaried. This could well be the flip side of capitalism, and even hasten globalization in a way that would not be in the best interests of the US. For this reason, the US may want to hold on to natural resources-endowed areas, such as Iraq. However, eventually even this policy of occupation may be unsustainable sociologically and politically.

As the US opportunistic-capitalism displays its true colors in terms of concern only for profits at the expense of national interests, the US industrial scene can become eroded and its economy could crumble. Then, the US will not be able to even service the interest on its debts. When the developing countries become alive to this disability on the part of the US, they will distance themselves from the US dollar-debt instruments, and make it impossible for the US to finance its debts and even its community services. Hence, in spite of all the make-believe propaganda of

US economic recovery, the US is quite likely to become a no-revenue, no-resource and no-work society. Who will then be buying the East Asian commodities exports? When the Asian countries finally wake up to this looming calamity, then and then alone will they form their own regional economic bloc, to continue to sustain their exports by enhancing regional imports and consumption capability.

While many East Asian countries have adopted this foreign investment route (FIR) to quick economic development, in India its home-based and non-resident enterprisers have contributed to its homegrown slow (but steady) economic development with efficient deployment of financial and intellectual capital. In fact, more and more American high-wage professional jobs (from architectural design and radiographic diagnosis to satellite survey analysis and funds management) are being outsourced to Indian IT companies. Make no mistake that the credit for this goes entirely to the Indian people, who have had to reckon with their government's and politicians' corruption and incompetency to enact constructive measures to assist their entrepreneurship (and still take undeserved credit for it). But for having to work against this pre-load, the Indian economy would have prospered much more. Sadly, Indian professionals can do little to rescue and take over their inefficient political machinery from the clutches of the professional political parties, whose only capability and occupation is to battle one another in elections. However, when the Indian intellectuals, information technologists and knowledge capitalists decide to also get involved in governance according to our advocated community sectorial representation in governance (leading to civilian democratic politics), then only will the lot of the poor masses improve. When this enormous social capital is transformed into knowledge capital, then only will we witness a quantum jump in the living standards of the population and the progress of the nation.

It is a distinct tragedy that Indian politicians (quite a few of whom are uneducated) have failed to provide any measure of governance, such as in modernizing primary-to-university education (for providing more knowledgeable social capital for their professional entrepreneurs), structuring the healthcare delivery system, improving community services (such as uninterrupted electrical power) and modernizing the rail transportation (and supply chain) system. Indeed, this progressiveness divide between India's civilian and governmental societies is typical of so many under-developed and developing countries. Hence, it is in their best collective interests that their civilian societies go one step further in entrepreneurship by taking over the governance, for real development of these countries. It is only when this vast human resource becomes self-actualized, that the developing countries can become developed countries and compete on even terms with the present-day developed countries. This is when real globalization will take place!

1.3 Functionally-sustainable communities for local economic empowerment and governance

A prime feature of Third World countries is under-developed rural areas, resulting in rural-to-urban population migration, poverty and lack of means to support community services. On the other hand, a prime feature of the discriminated and socially outcaste Fourth World communities is abject discrimination from living normally, as well as their persecution by the intolerant people of the establishment. In fact, worldwide, the social scenario is very disturbing, due to inter-ethnic strife, ethnic minorities' marginalization, and cultural suppression of minority communities within nations. All communities and people need to have unbarred opportunities to develop and progress. Hence, those culturally (as well as psychologically and economically) suppressed communities need to become autonomous and self-reliant, so that they can fashion their own destinies. All of these Fourth World peoples that have been marginalized can in fact get maximal opportunity to prosper by being constituted into self-reliant communities functionally-sustainable communities or FSC(s). So then what constitutes an FSC?

A functionally-sustainable and autonomously-governed community (FSC) is one that has adequate land and trade-specialities among its people, to be able to sustain the basic functional (revenue-generation, community-services, small-business and governance) sectors. In other words, the revenue generated by exporting its (natural-resource, agricultural and industrial) products should be able to sustain the services and small-business sectors of the community. An FSC is the grassroot unit of governance and functional socio-economic democracy. As such, it should have adequate qualified human resources, who could competently represent the various sectors of the community in governance by administering the portfolios of their sectors.

Hence, the key for Third World development and poverty eradication as well as the liberation of the Fourth World communities from oppression is to organize economic blocs in the form of functionally-sustainable (rural) communities (FSCs), so as to develop and manage local resources and industries. The resulting revenue generated from exporting agricultural and industrial products is to be utilized to sustain community services and small businesses. An exemplification of a functionally-sustainable community design (as provided in detail in Chapter 5) can be demonstrated to indicate how uniform living standards can be achieved for all the social sectors of the population, by some strategic organization of the community's population sectors.

The concept of a functionally-sustainable community can be relevant to not only economically backward as well as discriminated communities, but also to new communities that come about around natural resource sites. The dilemma is that if there are too many people working in the natural resource development industry in these so-called boom communities, or if there is an unduly high proportion of people engaged in agriculture in the poor rural areas of the world, then the lifestyle suffers for lack of living amenities. As a result, the younger people will leave the community, and over a period of time the sustainable resource development will not be possible.

So, there has to be adroit population distribution among the revenue-generating sector of the community, the community services-providing (and governance) sector, and the small business sector (to even include group professional, medical and legal practices). Chapter 5 provides such an optimal design, whereby the revenue generated from exports by the resource development and agricultural sector is utilized to sustain the community services sector and the small business sector, such that all the inhabitants can enjoy near-uniform earnings and living standards.

In a typical FSC (made up of economic units), the inhabitants would manage the local enterprises, with gains relaying back for their benefit and for local development. For this purpose, it is useful for medium and large scale enterprises to be cooperatively organized, so that the employees have a stake in their corporation's performance and success. The cooperatives in the various societal sectors (such as community services sector, healthcare sector, transportation sector, private business sector, etc.) would be organized into associations (such as of legal professionals, primary educators, etc.). Additionally, each FSC would have agencies (such as for trade and commerce, postal, municipal and transport services) and councils (such as township or neighborhood citizens councils for environmental and civil protection, and the sports council). Each of these associations, agencies and councils, together representing all the functional sectors of a community, would vote two of their most competent candidates to represent that sector in governance. The general public would then elect one of them to represent the sector on the local government legislature, thereby providing the framework of a truly democratic and knowledgeable (party-less) civilian professional-governance system (or PGS).

This verily constitutes a new concept of a people-centric democratic societal and governance system. This new democratic system would replace the current pseudo democratic system of governance management as a business undertaking, by the political parties securing public contracts (based on and legitimized by public votes) to manage the governance of the community. The political format of this neo-electoral and professional governance system is clearly delineated in more detail later on in this chapter as well as in Chapter 12.

It would also be in the interest of FSCs to cooperate with one another (and organize themselves into economic blocs) to share their know-how and trade in resources and technologies, in order to help one another to uniformly raise their living standards. This cooperation among FSCs, based on the neo-humanistic attitude of promoting the welfare of all peoples and communities (as opposed to merely eliciting foreign investment-based development and perpetuating economic colonization), can contribute to a new equitable Global Order. It would hence be economically beneficial for two or more FSCs to come together and form a self-reliant socio-economic bloc (SEB), while several SEBs would form a self-reliant economic zone (SEZ).

In the context of the present day setup, the SEZs would correspond to nations, while the SEBs would correspond to the states (and provinces) of nations. The FSC(s) will have the option of interacting with neighboring FSC(s) with whom they feel socio-culturally comfortable, to form self-reliant economic blocs or SEBs. An SEB would, in turn, need to have adequate land and resource density and diversity, such that it can function as a self-reliant agro-industrial and services-providing blocs.

1.4 Progressive socio-economic utilization system within FSCs

With regard to the socio-economic organization of a community, we reject both the communist and capitalistic systems (due to their shortcomings and failures), but incorporate some principles of a new socio-economic system (Prout),* entailing proper utilization and renumeration of all levels of human resources. Within FSCs, grassroots socio-economic development would be carried out by means of cooperatives, which will address business planning, factors of production cost and productivity, purchasing capacity and collective necessity. In our economic setup, cooperatively managed business enterprises and industries will enable work to be carried out in the spirit of coordinated cooperation, with due consideration for human rights and fair renumeration.

In FSCs, a cooperative economic system would be best able to utilize and provide fair renumeration to the locally available social-capital and knowledge-capital in the community, business-corporational and governance sectors. Especially, in poverty-stricken rural areas of developing countries, as well as within the FSCs of liberated Fourth World communities, the cooperatives will bring together producers, distributors and consumers in a coordinated partnership. These cooperatives (based on optimal or progressive utilization of human, natural and

**Proutist Economics: Discourses on Economic Liberation*, by Prabhat Ranjan Sarkar, (ISBN 81-7252-0034, Ananda Marga Publications, EM Bypass, Tiljila, Calcutta-39), 1992.

material resources) will function on the principles of individual liberty, equality and democracy, with sharing of revenue and profits by the cooperative members. Such cooperatives will be organized in all spheres of economic activity as well as social life, for the welfare of the people. The cooperatives will constitute an organization of people coming together, to help one another and save themselves from capitalist as well as communist exploitation.

The cooperatives will in fact constitute the catalysts of FSCs, wherein local people will generate revenue (through resource development, industry and trade) to in turn develop their own community services of water supply and sanitation, electrical power, healthcare, education and transportation. This cooperative system of economic development and management verily constitutes collective capitalism (or CCP, as opposed to subordinated capitalism). In this setup, the capital will be cooperatively generated, controlled and distributed.

For people to interact and live in peace, we need to make provision for their satisfactory economic means and livelihood, cultural and psychic expression, enlightened and benevolent governance system, so that they can maximally develop all of their potentialities. In order for them to have a fulfilling lifestyle, they also need to feel that they constitute intrinsic members of the community they are living in, and that they are contributing to its development. This people-centered and people-empowered system of CCP (collective capitalism) and SED (socio-economic democracy) along with the civilian professional-governance (CPGS) system will auger well for optimal utilization of natural resources, community services and human potentialities.

1.5 Alternative political structure for harmonious and peaceful psychology and living setup

Today, even in nations that have a disturbing record of human rights violations (according to Amnesty International), the concepts of globalization and human rights, anti-racism and anti-castism, democracy and disarmament are all rhetorically advocated and theoretically implemented. However, the end result is a perpetration of gross inequalities and divergent standards in all strata of human living. In older and big developing nations, there are several groups and communities who have no cultural and ideological commonality with the national culture and ideology. They hence prefer to be politically autonomous, and have their own governance system. However, their national governments regard this so-called separatist movements as subversive and forcibly (and militarily) suppress them. This non-compromising attitude on the part of their national governments is often motivated by these culturally distinct blocs having rich cultural resources. In the past decades, there have been, throughout the world, innumerable situations of inter-religious conflicts and ethnic killings, of the suffocating lot of under-privileged communities and castes, of freedom struggles by oppressed communities, of suppression of spiritual and religious groups, and mass killings in the name of cultural revolutions and patriotism. Throughout this abuse of humanity, the United Nations (UN) has had to remain a painful inept bystander.

In fact, the entire present day global order of community of nations has become corrupted and consolidated into distinct camps of industrialized nations, developing nations and poverty-stricken under-developed nations. Even the UN cannot alter this affluent hegemony of nations, because the UN is itself financially supported by the affluent nations. In the present day global political-economic order, the economically and militarily powerful (eg. G-8) nations have a big influence on the destinies of the weaker Third World nations. On the other hand, the prejudicial social attitudes and structures within Third World nations have caused marginalization of their own Fourth World populations. We can hence make a deserving case for marginalized and persecuted people to be brought into the fold of FSC(s).

For this purpose, as an alternative political-economic setup, it is advocated that in the Third World regions, poor and/or marginalized communities come together to form FSCs; this would enhance economic development, while also alleviating social discontent. What we are essentially saying is that it would be in the best interests of everyone, for dissatisfied communities to be given autonomy for their socio-economic development; this would eliminate the potential causes for unrest, separatist and freedom movements, and even terrorism. Similarly, it would auger well for peace and harmony between neighboring nations to rise above narrow ideological sentiments, and instead to cooperate with one another in all spheres of work and living. Hence, two or more states could come together to form an SEZ; such a cooperation would help to raise the living standards of their people, while also mitigating inter-nation border disputes and hostilities.

The governments of SEZs, analogous to present day nations (such as, say, countries of the Arabian peninsula), would constitutionally ensure implementation of decentralized planning and balanced development of all sectors of the economy in their constituent FSCs. The SEZs, of a region or a continent, would in turn be synthesized into regional federations or RFDs (such as the South-Asian Federation, in the vein of European Union or EU) under a world government, to constitute a neo-humanistic global order. A detailed methodology and mechanism for effecting this neo-political restructuring of nations is provided in Chapter 4. The role of this apex world government would be to monitor and ensure political and economic stability, social and physical security, protection of human rights and ethnic minorities, and equal opportunities for all the inhabitants of the world to progress and prosper multifariously.

In this neo-political structure, the FSCs would constitute the grassroots of socio-economic democracy, and enlightened governance. Thus, FSCs would provide their inhabitants progressive social, economic and governance systems. The FSCs would help socio-economically backward (and rural) communities to become progressive, and also help to provide freedom of expression and dignified living to marginalized cultural/ethnic communities. In fact, in our proposed world government political system, it would even be possible for similar ethnic neighboring communities located in separate nations or SEZs to beneficially come together and form one FSC.

1.6 Socio-economic democratic electoral and governance structure within FSCs

As indicated earlier, a prime feature of the prevalent social order is discrimination, on the basis of culture and language, skin color and physiogamy, literacy and poverty, gender and descent. In this century itself, those discriminated people (because of their race and physiogamy) have been enslaved (as in South Africa and Zimbabwe or former Rhodesia) and gassed (as happened to the Jewish population under Nazism), rendered homeless and virtually wiped out of existence (as happened to the native populations of America and Australia). The gender discrimination shows up in the form of women who are not allowed to participate in society functioning in certain societies riddled with religious dogmas (as in the case of some nations in the Middle-East and Western Asia). Those discriminated, because of their being born in so-called lower castes, have been debarred from all public participation sites, events and functionaries (as in the case of dalits in India). What is sad is that these culturally, economically and politically discriminated and suppressed people are not allowed to become liberated and self-governed.

All of these discriminated Fourth World people also suffer from discrimination in employment, education and healthcare. They live and die oppressed, suppressed and depressed. These discriminated peoples need to have their own FSCs, for them to develop their own economy, community services and governance. But they are not allowed to do so, they have no mechanism for voicing their grievances and plight. For these millions of people living in abject poverty, psychic oppression and cultural suppression, the only hope is that they be allowed to form their own FSCs, based on the (to be formed) constitution of the (to be formed) world government. They would then be in charge of development of their own community (within and with assistance from their SEZ), and be empowered to charter their own socio-economic destiny.

Indeed, the prime features of the present day democratic system are:

- socio-economic inequality, because of the subjugative work organization setup (in the capitalist system), involving employers and employees having grossly divergent social standing and economic benefits;
- the party system of political governance, whereby the political members of the parties are continually engrossed in election campaigns (subsidized by capitalist corporations) and political alliances, and which thereby constitute an enormous wastage of human resources and monies, and detracts from the legislators dedicating themselves to governance;
- impossibility for competent independently thinking persons from getting elected to the governance legislature; and
- non-involvement of public constituencies in public policy-making and economic development.

In contrast, our proposed political and socio-economic setup is based on FSCs, in which the community activities are cooperatively organized. As a result, all the people can be involved in all the functions of the community, and hence in its economic development. Now, in this setup, we are advocating a neo-electorate (and neo-political governance) system, wherein these community-activities' cooperatives and/or associations (such as teachers', doctors', lawyers', farmers' associations) elect their own representatives to the local government. This constitutes the basis of the new concepts of Collective-Capitalism (CCP) and civilian Socio-Economic Democracy (SED).This system will primarily result in only competent persons and experts, within the various sectors of community (with no party affiliations), being elected to political governance. These persons will be held solely accountable for their governance performance.

So then, let us reiterate what constitutes collective-capitalism (CCP) and socio-economic democracy (SED). In simple terms, CCP implies collective generation and sharing of capital. It also tacitly implies the equal importance of social, knowledge and financial capitals. In this system, the collective-capitalist corporations will primarily raise business-development funds from banks, instead of eliciting public investments, so as to eventually turn-off stock-exchanges, associated with stock and currency tradings and manipulations. The SED is the political counterpart of the CCP. Once the community is organized into social-capitalist corporations, it would be in a position to provide political and governance representation to its various functional sectors, through associations representing these sectors (making redundant the system and need of political parties), to constitute SED.

At the FSC level, the associations of cooperatives will elect their representatives to FSCs legislatures. The elected legislature members from local FSCs will in turn elect representatives to the state government (or SEB government) and the SEBs' governance members will elect representatives to the national government (or SEZ government). From these representatives will be elected governance officers to regional federations' government, and thence to the world government. This neo-electorate and governance system will be devoid of petty party politics, cronyism and corruption, and above all save colossal amounts of public monies from being misused to support extravagant election campaigns and party conventions. Chapter 10 provides the detailed mechanism of this electoral and governance system.

1.7 Stepwise global political restructuring

In light of our advocated neo-political order and grouping, what will happen to the prevalent political order and system of governance? In the economically and politically stable countries, the people may choose to retain the current setup of states or provinces within nations. However in developing regions, it would be more socio-economically viable to develop this neo-political order or setup of autonomously governed FSCs within SEBs, with two or more nations coming together to form SEZs within regional federations or unions (such as the Southeast Asian Federation or union or the Middle-East federation or union, etc.).

Hence, as a first step, in the under-developed regions, the present day political governance system could be first replaced at the local community level, by the new governance system. In other words, within the FSCs of an SEB, the governance would be carried out by elected representatives of sectorial associations (of professional groups and cooperatives). However, at the state level, the current political-governance system would either continue, or the FSCs would elect representatives in the various administrative portfolios to the SEB state government. This would constitute Stage 1. Nevertheless, even this process would need to be supervised and carried out under the aegis of the corresponding regional federation council.

Hence, we would first need to establish an interim regional federation council, made up of independently thinking and moralistic representatives from the representative nations or SEZs of the continent. This regional federation council would then legislate and supervise the formation of FSCs, and election of FSCs' associations' representatives to FSCs' legislatures. This regional council would also supervise the implementation of the governance system in the FSCs. Once a stable governance is achieved in all the SRCs, the regional federational council could plan for Stages 2 and 3 — the introduction of the new form of democratic governance system at the SEB and SEZ levels. Thereafter, it would implement Stage 4 — the formation and implementation of Regional Federation's governance system.

What we are proposing is intra-nation economic restructuring into FSCs, intra and inter nation groupings as SEBs, and economic regrouping of nations into SEZs. As indicated above, Stage 1 could be allowed to be consolidated for sometime. Then in Stage 2, the FSCs within nations (and even belonging to neighboring nations) would be constituted as SEBs and SEZs, under the supervision of the interim regional federational council. After that has been accomplished, the governance councils at the SEB and SEZ levels would be made up of elected members of FSCs legislatures. Of course, at that stage, some of the industrially and economically developed nations may also want to come together (and cooperate with one another) as SEZs, if they deem such a step to be economically viable and beneficial.

Assuming a nation (and in future, an SEB) is made up of n (=10, say) FSCs. Then in that SEB government, each political portfolio would be managed by the elected representative of the n (or 10) FSC managers of that portfolio. In other words, in the SEB government, the minister for (say) healthcare delivery would be the elected representative of the n (= 10) FSCs' legislators of healthcare delivery. The vacant seat in the FSC government, caused by this legislator now working at the SEB level, would be filled by the second elected representative of the healthcare delivery association of that FSC.

This development of the governance system at the state or SEB level and thereafter at national or SEZ level would be allowed to be consolidated over a couple of years, while the next phase of establishment of regional federations (RFDs) would be planned. This would be followed by the establishment of the governance system of regional federations, along the lines of EU (such as the African Federation, South American Federation, Southeast Asian Federation, etc.). Once that is done, the interim regional federation council would resign, and hand over governance to the elected representatives. Finally, the governments of the regional federations would elect their representatives to the world government council of governance.

With regards to the formation of local and regional governments, the FSCs' associations-of-cooperatives will elect their representatives to FSCs' governments. These FSCs' legislators will, in turn, elect their representatives to the SEB government; the SEBs' legistators will elect the SEZ governing council members. Finally, these SEZ ministers will elect their representatives to the regional federation, and thereafter to the world government. Thus, the world government will automatically have both regional representatives and population-proportional representatives, who will be required to provide competent governance conducive to the progress of all the regions and peoples of the world.

It is for grassroots implementation of collective capitalism (or social capitalism) and for the regional (and eventually global) implementation of economic democracy as well as for promotion of socio-economic justice, that we have proposed an alternative organization of the world regions. This new global order will: (1) prevent economic and political instabilities and colonization, and (2) promote global cooperation towards global peace and security, dignified living standards and progression to supra-aesthetic lifestyle. In this neo-setup, FSCs will be the basic grassroots unit of socio-economic-political democracy within nations (or SEBs). The nations would come together in the fold of SEZs, and SEZs into regional federations or unions, which will operate under a world government. Such a people-centric political-economic order (schematized below) will foster economic and political security, and help to transform the present day exploitative and armament-based economy to a cooperative and welfare-based economy.

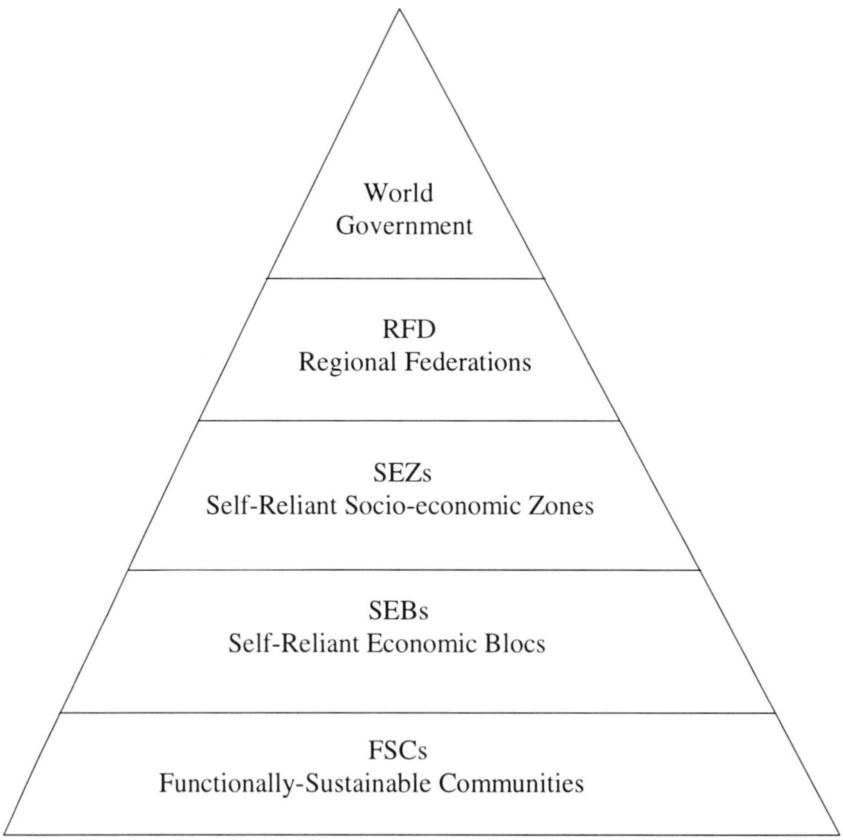

People-centric Political-economic order

1.8 The economic system to be implemented at the grassroots level within FSC

Let us now discuss the basis of a progressive societal setup in the light of human nature and need. No doubt, micro-psychic longings constitute part and parcel of human nature, and form the basis of capitalism. However, no amount of such finite acquisitions can satisfy the inherent tendency of human beings for uninterrupted mental fulfillment. A progressive society is one in which engineering and social sciences provide the requisite ambience for human beings to progress to their enlightened desideratum. From this, emerge the concepts of socio-economics of progressive utilization of human potentials, for the making of a knowledge-based society to optimize the development and utilization of physical and social resources, and eventually of a psycho-spiritual society to catalyze and guide intellectual potentialities development for collective welfare.

These progressive principles emphasize decentralized economic planning: resource identification as well as its localized conversion into products for public utilization, the organization of the industrial sector as cooperatives, and the government sector involvement in community services. In FSCs, economically sustainable development entails development by using local resources (physical, intellectual and spiritual) and initiatives, with the first priority of developing countries being to produce the basic necessities of living. The provision of 100% employment and adequate purchasing capacity of the stipulated minimum wage, to sustain basic living requirements, constitute priority goals of self-reliant development in developing countries. The business sector would be organized as key industries (public utilities and large scale industries), medium-sized industries and small scale private enterprises. The large and medium scale industries and enterprises would be organized and managed as cooperatives. The government sector would be primarily involved in providing community services (such as education, healthcare delivery, water supply and sanitation, electrical power and public transport), and of course be involved in public policy-making. Such a socio-economic setup will also be beneficial to the discriminated Fourth World peoples of FSCs. With the FSC being organized into cooperatives and with public policy being developed at the grassroots level (by associations of similar types of cooperatives, such as agricultural and manufacturing cooperatives), the Fourth World people would also be involved in economic development and management, and of course participate in economic gains.

At the level of an SEZ or within a regional federation, we would need to foster all aspects of economies: *people's economy* dealing with necessities of living, *psycho-economics* for development and maximal utilization of intellectual and para-psychic potentials of people, *commercial economics* dealing with banking and fiscal policy, and *general economics* dealing with industry and economic growth. Societal stability requires a universal social outlook and the uniform development of all sectors of economy as well as of the workforce. Sustainable local development and self-reliant regional economic development would deal with industrial organization, trade, fiscal and monetary policies. In the monetary system of an SEZ, money would have a stable standard linked to and backed up by a basket of commodities (such as natural resources of oil and precious metals). The central bank could provide banking for key industries, while the cooperative banks (and credit unions) would serve the industrial cooperatives. The government sector would also deal with minimum wage and income range (based on merit and social value of work), as well as tax levels and interest rates (linked to economy growth rate). The minimum wage would need to cater to a minimal living standard, that provides for housing, education, healthcare and purchasing capacity for consumer items.

In the new proposed socio-economic democratic system, all of the community's services and business enterprises would be set up and administered as cooperatives, which would essentially operate as collective capitalist corporations. The business cooperatives would take bank loans to set up and/or expand their business. However, the production would be tailored to the consumers' demand. Such a policy would address the issues of over-production, reduction in public consumption and consequential layoffs. The business cooperatives would take bank loans from the cooperatives banking system, and issue shares (in relation to the equity of the corporation) only to their employee members. There would hence be no need for stock market and currency players and manipulators. We would not have to contend with and worry about the phenomenon of stock trading and manipulation, stock market crash and economic collapse.

1.9 The financial aspect of intra and inter RFD development and trading

Within each RFD, there would be a common currency, printed by the RFD government. This would enable trading within each RFD using the RFD currency. However, what about trading among some newly emerging hitherto under-developed communities (or FSCs)? For this purpose, the RFD would provide, through its regional banks, loans to the RFD government banks, which in turn would provide loans to the RFD cooperative banks. These RFD cooperative banks would in turn give loans to the FSC cooperative banks to finance the cooperative enterprises (i.e. for the enterprise population sector) of the FSC. This would enable these enterprises to become functional.

At the same time, the RFD government would start providing funds to the FSC government, for developing community services, such as water supply and sanitation, electrical power, healthcare delivery and education. The cooperative enterprises as well as the small-scale enterprises (such as shops) population sectors would be able to pay for the community services as well as for daily living needs from these loans. This would enable the community-services government sector to recover its investment. The enterprise sector could also sell its produces or services, within and/or outside the FSC, for revenue generation. Initially, however, this could be difficult, because of a lack of adequate money in circulation. In order to facilitate this process, the FSC governments could initially buy off the produce and pay money to the producers. Then the FSC governments could either trade in commodities or pay money for buying them.

In fact, each FSC would function as a "government of cooperatives," while each SEB would function as a cooperative government of FSCs. The regional (and, later on, global) implementation of collective capitalism would auger for regional (and global) economic stability, and thereby enable all the regions of the world to converge to a near-uniform living standard. Chapter 10 details this economic system for eclectic utilization of human resources and potentialities, towards cooperative and enlightened living, as described by the inspiring shloka from the Rigveda at the very outset of this Preface.

1.10 World government and constitution for human rights and enlightened living

What constitutional guarantees should the society and governance provide to the people? Primarily, all the people should get equal opportunity to develop and express their potentialities, and the society should be able to utilize these potentialities. The socio-economic system should ensure equitable distribution of wealth, provide social security, and help to cultivate a neo-humanistic outlook. The constitution of an FSC should guarantee employment for all, formation of cooperatives, and utilization of all human resources in the functioning of community, and a minimum wage with adequate purchasing capacity to meet the basic living needs. The constitution of an SEB should support and guarantee education and healthcare in all its constituent FSCs, and ensure religious freedom and non-discrimination by caste or religion. The constitution of an SEZ would safeguard human rights as well as animal rights to life, incorporate measures for implementation of non-discrimination on the basis of race and caste as well as religion, ensure a secular society and freedom of religious practice, and provide for ethnic minorities' protection and tribal cultural preservation. The SEZ constitution would also endorse economic democracy and the proposed new electoral governance system by which capable people with adroit backgrounds get to be in charge of specific public governance portfolios. The constitution of a regional federation should primarily ensure human rights of inhabitants in all realms (such as to employment based on their credentials, to education and healthcare and to social and economic security), as well as to economic democratic organization and governance of the society.healthcare, and to social and economic security), as well as to economic democratic organization and governance of the society.

The constitution of the world government will define and guarantee all these principles and measures, to be adopted and implemented at the FSC, SEB, SEZ and regional federation levels. Above all, it will emphasize human rights in the most comprehensive way. This will include the rights to:

- employment and minimum wage;
- purchasing capacity for minimal living standard;
- primary, second level and college education;
- affordable medical and healthcare;
- social security and old age benefits;
- freedom to adopt religious faith and perform spiritual practices;
- freedom of expression and dignified criticism of public policy;
- security from terrorism and from the danger of weapons of mass destruction;
- physical security for all the inhabitants of the world, by declaring it to be criminal for anyone to indulge in terrorist acts on innocent people, as well as for the head of an SEB government to declare war on another SEB or to encroach on its territory or to invade it and destroy its institutions; and
- competent people-centered governance in accordance with the constitution.

The establishment of the World Government will:

- replace the present day hegemony of nations and multi-polar global order, not by a "family of nations," but by "a global family of communities of people;"
- usher in an era of global parity and sharing of multifarious resources among and by all the communities of the world;
- make all nations subscribe to the neo-humanistic governance concepts and ideas, and accountable to the world government;
- help to monitor and diffuse contentious issues between communities and blocs, as well as handle inter-community and inter-bloc litigations through its (to be established) world government;
- hold governance ministers and officers as well as individuals accountable for initiating and/or promoting inter-community violence and strife,

and for crimes against humanity, through the (to be established) world criminal court;
- finally result in tangible disarmament and redundancy of inter-nation militarism, in the wake of assumed and legislated global security;
- nullify the need for inter-nation intelligence services and covert operations;
- erase terrorism, by erasing the etiology and the germinating causes of terrorism;
- auger for ultimate safety and security of inhabitants of the earth against not only the danger of nuclear inter-nation and global warfare but also the danger of blowing up of nuclear and biological weapons' arsenals by natural calamities (such as earthquakes and pole-shifts);
- ensure people's empowerment in economic development and political governance; and
- pave the way for the present day politicians-centered and benefiting society, and governance system to be replaced by people-centered society and governance system.

Together, the formation of local self-reliant economic blocs and zones (intent on helping one another, instead of leveraging on their strengths and others' weaknesses) constitute the key to Third World and Fourth World liberation and development. In fact, in time, even the industrially developed nations would come to understand, appreciate and implement such a neo-humanist outlook, combined with collective capitalism, socio-economic democracy and professional governance system. Decentralized economic development in FSCs, neo-humanistic outlook in all regions of the world, economic and political stability for all the regions of the world functioning under a world government, will constitute the new global order, towards (what can be termed as) neo-humanistic and democratic globalization.

The dormant humanity can be awakened by a neo-humanistic ideological happening,

Coloring the minds with sweetness and charm,

To serve as kindled lights in the darkness.

Fourth-World dwellings on the other side of an open sewer behind houses, in the world's biggest democracy. This is why our present-day system of democracy is a farce. In our civilian–centric democratic system, the township sectors dealing with sanitation, cooperative-employment and residential dwellings would collectively ensure that there is a proper sewer system and that even the poorest of the poor can live in dignity.

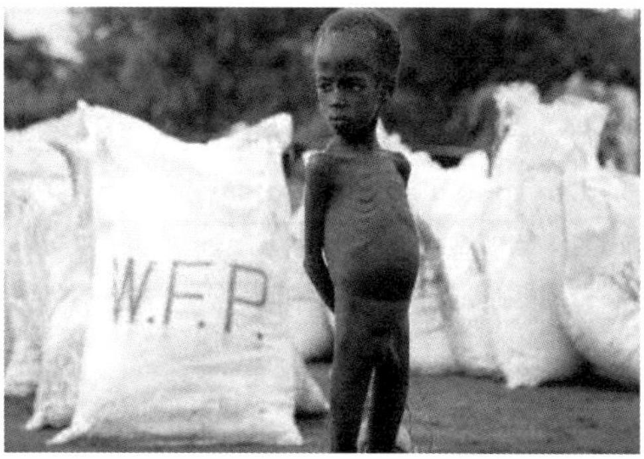

A young starving boy stands in front of relief food bags delivered by the World Food Program (9 August 2003) after an airdrop by the WFP in the village of Acumcum, in the Bahr El Ghazal Province of southern Sudan. To prevent these tragedies, each region needs to form an economic bloc, within which all the FSCs cooperate in helping one another in times of calamities and in preventing calamities by capacity-building for sustainable development.

2 Third World Under-Development and Need for Self-Reliance

2.1 Under-development

The Third World has had (1) a legacy of resource subversion, due to political and economic colonization by colonial powers and capitalist corporations, (2) a history of psychic suppression and persecution under some repressive regimes, and (3) incompetent governance (contributing to stifling of their citizens' potentialities) combined with bleeding of wealth by their corrupt political leaders. Even after the sun sets on colonial empires, psychic and economic exploitation and colonization continues to be perpetuated on the previous colonies, whose people's sufferings continue under their present governmental regimes.

The situation is further compounded due to the bleeding of wealth by the political leaders of developing countries, wherein a big percentage of the population is uneducated and devoid of political consciousness. For instance, the politicians cream off huge sums of foreign aid, take cuts from contracts to foreign agencies to supply armaments, and squeeze money from business enterprises for providing them export-import licenses. Some of them even set up pseudo companies (under management of their relatives) to elicit huge investment loans from foreign banks, to fictitiously foster indigenous development. Indeed, there is no limit to the ingenuity of these politicians of most developing countries; the people are virtual pawns in their corruption strategy and drive.

***Undeveloped Rural areas*:** Third World countries are characterized by vast undeveloped rural regions, with:

- unfulfilled basic living needs of drinking water, nutritious diet, electrical power, housing, healthcare and education;
- difficulty in retaining local literate, professional and labor population;
- unexploited natural resources, sustainable agricultural and farming productivity techniques, mining, trades and environmentally protective industrial development;
- inadequate revenue generated from the above to support community (municipal, healthcare and educational) services;

- non-availability of appropriate technology to address resource development, living needs and community services;
- a very pathetic standard of living.

Urban Slums: As the rural regions do not have facilities to either retain their professionally trained inhabitants or to even offer employment to laborers, there has been a continuous drain of human resources (both literate and illiterate, trained and untrained) from rural to urban areas. This has resulted in overloading and breakdown of urban community services (such as transportation, healthcare, education, water supply, electricity and housing), resulting in urban slums rife with disease, thousands of street dwellers, overcrowded hospitals, acute water and electrical power shortage.

2.2 Under-developed economy versus exploitative development

The indicators of an under-developed economy are: (1) low income per person, (2) existence of a high proportion of the population engaged in agriculture, using low-level technology, (3) a small and unsophisticated manufacturing sector, (4) a low level of education and literacy, (5) a low level of capital formation, (6) poverty, represented by not having the minimal living necessities, e.g. food and water, housing and clothing, healthcare and transport facilities, and (7) helplessness of the people, in having no means to improve their lot.

Third World under-development has been attributed to many factors: cultural peculiarities, over-population, bureaucratic mismanagement, corruption and the bleeding of wealth. Of these, the "bleeding of wealth," i.e. the systematic removal of wealth from the country so that it becomes impossible to maintain or build a capital base, has had a big influence on the current magnitude of Third World under-development. Additionally, the First World has devised, over several centuries, many colonial and neo- colonial schemes to expropriate wealth generated in the Third World.

Today, many years after independence, many countries that gained independence have stayed under-developed. This is also due to their own corrupt political leaders and regimes, who have bled their own countries (by manipulating banks into giving business loans to their relatives and cronies, or by obtaining kickbacks from foreign contractors, or by selling natural resources cheaply in return for kickbacks), and using this black money to buy into more businesses and siphon the hoarded black money into overseas banks.

Although First World economies have the appearance of strength, in fact their strength is derived from centuries of exploitation, and is substantially dependent on continued cheap imports and/or cheap labor utilization from the Third World, and the ability or willingness of the Third World to tolerate debt. The indicators of exploitative development arise from concentration of wealth, the economic power and political influence of these so-called multinationals, the economic warfare mentality behind it, and the unholy alliance of the third world political leaders with the capitalist cartels.

Exploitative development is associated with: (1) over-concentration of industries and wealth in a small segment of population, by means of takeovers and mergers; (2) dependence on cheap imports from under-developed countries; (3) buying of shares, land and commodities by speculators, with the sole purpose of selling these at higher prices; using these purchases as security to get bank loans, so as to buy off more and more businesses; (4) banks involvement in such shady businesses and loans. Additionally, the continued concentration of wealth into first world countries generates economic instabilities and cycles of inflation-deflation. Thus, the capitalist development option is seriously flawed.

The communist development option has already discredited itself, by imposing an unpsychological theory of state ownership, of agricultural land or a share in the business, the ruthless way of dealing with employees, denigrating spirituality, and having no conscience for unleashing terror among citizens through mass purges.

2.3 Economic colonization

In this hopeless condition, there emerged in the 1980s a model of capitalist economic colonization, which altered the economic destinies of most East Asian countries. In the early 1970s, to counter the huge increase in petroleum prices and the resulting high inflation, the United States industry shifted production to some third world Asian countries: Taiwan, Hong Kong, Singapore and South Korea. In 1980s, the US industry consumer products shifted to three more Asian countries (Malaysia, Indonesia and Thailand), to take advantage of their cheap labor force. While these seven Asian countries served as US economic colonies, the over-production of consumer items caused a crash in the price of these items.

In 1996, the capitalist currency traders decided to make money by betting against Thailand currency, which resulted in its fall and of the stock market. The currency traders then started betting against the currencies of other East Asian countries, resulting in the investors withdrawing their money. In Thailand, people even started sending dollars out of the country. The International Monetary Fund (IMF) prescribed remedial measures (such as curtailment of welfare schemes and food subsidies), which in fact added more hardships to the people of Thailand.

Thus, in short, Capitalism created economic colonies in developing countries. Then, the capitalists manipulated the currencies of these countries to additionally devaluate their indigenous industries, and make them vulnerable to be bought off by foreign investors at cheap prices. In order to solve the unemployment and economic crisis, these countries like Indonesia and Thailand were reduced to begging foreign companies to come in, and buy their factories at throw-away prices. It is this continued dependency on and vulnerability to Western investors that has caused the economies of these Asian countries to be unstable.

In short, for the last two decades, the capitalist countries pretended to develop the East Asian countries, by making them producers of technologies and gadgets for their own consumption, by using the cheap labor of East Asian countries. However, the economies of these East Asian countries were never grassroots-based. Hence, in the absence of a viable and stable economic infrastructure, some East Asian countries (such as Indonesia and Philippines) are still facing the same problem of rural under-development and urban chaos, just as in the case of the South Asian countries like India, Pakistan and Bangladesh.

US banks, that had given out huge loans to shady manufacturing and production companies in East Asia, Russia and South America, were having to forfeit these loans, and the IMF could not prop up these shady industries. The collapse of US banks (and possibly the American dollar) could have in fact caused a global economic crisis, were it not for the oil-producing countries keeping their monies in US banks and the IMF propping up the US banks in the guise of shoring up the economies of these developing countries. Globalization is the latest maneuver on the part of developed countries to exploit developing countries, by forcing developing countries to be open to MNCs (utilizing their cheap labor and technical human resource) and exports from industralized countries, in order to maintain their economic edge.

2.4 Political apathy and indifference

Within a few years after the East Asian economic crisis of 1997–1998, the East Asian countries have staged some economic recovery. But for the South Asian and African countries (like Ethiopia, Chad and others), the poverty and plight remain unaltered. It has been more than 50 years since most previously colonized third world countries became independent. Yet, many South Asian and African countries suffer from lack of housing, shortage of water and electrical power, healthcare and education, roads and transport. What makes it worse that these countries continuously suffer from drought, lack of fresh water (because of political ineptness and corruption) and floods (with loss of life and property).

It does no good to keep blaming the political colonialists and the neo-economic colonialists for the continuing abject poverty. The incapable and immoral politicians and bureaucrats of these countries are to be blamed for it. We can criticize the industrialized countries' multinationals for using the East Asian countries to fulfill their demand for consumer goods, then staging currency devaluation to cause a collapse of the manufacturing companies, and finally with the help of IMF buying up these companies at throw-away prices. Still the living standards of these East Asian countries are much better than those of South Asian countries, that did not subscribe to the industralized countries' multinational companies. That does say something for the incompetency of South Asian countries' governments!

In India, for instance, all the rural development schemes and budgets set aside for rural development have failed to benefit the people. During elections, it is a common complaint among the villagers that the politicians only visit them to canvass for their votes at election times, without even addressing their common age-old problems of lack of water and electricity, medical clinics and schools, roads and means of public transport. This plight of rural population is due to the political party system of governance, whereby the elected legistrators are impervious to the welfare of the people. It cannot be solved by globalization and free trade. The answer lies in (i) organizing the local rural populations into cooperatives, with government start-up fundings directly made available to these cooperatives, (ii) having the associations of these cooperatives in all the community sectors elect their most competent representatives to the legislative assembly, and (iii) making these political parties and their politicians redundant.

2.5 Globalization: a neo-economic colonization?

There still remain the unsolved problems of: (1) developing countries being forced to sell their resources cheap to the developed countries, (2) having their forest reserves to be destroyed and their environment polluted by their foreign-owned factories making export items, (3) having their people make clothings and consumer items at meagre salaries for these goods to be sold expensively abroad under the label of these multinationals, and (4) of the developing countries being given IMF and World Bank loans at exorbitant unpayable interests with the stipulation of opening their markets to open trade.

Indeed, is this what globalization is all about? In the true sense, globalization should imply that all the nations function as autonomously-governed but cooperating states of one apex government, that people of all nations have equivalent opportunities to develop and express their potentialities, and that people all over the world doing the same skill level of work get identical salaries. In other words, the people working in the Philippines, Pakistan and India to make fashion clothing, computer software and even medical instruments should be atleast paid reasonable (if not equivalent) salaries as their counterparts in developed countries. Only then will their living standards improve. Otherwise, it constitutes economic exploitation. So in the hands of rich countries, globalization is another instrument of perpetuating economic domination and inequalities.

In the Group 77 (now 133) Summit (in April 2000 in Yarana, Cuba), solutions were adopted to shake-up the world's financial systems:

- to give developing countries greater say over economic and trade policies;
- for forgiveness of foreign debts;
- for increased foreign aid;
- to evolve a new global human order aimed at reviewing the growing disparities between the rich and the poor, with the countries of the South given the right to participate on an equal footing in decisions affecting them.

While the resolutions at the G-77 summit may sound decisive, it is not only wishful thinking but in fact foolhardy to expect the developed countries to alter their stance, and think benevolently in terms of one human family. So then what is the alternative? The answer is in the developing countries taking charge of their own destiny; this could entail that:

- the developing countries (in various regions of the world) work together and assist one another to become self-reliant at micro and macro regional levels;
- at the grassroots level, all their communities' sectors' functions and developments be structured as cooperatives;
- socio-economic-political planning, development and functioning be carried out at the local (and regional) levels, by the local people using local resources, to constitute economic (and not just political) democracy;
- even governance be organized as a cooperative endeavor of the governance executives with the community sectors' representative associations;
- further, the developing countries can form their own "commonwealth of developing nations" with their own monetary funds, and develop beneficial trade policies among themselves;
- the G-133 and (politically and economically) non-aligned third world countries start evolving a new global order of inter-nation self-reliant blocs, within regional federations;
- the developing nations who make up the majority of nations in the UN, work towards the concept of a world government.

All of these measures will be discussed at length in the subsequent chapters.

2.6 The "totally neglected Fourth World" of culturally suppressed communities and destitutes

While economic labeling of world nations (as First World or Third World as well as North or South) has held center stage in global economic politics, even more lamentable and pathetic are the living conditions and psychology of communities (within developing countries) that are psychologically suppressed and politically subjugated because of their social cultural, ethnic, religious backgrounds.

These people include:

- all the native populations (of the world regions), whose cultures have been suppressed, who have been deprived of their habitats, and who have been rendered misfits among the people who have displaced them;
- people who were displaced by political upheavals (and/or unscrupulously planned land and property occupations), and have been living as refugees;
- people who have been prevented from following their religious practices, and have been culturally suppressed, as for example several nations and communities under repressive communist and intolerant religious regimes; and
- people who have been socially relegated to the category of "backward classes" by the oppressively rigid caste system, and have been living in social oppression and as economically backward communities.

How can we relieve these discriminated and marginalized suppressed and repressed people and communities? In the first place, we can formulate constitutional safeguards for them, both preventive and punitive. Further, in order to "rescue" people who have victimized and outcasted (by virtue of their race, caste and social standing), a solution could be a UN legislated mandate for these nations' judicial ministries to set up an independent Network of People's Courts (PCN). This PCN would entertain appeals from individuals and groups. Their decision, in the case of legitimate cases of victimization, could range from reparation (to be provided by their oppressors) to provision of an autonomous micro-community status for a big number of victimized people. However, in the UN framework, at present there is no scope of appeal by the victimized communities of nations, unless this appeal is made by other nations on behalf of those communities. Unfortunately, in the present set-up, the UN cannot be restructured to also represent people and not just nations' politicians; such a move would be opposed by its member-nations' governments. This is why we need Regional Federational governments (under a World government), whose ministries are not dominated by party-politicians but are open to receive and act on dissents by suppressed and oppressed groups.

Now in addition to these suppressed and oppressed communities, we have a big number of people who have nothing and who survive by begging. The South Asian countries below the Himalayan mountain range, and particularly India, have probably the biggest proportion of these poor beggars. Their plight is the worst among all the suffering humanity. They have no home, live on the roads, and beg for food day in and day out. They cannot afford to relax (let alone rest), but have to be alert and begging for their meals. Most of these beggars are also handicapped, blind and/or lame and rife with disease (such as leprosy). It is difficult to imagine the psychology of these beggars, who go to sleep and awake with no hope. They have mentally accepted this life of misery until death. Some of these beggars are couples with children, who are also consigned to a lifetime of destitution.

These beggars are the totally forgotten and saddest portrayals of our apathetic and degenerate society. They live and die on the road. No government cares for their lot, because they have no ballot value — is this not shameful? This is the tragedy of the so-called democratic (capitalism-supportive) system of political governance, in which on the one hand some people die of obesity-related diseases while others die of starvation. The beggars constitute the most neglected and forgotten Fourth World community, so much so that no one (certainly not any politician) even mentions them or even recognizes their existence. However, they constitute a big segment of the Third World population, especially in India. So to ignore them is immoral!

It is verily the moral duty of the local governments and the community inhabitants to bring the socially discriminated people into the main stream of community living, and to rehabilitate their beggar brethren, to also bring them into their fold, and transform them into functional members of the community. In this regard, the cooperatives system can very well cater to this task, because the cooperative members could decide to share the initial financial burden of involving these Fourth World people into their work and living cooperatives.

To start with, they need to be accommodated in specially arranged "homes-for-destitutes" (HFDs), wherein their primary living needs can be taken care of. In these HFDs, there would be cooperative living. In the next stage, to enable them to live in dignity, they could even be engaged in some cooperative works, as per their aptitude. They would also need to be included in the community healthcare delivery scheme, and thereby be entitled to socialized healthcare coverage. This entire project of rehabilitation of the destitutes would belong to the category of "social services and security", and would constitute a legislative (or policy-making) department of the local FSC government. In the third stage, they could be employed by the cooperatives, and thereby start living as regular members of the community.

2.7 Neo Socio-economic-political order

The 20th post-colonial era of the century has witnessed the domination of exploitative development systems of capitalism and communism, which are based on subordinated-cooperation and tyrannical-regimentation, respectively. Under so-called capitalistic-democracy, the corrupt and self-serving politicians have let their people down. We can also include the apartheid regimes in the capitalism category, because they were recognized and legitimized by democracy-trumpeting capitalist countries. As regards, communist regimes (such as of Russia and China), they were so ruthless that they ordered genocides of their own people in the guise of ideological cleansing. It is indeed difficult to understand the terror in which their people lived.

It is no wonder that these exploitative economic systems have failed to develop Third World countries to be independent and self-reliant. In fact, to date, no developing country (say, in Africa, Asia or South America) has successfully eradicated poverty, and made the transition to a developed country by employing communist or capitalistic economic model. Third World development can however be brought about by a new socio-economic-political order, based on the foundations of neo-humanism and grassroots socio-economic democracy (whose grass-roots base is a functionally-sustainable community).

Neo-humanism raises ones' consciousness above narrow geo and socio sentiments. Neo-humanism recognizes that the destinies, progress and economies of both north and south regions of the world are inter-linked. Neo-humanism can inspire developed countries to abdicate the time-honored policy of exploitative development and to facilitate (knowledge-based economy) development of Third World countries. On the other hand, socio-economic democracy (based on the concepts of collective capitalism and optimal utilization of physical, intellectual and even spiritual resources), adopted within functionally-sustainable communities (FSCs), can cater to local interests and needs by fostering local development of people's resource and enterprises, to provide for community services and improved living standards.

The problems of developing countries are multi-dimensional. On the one hand, one needs to provide decent living facilities in villages, by cultivating and harnessing the local resources. On the other hand, the urban centers urgently need proper planning for coping with the overloading of their basic services. So, in order to address the needs of both urban and rural communities, the key factor is decentralized development and local management of local resources and industries, so as to support the services sector of the community and also sustain its small business sector. This, in turn, can help to provide employment of the local inhabitants in the resource development sector, community services sector, the small business sector as well as the governance sector.

In the following sections, we will discuss neo-capitalism and neo-democracy of the neo socio-economic, for the upliftment of developing countries.

2.8 Collective capitalism and Socio-economic democracy

At the grassroots level (of FSCs), involvement of the people in economic development (and in sharing of economic benefits) can come about by the formation of producers', distributors' and consumers' cooperatives, as well as professional group-practice corporations (as for instance of lawyers, doctors and engineers). When this cooperation (within cooperatives and group-practice corporations) involves equal rights for the participating members, equal *locus standi*, mutual respect for one another and catering to mutual welfare, it results in coordinated cooperation of (what we term as) collective capitalism or CCP.

Both the communist (commune) system and the capitalist system involve subjugative cooperation and not the coordinated cooperation concept. The cooperatives system (of collective capitalism) will empower local people to develop local resources and materials, as well as local industries based on these materials. The cooperatives system would be able to respond to market needs as well as adjust to economic downturn without retrenchment. Cooperatives will not only address the work setup, but also the living setup in terms of community services (especially in rural areas): water-supply and stimulation, electrical power, primary healthcare and education.

Today, many neo-technological (particularly software) companies are providing shares to their employees, and thereby making them participants in company growth and profit-sharing. However, our cooperative system will involve cooperation in all aspects of community living, from education and healthcare to business and even community governance. The cooperative system will involve synergistic cooperation, in thc spirit of all for one and one for all. This will address the issue of unemployment, as well as motivate the people to work for and contribute to society to the best of their abilities. The cooperative system of societal organization and governance will usher in a new era of human rights, security, peace and prosperity.

Once, collective capitalism has been established, then its institutions (namely the associations of cooperatives representing all the sectors of the FSC) can elect their governance representatives, to constitute a civilian professional governance (CPG) system. Thus, collective capitalism (CCP) acknowledges and effectively utilizes social, knowledge and financial capitals. The CPG system entails governance by most competent elected representatives of CCP. Together, this economic-political system of CCP and CPG constitute socio-economic democracy.

2.9 Optimal utilization of resources within self-reliant communities

Socio-economic democracy (SED) entails people-participatory economic development in the form of grassroots community organizations (cooperatives, professional associations and community agencies), and these organizations electing their representatives to local governance. Socio-economic democracy promotes local self-development and self-reliance. It is our advocated avenue for Third World development (in preference to inviting multinationals to set up their businesses), so as to provide local people's employment and a decent living standard. Local self-development (through, if necessary, training of local inhabitants by outside experts) can help to culture indigenous capabilities and skills, innovation and enterprise. On the other hand, inviting foreign businesses to set up establishments may constitute a short term quick development formula. However, it results in technological dependency, crippling of local innovation and economic neo-colonization.

Hence, the preferred advocated modality of poverty alleviation and uplifting the living standards of the (rural) masses of developing countries is to design and establish functionally-sustainable communities, wherein one segment of the population is cooperatively engaged in agriculture and farming and/or natural-resource development (such as mining and/or agro industry), so as to bring revenue into the community with which to (i) support a second segment of the population that is engaged in governance infractructure and in providing community services (water supply and sanitation, roads and public transport, electrical power from renewable energy sources, primary healthcare and education), and (ii) sustain a third segment of the population that is engaged in small scale enterprises.

The concepts of neohumanism-promoting system of optimal and democratic utilization of land and industrial resources as well as of intellectual and supra-intellectual potentialities for the progressive development of society are embodied in the Progressive Utilization (Economic) Theory.* Further, in this framework, the natural resource industry would be organized as public utilities, medium scale

**Proutist Economics: Discourses on Economic Liberation*, by Prabhat Ranjan Sarkar (ISBN 81-7252-003-4, Ananda Marga Publications, EM Bypass, Tiljala, Calcutta-39, 1992).

industries and businesses as cooperatives, while small scale enterprises could be privately owned.

In the cooperatives system, it can be possible to provide near-full employment as well as a guaranteed minimum income (adequate to fulfill the minimal living requirements), as a constitutional requirement. Further, our objective would be to ensure adequate and (ever-increasing) purchasing capacity to satisfy all basic living needs (food and shelter, healthcare and education, water and sanitation, electrical power and public transport), as well as afford amenities for liberation from physical drudgery, and utilize one's potentialities for a development of higher faculties and a progressive society.

The distressed and oppressed humanity has been awaiting the crimson hues of the dawn of neo-humanism,

to dispel the darkness of narrow sentimentalism and dogma,

for all human beings to have enlightened living,

to experience mind transcendence, so as to obtain relief from its afflictions,

So that humanity can move on and on in its journey beyond relativism!

Two starving boys cling to each other outside a feeding center (9 August 2003) in the village of Acumcum, in the Bahr El Ghazal Province of southern Sudan. Many children were abandoned, as their parents went in search of food for themselves, when the province was hit by a devastating famine.

It is a disgrace to our present-day civilization and to the UN that these human disasters are allowed. The problems of Third World countries are totally different from the issues occupying the attention of G-8 countries. The Third World countries need to realize that they themselves will have to address their problems by forming self-reliant regional blocs, to invoke a regional cooperative approach (involving aid plus technological capacity building) to the problems facing the communities within each bloc. We can only say that we are civilized when we concern ourselves with one another's problems. Our World people-centric (instead of nation-centric) government will not allow such disasters in any part of the world.

3

Functionally-Sustainable Communities: Socio-economic-political Framework

3.1 Etiology of under-development

The Third World involves a legacy of colonization and exploitation, along with one or more of: suppression of people's potentialities, persecution of minority communities, apathy and neglect on the part of its own political leaders. Even after the end of political colonial empires, economic colonization continues to be perpetrated. On the other hand, cultural, ethnic and religious persecutions continue unabated in many developing countries.

The present global economic order is characterized by: (1) the developed countries of the world taking advantage of cheap natural resources and labor of third world countries, (2) professionals from developing countries migrating to developed countries for better work and living prospects, (3) multinationals fostering local industrial development, while being unwilling to support local technological incubation and training so as to continue dependency, (4) fictitious market boom creation and over-investment, leading to industrial and economic collapse, (5) as a result of all of which the gap in living standards between the developed and developing countries keeps widening.

The subordinative and regimentative socio-economic systems of capitalism and communism have failed to develop Third World countries to be independent and self-reliant. Additionally, the present social order is equally unfair and unjust, with certain religious and cultural communities (depending on the majority religion and culture in the nation) being either (1) psychologically, politically and economically marginalized, or (2) discriminated from having fair and just access to education, employment and healthcare, or (3) prevented from following and performing their religious beliefs and practices.

3.2 Background and development strategy

Scenario of urban and rural communities: Rural undevelopment, urban-to-rural population migration, and urban degradation have resulted in a multitude of problems for all the categories of Third World communities. The most serious problems are abject levels of poverty, joblessness and total absence of basic services to the community, namely housing, education, transportation, garbage disposal and sanitation, and healthcare.

Difficulty for a developing country to be self-reliant on its own: Individually, it is difficult for any developing (South Asian or African) country and any Third World community to raise its socio-economic level and provide (i) dignified living standards (of food, housing, healthcare and education), and (ii) freedom of cultural and religious practices for its inhabitants through natural resource, agricultural and industrial development.

For a developing country or a marginalized third world community to come up, it is not wise to merely open itself up to outside investors, for creating employment and industrial infrastructure development. This approach tends to cripple indigenous initiatives and industrial development, and to in fact promote exploitative development. Rather, the development and economy should be grassroots-based, involving growth of local enterprises (and economy) using local resources in a climate. This approach fosters local initiatives and industriousness for collective welfare. For this purpose, it might be necessary for a developing community to obtain loans from even international banks, and utilize it to invite experts to culture indigenous development, rather than allow its industrial and economic development sector to be totally taken over by foreign companies.

The same principles of development apply for the economic development of culturally suppressed communities. However, these communities additionally need protection from suppression and persecution, by being given autonomous status and hence unbarred freedom (1) for following their cultural practices, (2) of political governance autonomy, and (3) to develop industrially and economically.

The defining characteristics of a sustainable and regionally-developed economy are: (1) decentralized economy involving local planning and development by local people; (2) maximum utilization of all local material and human resources; (3) balanced development of all sectors of the economy; (4) equitable distribution of wealth, by organizing all the work sectors into cooperatives; (5) ecological, economic and homeostatic sustainable development; (6) use of appropriate cost-effective technology; (7) export of mostly manufactured goods, with minimal export of raw materials; and (8) constant endeavour to increase effective purchasing capacity of the people.

Then, to develop a self-reliant economy of a developing region (made up of a number of self-reliant communities) and promote uniform living standards within the region (while countering exploitative development), it is necessary to foster cooperation among its functionally-sustainable communities (FSCs) by weaving them into self-reliant economic blocs, zones and federations. Hence, on the basis of neo-humanism, we are advocating cooperation within FSCs and among the

FSCs of socio-economic blocs (SEBs) and self-reliant economic zones (SEZs). The concept of progressive (natural and industrial) utilization of human resources (PROUT) can be implemented by means of this coordinated cooperation among the members of a community as well as between communities, and eventually even between the North and South regions of the world, as the basis of a new world socio-economic order.

3.3 Functionally-sustainable communities

In the Preface itself, we introduced a broader categorization of Third World, to include both industrially under-developed and economically lagging nations as well as culturally and psychologically (and hence) socio-economically suppressed communities. What we have endeavored to convey, herein, is that these Third World communities and nations had been bled by political colonization. Later, some nations have continued to be economically exploited in the framework of international capitalism (by multinational corporations), while other nations were stifled and stagnated by repressive communist regions. Even within nations, some ethnic minorities have been neglected, discriminated and suppressed. This civilian suppression by repressive ruling regimes is not just a feature of the past few decades. The history of past and even present-day human civilizations is in fact characterized by:

- gross abuse and terrorization of the civilian populations by the ruling regimes;
- gross and abashed abrogation of human rights;
- ethnic conflicts and persecutions;
- struggles for independence and autonomous governance;
- bleeding of wealth from communities by their colonial rulers as well as by their own political leaders after independence of the colonies;
- continuing endeavor of economic exploitation of poor and under-developed countries, most recently in the form of globalization, involving exploitation of cheap labor and pulverization of indigenous trades.

One aspect of Third World development involves fulfillment at the grassroots rural level of making available and providing access to: food and drinking water, transport facilities and environmental hygiene, primary healthcare and education, purchasing capacity for the minimal necessities of life, and basic amenities to lead a healthy and fulfilling life for development of one's physical and intellectual potentials as well as aesthetic and psychic potentialities. This grassroots development cannot be achieved and sustained by (if necessary) inviting outside (or foreign or multinational corporations) investment and enterprise, in order to provide employment for and thereby increase of the living standards of local people. This is because the level of literacy and education, social awareness and technological capabilities of the rural local people is not at a level that can be made use of by the multinational corporations.

Herein, the term "third world" refers to developing countries that have a low standard of living. It also includes people who have been marginalized and/or functioning in the subjugative-cooperation system of capitalism or the autocratic system of communism as well as communities that have been culturally and politically suppressed. In general, people should not be working for the benefit of their supervisors and owners; the concept of a "job," to which a person is harnessed, is indeed a primitive and uninspiring concept. Nor can people live and progress intellectually, as well as psychically and economically, when their culture, thinking and psychology are suppressed. In an enlightened society, everyone should be able to have the satisfaction of being able to utilize their potentials for the maximal benefit of the community. This kind of fulfillment can be had through (i) our socio-economic democratic system of organizing the community in the form cooperatives, and (ii) of civilian professional governance by the most competent representatives of these cooperatives.

The solution to this externalized and internalized crippling of people's potentialities is grassroots and decentralized community-centred sustainable development, by forming functionally-sustainable communities (FSCs), interacting to form economically self-reliant blocs. Within each FSC, the organization of the society would be in the form of work and living cooperatives, to (i) jointly manage land and water resources, (ii) provide food and social security, healthcare and educational amenities, and (iii) provide diverse livelihood opportunities (to satisfy cooperatively the diverse potentialities of people) through sustainable micro-enterprises and professional services (e.g. medical, legal, educational, etc.). Further, the governance of all the community functional sectors would be in the hands of well-qualified community representatives (of sectorial cooperatives, professional associations and agencies as well as people councils), thereby eliminating malevolent governance by political parties, mismanagement of community resources (by political parties) through incompetency and corruption, and seeding of sentimental prejudices of political parties among the people.

The primary need is for welfare economics, in order to cater to the economic upliftment of the deprived and depraved masses. However, welfare economics is not just about satisfaction of physical needs. Herein, we are providing a new dimension to welfare economics, to also include psycho-economics (to promote peoples' psychic potentialities) as well as a neo-humanistic outlook (to be liberated from narrow and parochial divisive sentimentality). It is the neo-humanistic outlook that can provide the incentive for coordinated cooperation among people of different castes as well as ethnic and social backgrounds, and eventually form the basis of North-South cooperation towards genuine or democratic globalization, accommodating the collective needs of both developed and developing nations.

3.4 FSC development through local empowerment

We need to firstly delineate the geographical jurisdiction of an FSC. In a rural region, when we find villages and townships struggling on their own to provide the basic community services to the inhabitants, it is prudent to coalesce several villages and townships surrounding an urban center into an FSC. Alternately, we can "rehabilitate" a marginalized community by making it into an FSC, to enable their people to model their own future while living freely without restraints and/or psychological impediments.

The governing principle of a functionally sustainable community is not that the community can survive by itself without any interaction with the surrounding communities. Rather, it is required that the coalesced micro-communities of an FSC can collectively cater to their inhabitants' living needs of: food and provisions, and capacity building of human resources for operating community services (maintaining housing colonies, water-supply and sanitation, roads and public transport, healthcare delivery and education).

We are primarily emphasizing that, collectively, the communities need to at least have: (1) the human resources for agriculture and/or cottage industries and/or basic small scale manufacturing, (2) adequate skilled population to work in community services as delineated above, and (3) some professionals, e.g. doctors, engineers, lawyers, educators and bankers. Thus, if there is this reasonable diversity of requisite human resources, their combined acumen and skills will be able to organize the combined communities into an FSC. Within such an FSC, the revenue generated from the export of products can be utilized to (i) build healthcare and educational centers, water-supply and sanitary plants, electrical power plants, etc., as well as (ii) import other necessities such as pharmaceuticals.

In most developing regions, the problem at hand is two-fold. On the one hand, one needs to provide decent living facilities in the rural areas, by cultivating and harnessing the local resources. On the other hand, the urban centers urgently need proper planning for coping with the demand for basic services. What is needed is designing, planning and administering the various interactive and mutually-influencing sectors of the community, namely revenue generation sector, services-providing sector and small business. We have termed this discipline as Community-development Engineering (CDE), entailing:

- providing training to the local inhabitants in resource development, trade and commerce, community services and small business; and
- econometric analysis of the above three sectors, such that the revenue generated from selling products outside the community can be employed to support and sustain community services and small businesses.

An illustrative example of FSC design is provided later on in Chapter 5.

3.5 Community development through cooperatives

For Third World nations, indigenous industrialization could be a slow process for uplifting the living standards. Hence, inviting multinationals to set up their businesses could provide a quicker route to provide employment and a decent living standard. However, there needs to be an agreement with MNCs to technologize the local universities' laboratories, so as to develop indigenous capabilities and skills, innovation and enterprise. In the long run, inviting foreign businesses to set up establishments could result in technological dependency, crippling of local innovation and economic neo-colonization. Hence, an arrangement for gradual technology-transfer also needs to be put in place.

Multinational companies can only set up their operations in the urban centers of developing countries, where (because of the presence of tertiary-educational institutions and colleges of technology) there is availability of technologically skilled human resources. Nevertheless, in rural areas with undeveloped resources and human potential, the way to develop means of livelihood for all and to rescue people from poverty is by establishing cooperatives in farming, manufacturing, product distribution and community services. Cooperatives would apply for loans from cooperatives' banks, to get started and bring to bear better amenities and modern methods of farming and production, which would have been out of reach of individual members. Cooperatives will provide shares to employee members, and even provide short term loans to them, to facilitate productivity and to help tide over financial difficulties. Producer and purchaser cooperatives will work coordinatedly, to ensure economic stability and employment security even in times of economic downturn.

Cooperatives involve people working together, sharing working and living functions and roles. In this way, they can enhance their work renumeration, eliminate owner profit, and promote more cost-effective living through elimination of extra paid labor. We can have cooperatives in all sectors of community function. For instance, farm-labor cooperatives can help to command better wages for the farm laborers and also provide better quality of life in terms of housing, healthcare and children's education. Ideally and in time, it is hoped that the farmers and their laborers can constitute one common agricultural cooperative.

Municipal services (of water-supply and sanitation, sewage disposal and environmental protection, roads development and public transport) can also be organized as cooperative endeavors of all the people working in these services. Likewise, cooperatively owned and managed primary care polyclinics can provide more cost-effective healthcare, through direct client registration and medical coverage, with payments made on a monthly or annual basis.

Cooperatively owned schools can elicit more dedication on the part of the teachers in return for better salaries (due to elimination of owner profit), by incorporating tutoring in the school teaching program, and thereby not requiring parents to send children to coaching classes which is the bane of the present-day education process in many developing countries in Asia.

In general, cooperatively owned and managed small and medium size enterprises can yield better salaries for employees (for both managers and work-subordinates) and better pricing for consumers. By eliminating capitalist owner's profit and incorporating employees welfare fund (for medical care, education and housing), a cooperatively owned and managed company can be more competitive relative to an owner-based company while at the same time have more dedication on the part of their employees.

3.6 Towards a stable socio-economic democracy for a progressive society

Some of the obstacles to progress of developing countries are poverty, absence of a high level of educational and professional infrastructure, high level of illiteracy, religious (non-secular) state with its constitution based on religion, religiosity and religious dogmatism, corrupt and incompetent political-party based governance system and political society, inter-ethnic and inter-religious tensions and strife, lack of opportunities for the educated and professionals to develop and fulfullingly utilize their potentialities. The key to overcoming these setbacks and background attributes is education and rationality (imbibed through neo-humanism) along with socio-economic democracy, which would enable progressive-minded people to be involved in governance!

Socio-economic democratic system can be instituted at the grassroots level through the formation of socio-economically sustainable and autonomous communities (FSCs) within and among nations. Especially in developing regions, FSCs would enable economically struggling rural villages as well as culturally suppressed (and marginalized) micro-communities to come together and form these autonomously-governed macro-communities. Now, within these functionally-sustainable macro-communities (FSCs), socio-economic democracy can be instituted by facilitating the empowerment of the local people, to participate in all the community's functions as well as in economic development and gains, by forming cooperatives in all sectors of community function. Examples of cooperatives would be work cooperatives (producers, suppliers and users) and living cooperatives (also involving schooling and clinics).

In this new socio-economic democracy setup, all business enterprises will be organized as cooperatives (such as for instance agricultural, manufacturing companies cooperatives, distributors cooperatives and even purchasers cooperatives), thereby involving the people in all aspects of economic activities and gains. The producers cooperatives will monitor and cater to the consumer cooperatives needs, and not over-produce. Also, the work cooperatives would get start-up funding from cooperative banks, and not issue public shares. In other words, people not involved with the business corporations will not be allowed to own shares and/or control the economy of the companies. There would hence be no real need for stock markets, obliviating concerns about stock market (and currency) manipulators and stock market crash. This system would safeguard the people from their hard-earned money being misappropriated.

Cooperativers of each sector will be organized into an association of that sector. The role of this association will be to provide a helping hand to the cooperatives, by providing them data on supply and demand as well as guidance on price-setting and profit expectancy. Hence, in this socio-economic democratic setup, there will be a stable economy. In this setup, it will be the corporations employees who will be the generators and hence owners of capital; this will give rise to a new system of collective capitalism. Further, all the FSCs will essentially function and also cooperate with one another globally, to function as a cooperative (self-reliant) bloc.

Within each FSC, grassroots organizations will be formed, to represent all the operational sectors of the community. For example, we would have associations of lawyers practice groups and healthcare management corporations, energy-supply and telecommunication corporations or agencies, agricultural cooperatives, and even residential cooperatives in the form of neighborhood development councils. All these grassroots organizations will elect representatives to the local legislative assembly or government. In this way, the local governance will be carried out by the people's representatives in all sectors of the community, resulting in a truly democratic governance system.

The local government will hence consist of elected representatives of, for instance, primary-healthcare system, primary-education system, industrial enterprises, village-Bank, etc. Then, all these selected, appointed government members will have the adroit credentials for their portfolios. They will be expected and able to totally concentrate on their roles and functions, without having to reckon with inter-party sledging and squabbles. These representatives will be appointed for a three-year governance-term. They will be totally responsible and accountable for their departments' performance. Their re-election on the governanc board will be based on their performance. This system of governance will ensure that governance board members have adroit qualifications for their posts, while also being totally accountable for the performance of their departments. This new *governance system will do away with the multiple party system of make-belief democracy, money-wasting mechanisms, corrupt governance and introduce real democracy.*

3.7 People-centric governance

To run a people-centric government is surely the most difficult job in the world. Yet we have the most incompetent people in these positions, primarily because they desperately want to be in these positions and have the political clout for it. In the current democratic political set-ups, the secretaries of the various ministries administer the portfolios of their ministers, who most often have no competence or acumen in governance. However in our neo-political set-up, the governance executives (GETs) would need to have the background and competence to administer their portfolios: to comprehend issues and develop reforms and public policies, to direct the formulation of appropriate policy models for forecasting outcomes, to understand the interdependence of the various sectors of the community and their ministries, to be able to assess how public policy of each sector will impact the other sectors, to be mindful of the legal implications of their enacted policies, to coordinate with the education sector in human capacity and social capital development for their sectors, and above all to provide the most beneficial public policies for the people.

Governance executives are managers of their respective public sectors. They not only need to be specialists in their particular portfolios, but also need to have knowledge of the political economics of their sectorial ministries. In our proposed people-centered governance system, the GETs need to enact reforms and policies that reflect the voice of their community sectorial associations. At the same time, they need to closely coordinate with the GETs of other sectorial ministries to ensure that their respective policies are beneficial to all the sectors of the community. For that, they need to have an innate pulse of democracy-in-action, local and regional laws, people's rights and expectations, and a visionary concept of good governance.

In developing countries, it is important to develop a vision of where the community needs to be in the short and long terms. For instance, the 20-year goals could be employment for all, food and water for all, housing for all, healthcare for all, high school education for all, and public transport for all. These may be termed as the seven basic goals (SBGs) of a developing community. Poverty reduction and its eventual eradication constitutes a key governance mission for many developing countries. This requires formulation of a minimum living standard (MLS) in terms of the minimum requisites for living, and setting up of a minimum wage and its purchasing capacity (MW & PC). Finally, this has to be translated into governance.

3.8 Community-development politicization (CDP)

Let us say that the community comprises of the following sectors:

1. agro-industrial (revenue-generating) sector (RGS)
2. community services providing sector (CSS)
3. small-business sector (SBS)
4. education sector (EDS)
5. governance sector (GOS)
6. natural recourses industrial sector (NRS), in which the natural resources would be sold to the RGS so as to convert the natural produces into commodities.
7. law and jurisprudence sector (LJS)

Now, as per CDP, the econometrics of a functionally-sustainable community (FSC) should make it possible for the revenue generated by exporting agro-industrial products (to other FSCs as well as to other socio-economic blocs), to support the CSS and SBS as well as the governance sector (GOS). Hence the governance executives (GETS) would have to work out the budgets of their own sectors, in conjunction with the budgets of the other sectors, so as to satisfy the community-development engineering (CDE) criterion of the generated revenue being able to sustain the other sectors: CSS, SBS, EDS, GOS, NRS and LJS.

The sectors that need to closely interact with all the governance sectors are the education governance sector (EDS) and the law and jurisprudence governance sector (LJS). The EDS has the responsibility for adequately educating and training appropriate human resources to work in the various sectors. Also, the EDS has to, in conjunction with the other sectors, forecast the growth of the various sectors, and accordingly tailor the educational programs to cater to this growth. An excess number of human resources in a particular sector would lead to unemployment, whereas an inadequate number of human resources in a particular sector would prevent development of that sector. As regards the LJS, it has to coordinate with all the other governance sectors to introduce and pass legislations towards a people-centric society. This sector also needs astute political judgment and a clear vision of the human rights agenda and crimes against people (including racial discrimination).

Among the other important community service sub-sectors are those involved in urban progressiveness. Most cities of developing countries have inadequate facilities and provision for electrical power and drinking water, sanitation and sewage systems, garbage pick-up and disposal preventive and curative medical care, roads maintenance and public transport, parks and ecology maintenance. The residential and office buildings constitute big slums, and are prone to disease. Hence, a special urban municipality needs to be set up, to bring together and coordinate the various sub-sectors associated with all the urban community services sector. Hence again, the urban management econometrics requires fiscal sustainability of urban community services. In other words, tax revenues generated from the urban industrial sectors (comprising businesses and shops) need to be properly utilized to maintain the above-mentioned urban community services and slums upgrading.

Developing nations' cities have not only slums of legitimate dwellings but also of homeless dwellers residing in open spaces and on pavements; one only has to visit Mumbai, the financial capital of India, in order to comprehend this phenomenon and the political apathy associated with it. Millions of people live in terrible unhygienic conditions on the edge of streets, on pavements, in garbage dumps and alongside railway tracks, with no sanitation facilities. Only a few of these people may have jobs, some make and sell small handicrafts, while others beg for a living. To make matters worse, they often have to pay the mafia and the police to be allowed to dwell in this way. The city governments have no plans for slums improvements, while the party politicians ignore them because they are not election vote providers. So what can be done to rehabilitate them?

In order to provide semi-dignified living conditions to these homeless slum dwellers, occupational rehabilitation is the foremost requirement. The sheer number of these homeless slum dwellers who need to be employed and functionally rehabilitated necessitates the formation of a special slum eradication unit (SEU). The mammoth task of this governance unit is to coordinate with the other governance units to (i) find employment for these jobless homeless slum dwellers, (ii) construct modest dwellings with water and sanitation facilities, (iii) help develop cooperative nano communities among themselves, wherein some of them get set up, as vendors, craftsmen and school teachers, while others are engaged in physical maintenance of the communities, financial management, and so on.

Politicization Index

	Indicators (I_j)	M_{i1} (+20)	M_{i2} (+10)	$M_i = (M_{i1} - M_{i2})$
1.	Capital for government operation	Capital from taxation of industries	Capital from taxes on people	
2.	Attitude to people	Responsive to needs*	Self-serving†	
3.	Community economic system	Cooperatively structured corporations and collective capitalism	Unfair salary and economic distribution.	
4.	Electoral procedure for governance legislators	Community sector-based	Political party-based	
5.	Education	Subsidized primary to tertiary education	Self-financed university education	
6.	Healthcare	Cost-effective health care delivery	Inequitable healthcare delivery	
7.	Poverty	Increasingly smaller standard deviation in the wealth distribution of the population	Big gulf between the rich minority and poor majority, with a big standard deviation	
8.	Employment	Government involvement in employment creation	High unemployment	
9.	Public transport	Facilitating and subsidized	Limited or no public transport	
10.	Relations with neighboring countries	Positive attitude to forming a self-reliant economic bloc with its neighboring communities	History of disputes with neighboring countries	

*A more responsive government will get more marks.

†A more self-serving regime will get more marks.

$$\text{Politicization Index (PLI)} = \left(\frac{\sum_i M_1}{2} \right) \%$$

As per the above table, the indicator in each row can have marks ranging from zero to 20. Now PLI is made of ten indicators. Hence, based on the above formula, its value will range from zero to 100. An index value of 50%–70% can be considered to reflect tolerable governance, a value >75% would be considered to be good governance, while an index value < 50% would be considered to be unacceptable.

Human society may be regarded as a macro-cooperative of micro-cooperatives of all societal sectors (agro-industrial, community services, healthcare and jurisprudence, etc.),

functioning as "all for one and one for all."

For enlightened living and all-round prosperity, we need

socio-economic democracy (SED), along with its civilian professional governance (CPG) of a functionally-sustainable community (FSC).

Migrant worker's dwellings (Pune, India)

One of the reasons why the middle and upper class get to enjoy a high standard of living is because of exploitation of cheap labor. In countries that employ cheap construction labor from poor countries, the agents consume a big percentage of their salary while their construction companies are guilty of always being in two to three months arrears with their salary payments. These workers toil and live (away from their families) in pathetic conditions. However, because their own countries benefit from the foreign exchange reserves derived from the dollars repatriated by the workers to their families, their foreign-affairs ministries do not bother to discuss improvement in the working conditions of the workers with the labor ministries of the countries of their employment.

In developing countries, poor migrant workers are engaged at public construction sites. They build for themselves these shanty dwellings during the period of their employment, and move from one construction site to another. Naturally, their children cannot attend school. Infact they are deprived of most essentials of living, while the politicians authorizing these constructions live in comfort and prosperity. When the construction is completed, local politicians come to inaugurate it. However, they never enquire about the migrant workers who built this site. They just do not care for all of the poor people. This is why we need a civilian democratic governance of a functionally-sustainable community, wherein our collective-capitalistic economic system of cooperatives will not let any group be neglected.

4

Neo-global Political Governance Structure

4.1 People's dilemma and future

Today, humanity is ill. In developing countries, so many are dying of starvation and disease, and yet we never hear political leaders expressing any concern about this colossal loss of life. Once AIDS becomes an epidemic, even these non-caring politicians will not be immune to this auto-immune disease. The root cause of human misery is that incapable people have been at the helm of governance. Posing as leaders, they have hijacked and pirated their nations, and even formed international cliques to safeguard their positions. They are not bothered with the welfare of the people, except in projecting themselves as leaders.

Humanity has, thereby been rendered helpless and too depressed to even utter protest against ruthless political opportunism and deceit. People are eagerly waiting for some neo-humanistic-minded persons to embolden them to reject this political party-based democracy, to adopt collective capitalism and socio-economic democracy, and liberate them from this subjugative mode of living.

No physical structure, town or empire can survive the ravages of time. Only noble ideas and deeds done for the welfare of this planet will be remembered and cherished. So, what does humanity need: social and economic security, access to healthcare and education, an enlightened system of governance, constitutional guarantee of human rights in the broadest sense, and inspirational environment to induce mind-transcendence in order to conceive and implement noble concepts.

In this situation, humanity needs an enlightened education system, to provide:

- knowledge of nature and environment, human psychology and social framework;
- the know-how for living and earning;
- the know-how for sustainable development;
- the basis for sustained peace;
- and the means for depropentisizing the mind to making it conductive to receive lofty ideas from Consciousness.

In the world of money-oriented competitive capitalist democracy, it is important to become acquainted with the depressed psychology of the unemployed persons.

They feel so humiliated at not being able to support their families, that they often commit suicide. What is the reactive psychology of the party politicians? Most of the time, in most countries, they are non-caring, except when it comes to election time. Some of them have the gumption of asking people to learn to live with less or to get re-trained, to accept less salary and lower living standards, while they themselves continue to enjoy a plush lifestyle. We will, hence, create a separate ministry for employment in our civilian professional governance (CPG) system. Only civilian members can understand and empathize with the problems and woes of civilians. The members of the elite political-parties society have long forgotten the day-to-day problems of civilians. This is why we urgently need a civilian governance system.

It is easy for prime ministers and presidents (as well as defense ministers and secretaries) to talk tough and declare war, especially when they only have to monitor it from the cozy confines of their living rooms. If the people demand that whosoever declares war must also participate in the war and lead from the front, these virtual and cowardly paper-generals will think twice before putting their feet in their mouths. As dark clouds of war drums move inland from the stormy seas, all that the common citizens can do is to wait and accept their destiny imposed upon them by the whims of their political leaders. It is for the concerned and caring idealistic youth to recognize that they need to come forward and demand sustained peace as a human right.

The majority of people have been bounced around by and among the exploitative minorities of ruthless wealth acquisitioniers, religious dogmatics, racists and casticism propagators, corrupt and ruthless megalomaniac political leaders. So what is their future? Verily, the tortured and abused majority will need to become unified in purpose. They should form economic work cooperatives to jointly own their business. Through their societies and neighborhoods, they should own their own lands and its resources. They should form their own sustainable micro-communities and macro-communities (or blocs), for local and regional self-governance. They should enlighten themselves in cognitive science, as to prevent themselves from being deceived by religiosity propounders. Through it all, they should form the mainstream of people moving on the avenue to physical and psychic freedom, leaving behind their exploitators on this trail.

Political-science research has been stagnant. Otherwise, how can one explain the perpetuation of the same old outmoded systems of governance, recycling from monarchy to communism to capitalist democracy to theocracy. Why could not political scientists have conceived of governance systems to exhilarate people's lives. Political-economics needs to incorporate human psychology: what type of system makes people happy and progressive without being lost in hedonism, as well as forward-looking without being embedded in the struggle of survival. Political-economics should be concerned with how to live cooperatively, to satisfy one another's living needs. It should be concerned with the creation of real wealth by and for all people, in what may be termed as collective capitalism.

The sovereignty of the people, straining to proceed on the ethereal pathways to glory, cannot be suppressed indefinitely, even by the quack constructs of those pretending to be deliverers of humanity. Humanity feels jaded. It is fed up of stifling dogmas and religiosity (imposed by clerics), outmoded societal frameworks and imposed thinking. It needs a new inspiration, a soothing but sublime ideology of cooperative living and an enlightened governance structure, that can enable all people to develop their full potentialities and to have unbarred expansion of their minds to full effulgence. To this end, in this chapter, we will delineate the neo global political structure, from functionally-sustainable communities up to the world government.

4.2 Formation of functionally-sustainable communities

We are proposing that, in order to end economic colonization and especially to foster Third World development, the regions of the world be divided into functionally-sustainable communities (FSCs), to be organized and coalesced into self-reliant economic blocs (SEBs). Two or more nations or SEBs could form mutually benefiting self-reliant economic zones (SEZs), to be in turn integrated into Regional federations (RFDs), under a world government. This is based on the assertion that self-reliant local and regional development augurs best for maximal development of regional economy, culture and potentialities of the local people.

An FSC is deemed to be the basic grassroots unit of socio-economic democracy and political governance structure. How do we form FSCs, while preserving national territorialism? We have indicated, earlier, that it would be beneficial from a socio-economic viewpoint for separate "struggling" villages and townships as well as for marginalized and culturally suppressed communities to be molded into FSCs. An FSC would have its own socio-economic democratic governance setup.

It should be possible, in the framework of a neo-charter of human rights (to be developed initially as a United Nations statute and later on as a World government statute), for a sustainable community to be constituted as an FSC, in order to provide freedom of expression, religious pursuit, economic development and political governance. In the interest of human rights and dignity, such a charter should take precedence over any national regulation.

In other words, by virtue of this to-be-constituted UN charter-of-rights, no country would get away with perpetrating cultural suppression and oppression on a community, and still obstruct (the recommendations of the UN committee for) the formation of that community into an FSC, on the basis of this being an internal problem. In fact, from an economic viability consideration, it should be possible for two similarly ethnic marginalized neighboring communities of two nations to first become FSCs within their nations, and then to also come together to form an SEB.

4.3 Self-reliant economy

An SEB is to be a socio-cultural entity as well as a politico-economic unit that strives for economic independence and self-reliance in the form of balance of imports and exports. It is to be a unit of monetary management and economic planning. Within each SEB, there will be decentralized planning down to the FSC level. When each FSC develops its economic potential by increasing the people's purchasing capacity, then the entire SEB would rapidly achieve economic self-reliance. Among the FSCs belonging to an SEB, there would be free trade and sharing of resources, so as to maintain a near-uniform standard of living throughout the SEB.

Self-reliant regional development (SRD): Self-reliance means relying on regional agro-industrial productivity, social capital and initiatives to satisfy the living needs of the people. It is also implies that there is adequate regional resource capacity and diversity, so that intra-SEB trade can to a large extent sustain the FSCs. SRD enables a region to determine the course of its economic well-being, free from the external coercion. The self-reliant economics of SEBs (within an economic zone) can provide multiple economic stimulants, so that economic stability can be maintained within the region and be somewhat impervious to economic shocks from other regions of the world.

Balanced economy: Within an SEB, all the sectors of an economy (namely, agricultural, industrial and community service sections) are to be developed in balance. The excessive concentration of the workforce in any one sector of the economy will result in either (1) inadequate revenues (if the revenue generating agricultural and manufacturing sector's population is low) to support community services and sustain small business enterprises, or (2) social dissatisfaction due to inadequate community services (if this sector is poorly populated).

Industry location close to resource location: For cost-effective productivity, local industry should utilize local resources and raw materials. Further, industry should be established where resources are readily available. Maximum productivity depends upon having local industries (for converting locally available natural resources and agricultural produces into manufactured products), obviating the need for expensive packaging and transport.

Living standard: In a developing country, the living standards of the people is to be continually improved by: (1) periodic increase in salary, which is only possible through cooperatives organization of the work sectors, (2) by first increasing the production and provision of minimum necessities and thereafter by the provision of commodities, (3) preventing concentration of income, which is implicit in privately owned medium and large scale enterprises, as opposed to cooperatively organized enterprises, and (4) thereby progressively enhancing the purchasing capacity of the people.

4.4 Neo-organization of world political structure

In order to have a stable and equitable global order benefiting all nations, and especially enabling development of Third World nations, we are proposing that at the local level, we have functionally-sustainable communities. The area of jurisdiction of an FSC is dictated by geographical features and/or cultural homogeneity. Each FSC will be functionally organized into cooperatives, and democratically governed by elected experts of professional associations.

A number of FSCs can decide to form an SEB (or a nation), while like-minded nations and SEBs could form an SEZ. The size of an SEZ will again be dictated by geographical and cultural factors. Then, a number of SEZs will be brought together under a Regional federation (RFD), such as a South Asian Federation, an East African Federation, a Caribbean Federation, a Central American Federation, etc. Finally, all the RFDs will come under a world government. However, each FSC will function as an autonomous economic democracy.

Local self-reliance development is a bottom-to-top approach to Third World development. Even then, individual SRCs of a Third World region cannot hope to compete and trade on equal terms with developed countries. It is hence also necessary for local FSCs to come together under the fold of SEBs, and thereafter into SEZs, and eventually regional federations (such as South Asian Federation, West African Federation, etc.) under a world government.

This will:

- enable trade and sharing of resources among the FSCs of an SEB as well as among the self-reliant economic zones (SEZs) of a federation, so as to eliminate deficiencies and eradicate poverty within a regional federation;
- prevent manipulation by developed countries to exploit cheap labor and resources of developing countries (in the guise of globalization);
- help to locally retain skilled workers, scientists and engineers, doctors and professionals (and make it unnecessary for them to migrate from developing countries to developed countries in search of a better living standard);

- provide protection of minority nations, ensure their economic progress and self-reliance, and involve people's participation in economic development and management as well as in political governance.

At the SEZ level, we also need a constitution that will protect human rights, guarantee purchasing capacity for basic living amenities, provide social security, ensure economic democracy, provide for a party-less political democratic system wherein specialists would be elected (by the respective cooperatives and associations) to administer specific portfolios, ensure independent judiciary and local government support for education without political interference.

The grouping of SEZs into regional federations will ensure coordinated cooperation within and among SEZs, and eventually even between the North and South regions of the world, as the basis of a new world order. This new global order will, in the neo-humanistic spirit, recognize that the destinies of all the regions and peoples of the world are inter-linked. For this purpose, conducive trade, monetary and fiscal policies will have to be developed in the SEZ, in order to foster cooperation among the FSCs of a region. This includes:

- resource management, organization of industrial and government sectors, policies on pricing and incomes within an SEZ;
- trade, monetary and fiscal policies within a Self-reliant Economic zone of member SEBs;
- fostering indigenous development and local self-reliance, towards economic democracy.

4.5 Illustration of the SEB-SEZ concept

Figure 4.1 illustrates a scenario of four states: A, B, C and D. Even though each of these states have provinces, yet from socio-economic progressive considerations, it would be more viable to organize A, B, C and D into SEBs, as illustrated in Fig. 4.1.

Now, because both the States A and B have marginalized ethnic communities AP and BP (having the same culture), it would be more appropriate, from the consideration of the charter-of-human rights, for each of them to first of all be designated as FSCs. Thereafter, by virtue of their being neighbors, it would be logical for them to even form an SEZ, across the boundaries of States A and B.

Likewise, SEBs AS-1 and AS-2 could decide to form an SEZ. However, it should also be possible for SEBs CS-2, CS-3 and DS-3 to form a common SEZ, from a socio-economic benefit consideration. Likewise, SEBs BS-1, BS-2 and

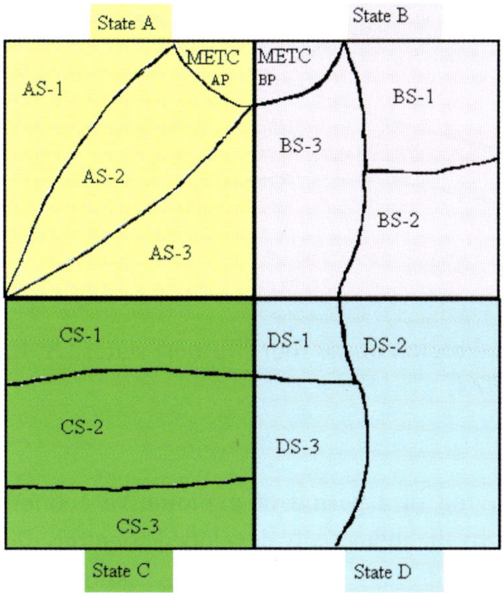

Fig. 4.1 Illustration of States A, B, C and D organized into SEBs: AS-i(s), BS-j(s), CS-k(s) and DS-l(s). Both the states A and B have marginalized ethnic communities (METCs) AP and BP, which have been culturally suppressed and are economically backward compared to other parts of A and B.

DS-2 may decide to form an inter-state SEZ. The re-organized states into SEZs (to belong to a regional federation) are illustrated in Fig. 4.2.

The re-organized communities and economic units would, then, auger for better economic as well as socio-cultural quality of life for the inhabitants of the region of the four countries.

4.6 Towards global stability

We have dealt with:

- the socio-economic principles and mechanisms as well as industrial and trade planning and policies;
- for generating local revenue for the development of community services and for sustaining small businesses;
- to foster indigenous development and local self-reliance;
- to thereby develop self-reliant economic blocs, ultimately contributing to regional federations operating under a world government.

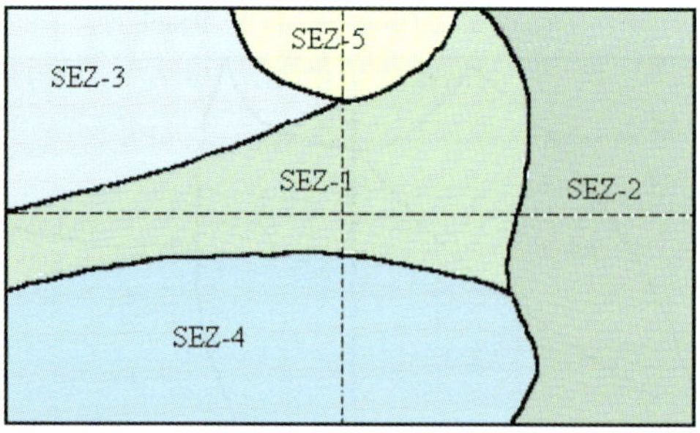

Fig. 4.2 Re-organized region of the four (former) states (A, B, C and D), showing the newly formed SEZs.

We have been living in a period of exploitative economic development of developing countries, by the industrially developed countries, through multinationals and attempted unfair trade and market schemes. Additionally, there have been unholy alliances between politicians and capitalists corporations, resulting in the demand for economic colonies. Herein, we offer a new socio-economic governance model, involving CCP and SED at the level of FSCs. The formation of economically self-reliant regions, organized as SEZs and regional federations under a world government, constitute the key to Third World development and a new global order.

4.7 Formulation of the neo-political organization and governance system

Throughout the world, democracy has been portrayed (and beleaguered) in the form of the so-called pseudo political democracy, involving people voting for political governance candidates. However, this procedure neither involves peoples' participation as partners in the socio-economic life and activities of the community (which gets centered in the hands of capitalists, corporations and politicians) nor does it make possible for truly competent people to get elected to public governance offices.

The present pseudo (political) democratic governance system is in fact a big impediment to grassroots and sustainable development, because it allows non-community and uncommitted people to run for elections and get elected as political parties' nominees for communities. These people have no roots within the community and hence no dedication to it, aside from being incompetent (their only credential being a loyal party member). It is no wonder that, in many developing countries, community problems remain unaddressed election after election. Secondly, since the governing political parties have to make the optimal use of their elected representatives, they appoint to local governmental portfolios elected members with no background in and competency to manage these portfolios.

Thirdly, because the elected candidates spend disproportionate amounts of money to get themselves elected, they look upon their term of public office as a means of not only recovering their expenses, but in fact in over-consolidating their finances so as to arrange for lifetime financial security for themselves and for their families. In fact, exploitation and bleeding of local resources and wealth by the politicians are the biggest reasons for continuing under-development in Third World countries, to the point that everyone recognizes it but feels helpless about it.

The biggest drawback of the political-party system of democracy is blind allegiance of politicians to party dictates, total involvement in party politics at the expense of societal interests, obsession of politicians with their party getting majority votes in local and regional governments, intra and inter party petty quibblings. All of this constitutes a colossal wastage of time, money and talent. In fact, in this party system of governance, it would be impossible for intelligent, competent, moral and independent thinkers (without financial assets) to enter politics.

In our socio-economic setup, FSCs would constitute the grassroots basis of socio-economic democracy. Then, the grassroots organization of an SRC would be in the form of (1) work and living cooperatives (WLCs), (2) neighborhood citizens' councils (NCCs), (3) agencies for community (municipal, postal and transport) services, and (4) professional group practice corporations (GPCs), in which there would be coordinated cooperation and economic-sharing among all the members. These WLCs, NCCs and GPCs will elect their own representatives to function as legislators and/or policy executioners (with the policies being formulated at grassroots WLC, NCC and GPC levels). The general public will then vote for one of these two representatives for the corresponding portfolio in the SRC legislature.

The legislators of all the FSCs of an SEB belonging to the common portfolio (such as education, healthcare, etc.) will, in turn, elect their representative to function as the minister-in-charge of the portfolio in the SEB government. Likewise, all the SEB ministers of each portfolio will elect their respective representative to the SEZ government. The SEZ ministers will, in turn, elect their portfolio representatives to the RFD government, whose ministers will then elect the world cabinet ministers.

The FSCs, SEBs, SEUs, RFD and the world federation will also have their respective constitutions having status promoting non-discrimination and all-round welfare and progress for all cultural communities, education and healthcare, social justice and physical and economic security. An added feature of these constitutions would be the (judicial) accountability of the elected governance legislators and ministers to their respective constituencies (WLCs and GPCs). This would auger for competency and honesty on the part of the elected governments' legislators and ministers.

4.8 Present-day lamentable societal setup versus neo societal order

It is indeed a sad commentary on the status of enlightenment and evolution of present day human beings, for:

- business to be carried out with the primary motivation of profiteering, as opposed to providing benefit for the people and earning a fair renumeration for the goods supplied and/or services rendered;
- relations between developed and under-developed populous countries being based on bussiness opportunities, instead of on the basis of a genuine desire to help upgrade the living standards of developing countries in the neo-humanistic spirit;
- people to spend their lives struggling to make ends meet, and to be engaged in de-inspiring jobs to enhance the wealth of employers, instead of their having the fulfillment of providing community services and be renumerated for it.

It is even more shameful that even today a smart minority of human beings (exploitative politicians, unethical business people, and conniving mean-minded political despots) continues to:

- cunningly exploit the majority of people engaged in labor jobs, devoid of the ability and means to find alternative means of livelihood;
- deprive the weak majority of people (in developing countries) of human rights — to dignified working conditions, to be paid in proportion to their labor intensity and skills on a par with people of developed countries, under the aegis of globalization; and
- be oblivious to the plight of the poor segments of the world population, to let alone be deprived of education and healthcare, but to not even have a roof over their heads and even a loaf of bread during the entire day.

It is out of lament for the plight of the suffering humanity that this book has been written. However, being sympathetic to their plight is not enough, and not justifiable. We in fact need to provide a new and just living modality and society, involving:

- a more enlightened system of collective living and community governance, in the form of socio-economic democracy and the system of cooperatives in all aspects of community living;
- community governance, involving the most capable people to be elected to public offices by the cooperatives and professional associations, in order to implement a dignified system of collective living and human rights;
- autonomous communities, operating in the framework of the socio-economic democratic system;
- regional federations providing the setup for free flow of commodities and human resources among their economic and zones, so as to ensure uniform living standards throughout the region;
- a benevolent world government, to ensure local, regional and global peace, dignified lifestyle, and all-round prosperity; and
- a neo-humanistic outlook, to help humanity to progress from a materialistic lifestyle to a more enlightened living as a collective family (all for one and one for all), and to advance humanity beyond the concept of so-called knowledge-based economy to the more lofty and dignified concept of supra-aesthetism.

Together, the formation of locally sustainable communities on the one hand and regional federations on the other hand constitute the key to third world development. Decentralized self-reliant economic development, neo-humanistic outlook in all the regions of the world, economic and political stability for all the regions of the world functioning under a world government, will constitute the new global order.

While sharing one another's distress, our hearts got softened.

Then, inspired by the cooperative spirit at work in nature, our minds got uplifted.

Why cannot we develop such a cooperative human society?

Slums encroachments on the banks of Bagmati river in Nepal

Squatters on polluted rivers in Jakarta (Indonesia)

When people live amid sewage-filled streams, they use the waters for bathing and washing, urinating and excreting, drinking and cooking. Those deplorable living conditions are attributed to the non-caring political society. It is only when the civilian professionals get involved in governance that we can expect more civilized living conditions for the civil society.

Let us evolve a people-centric socio-economic-political framework, involving a cooperatives-based FSC economy and civilian sector's representations in FSC governance, regional economic blocs (of cooperating FSCs) and their governance (such as the S. Asian Parliament). Let all the FSCs within each region cooperate, through free-trade and by sharing their know-how, so as to collectively raise the living standards of all the people in the region.

5 Functionally-Sustainable Community (FSC) Design

5.1 For poverty eradication and Third World development

Functionally-sustainable communities (FSCs) within a region: The keys to Third World development and poverty eradication within a developing country are: (1) urban slums transformation and provision of essential community services, and above all (2) rural development, by organizing multi-sectorial and rural FSCs, whereby the local population can obtain employment and enjoy a decent quality of life.

Regional self-reliance: The rational solution for developing countries to attain regional self-reliance, is by pooling their efforts and resources to:

- design culturally compatible FSCs, cutting across states' borders if necessary;
- cooperate in natural resources, agricultural and industrial development;
- institute cooperation in trading among FSCs, so that a regional block of FSCs has availability of natural resources, agricultural produce and industrial products required for socio-economic development; and
- through it all to attain the objectives (by the year 2010) of food, housing, healthcare and education for all — as the basic living requirement.

For this purpose, we are proposing that FSCs, in a geographically and culturally related region, come together and form a self-reliant socio-economic bloc (SEB).

5.2 Planning for self-reliant regional development

The principles of planning for self-reliant regional development are as follows.

Decentralized planning: Economic development should be decentralized, and grassroots-based. The closer a planner is to the site of planning, the more likely the plan is to succeed.

Pyramidal planning: There should be multiple levels of economic planning from community to bloc to zone levels with coordination and cooperation between levels. Small-scale industry can be set up locally, medium-size industry at the community level, with large-size industry at the bloc level.

Balanced economy: There should be balanced development of all the sectors of an economy (namely agricultural, manufacturing and community services sectors) and of both rural and urban areas. This, along with the organization of medium and large scale enterprises as cooperatives, will allow for a more even income distribution.

Development and purchasing capacity: Factors for development planning include maximizing productivity by locating local industries to utilize locally available resources, catering to the necessity for key and essential commodities, and constant endeavor to augment the purchasing capacity of people.

Development economy: Development needs to address all the components of the economy: (1) people's economy, dealing with essentials for daily living; (2) knowledge economy, involving development of intellectual capital; (3) commercial economy, involving a fair trading system, efficient movement-chain of resources and goods, through purchasing and distributing cooperatives; (4) general economy, involving bringing to bear a legislated approach to cost-effective business operations and fair-priced products, at all levels (primary, secondary and tertiary) so as to benefit both the business corporations as well as the purchasers of commodities, and thereby maximize living standards in all the population sectors of the community.

5.3 Community development engineering and SRC design

Community development engineering entails application of systems analysis and operation research methodologies to the planning and administration of both urban and rural communities. The key factor is decentralized development and management of local and regional resources, so as to support the service sectors of the community and also sustain its small business sector, to thereby bring to bear maximum benefits locally and regionally.

For this, we need to develop the concept of a functionally-sustainable community (FSC), entailing development of local resources by local population, to thereby provide employment for the local inhabitants in the resource development sector, community services (and governance) sector and the small business sector.

Functionally-sustainable community design

A community made up of a number of villages can be made functionally-sustainable with improved and near-uniform living standards/quality of life for its inhabitants, by

- delineating the various functional sectors of the community,
- forming cooperatives of people working in these community sectors, and
- designing the community sectorial population distribution, in such a way that the revenue generated by the agro-farms producers and/or factory cooperatives, by exporting/selling agricultural produce and/or small manufactured items to outside the community, can be employed to support community services as well as sustain small scale enterprises.

Let us divide the rural community (or township) population into the following three sectors:

- Revenue-generating sector, comprising of agricultural, dairy farming cooperatives and industrial cooperatives;
- Community services sector, comprising of municipal, primary healthcare and primary education cooperatives;
- Small and individual enterprises sector, comprising of provision stores, chemists, electricians, plumbers, etc.

In a functionally-sustainable comunity (FSC), the revenue generated by exporting agro products and/or manufactured items is circulated to support community services as well as to sustain small scale enterprises.

Functionally-sustainable Community (FSC) model illustration (to demonstrate how near-uniform living standards can be effected among all sectors of the population)

Let us consider three basic categories of population groups in a community:

Category A, of revenue-generating (cooperatively owned agricultural and manufacturing) sector, that generates or brings in income for the FSC (from outside the community) by exporting commodities;

Category B, of cooperatively managed community services sector, that is engaged in service work for the community residents (and is comprised of doctors, nurses, teachers and municipality employees), and is responsible for the following community services: water-supply and sanitation, electrical power and public transport, healthcare and education;

Category C, of small business sector, that operates small businesses as well some as cooperatively owned medium sized businesses.

Population distribution and money transactions basis: Consider the community population to be distributed within each of the above three categories as follows: Category A (20%), Category B (40%) and Category C (40%). Let us assume that the community population is 100. Then, the number of persons in Categories A, B and C are 20, 40 and 40, respectively. Assume, also, that an average person in each of the Categories A, B and C earns 100 monies (m) per month. We further assume that:

- the revenue-generating (manufacturing/agricultural) sector A generates 1000 monies (m) from outside the community;
- cost of community services (provided by sector B) = 40 m per person;
- cost of purchasing groceries and household commodities (from business sector C) = 50 m per person;
- the business population C buys, in bulk, items (such as food and products) from the agricultural and manufacturing sector A, of the amount of 1000 m;
- no community member pays income tax; however, each member pays 40 m for community services (including education and healthcare).

Incomes and expenditures of population categories A, B and C

Category A: The total money generated by the 20 persons of Category A is 2000 m, comprising of 1000 m from exports to neighboring communities and 1000 m from the bulk purchases made by the business sector C. The earning of each of the 20 members of Category A (revenue-generating population) is hence 100 m.

As indicated earlier, a person in any category (including Category A):

- spends 40 m out of the income of 100 m (or a total of 800 for the 20 persons in the entire Category A) for obtaining community services from population Category B;
- spends 50 m out of the income of 100 m (or a total of 1000 for the 20 persons in the entire Category A) for purchasing commodities or doing business with population Category C;

Table 5.1: Distribution of sectors' population, incomes and expenses in a model SRC (unit of money is m).

	1000 from revenue generated by exporting producers or commodities								
Category A (20 persons) or Income-generating sector	+1000 +1000	−800 (at 40 per person)	−1000 (at 50 per person)				−200 (at 10 per person)		
Category B (40 persons) or Community services sector		+800 (providing services to Cat. A)		−2000 (buying commodities from Cat. C)	+1600	±1600 (services to one another in the sector)		−400 (at 10 per person)	
Category C (20 persons) or Income-generating sector	−1000 (bulk purchase from Cat. A)		+1000 (selling commodities to Cat. A)	+2000	−1600 (for community services from Cat. B)	±1600 (services to one another in the sector)			−400 (at 10 per person)
Savings and loans							+200	+400	+400

- gives 10 m of the income of 100 m (or a total of 200 for the entire Category A) to the savings (and unemployment) and loan fund of the SRC.

Category B: The total funding to pay the salaries of the 40 persons in Category B (or the community service sector) would come from the following sources:

- from sector A (at 40 m/person from 20 persons in Category A) = 800 m;
- from sector C (amount of 40 from each of the 40 persons) = 1600 m;
- 1600 m from one another in Category B itself (= amount 40 m × 40 persons).

Category C: All the 40 persons in Category C can likewise:

- earn a total of 1000 m from Category A, at 50 m/person from the 20 persons of Category A;
- earn a total of 2000 m from Category B, at 50 m per person from the 40 persons of Category B;
- earn 2000 m from one another in Category C (= 50 m × 40 persons);
- spend 1000 m to buy bulk purchases from Category A.

This provides population Category C with a total earning of 4000 m (or 100 m per person), out of which a total of 400 m (or 10 m per person) is given to the savings and loan fund. Table 5.1 illustrates this scenario. It is seen that:

- each person in the community would earn 100 m;
- each person would spend 40 m (i.e. 40% of the income) on community services, such as healthcare, education and municipal services;
- each person spends 50 m (or 50% of the income) on purchases from the business sector of Category C;
- every person deposits 10 m (or 10% of the income) into savings.

The total monthly input into the savings and loan fund would hence be 1000 m for 100 persons. This would be utilized to provide loans to the members of the community for starting new business or to the new unemployed persons in the community. It is seen that a uniform standard of living can be attained among the three population categories of the community, as illustrated below.

For population Category A (of 20 persons), we have total income = 2000 m, expenses = 1800 m and savings = 200 m. The income per person or for an average person in this category = 100 m and savings per person = 10 m (or 10% of income).

For population B (of 40 persons), the total income = 4000 m, expenses = 3600 m and savings = 400 m. The income for an average person in this category = 100 m and savings per person = 10 m (or 0% of income).

For population Category C (of 40 persons), the total income = 4000 m, expenses = 3600 m and savings = 400 m. The income for an average person in this category = 100 m and savings per person = 10 m (or 10% of income).

Therefore, we have been able to achieve a uniform standard of living among the three population sectors, by adroit distribution of the community population among the three sectors.

5.4 FSC implementation through collective capitalism and socio-economic democracy

Starting from grassroots, how does one develop a rural FSC? This can be done by forming agricultural cooperatives, industrial cooperatives, community-services cooperatives and consumers' cooperatives. The agro-industrial cooperatives will take loans from central or overseas banks, to start cooperatively owned and managed crops and dairy farming on the one hand, and factories to make food products on the other hand.

The community-services cooperatives will undertake to develop housing and community services (hospitals, water and sanitation, electrical power, schools and transport facilities) for community, as well as help to start cottage industries and consumers' cooperative stores, so as to help provide employment for all.

Socio-economic democracy constitutes the basis of FSC design. The concept of truly democratic form of governance naturally follows from the organization of a community functioning in the form of cooperatives. The various cooperatives (industrial, trade, business, municipal educational, healthcare, legal, and sports cooperatives), professional associations (such as teachers', doctors', lawyers' and engineers' associations), community-functional agencies and people's councils would be best able to elect their most competent representatives to the various governance offices of the community. The socio-economic democratic (SED) system of organizing all aspects of community life in the form of associations (of cooperatives and group professional practices), community functional agencies and township citizens' councils will enable only well-qualified representatives of all the sectors of the community to be elected by the general public to the legislature.

This format and electoral system will provide equilibrium and equipoise in community life and ensure genuine democracy. These elected representatives, of the various sectors of community functions and living, will naturally be well qualified to administer their respective portfolios, and will be totally accountable for their performance. This compartmentally screened and peoples participatory system of election into governance will be more efficient, economical and transparent, and replace the political party system of governance.

5.5 For local and regional development and self-reliance

Our objectives are to:

- eradicate poverty locally and regionally;
- cater to provision and availability of the basic living needs;
- uniformly raise the living standards of people, locally and regionally.

Local development and self-reliance will involve the application of community development engineering (CDE):

- for the development of rural communities (entailing development of local resources and industries, to support community services and sustain small businesses within the community) and for urban re-development (involving provision of adequate community services of housing, healthcare, electrical power and transportation);
- for revenue generation (by means of natural resources and agricultural as well as industrial development in rural macro-communities, and trade development in urban slum populations), to support community services (education and healthcare, civic and municipal) and sustain small business enterprises.

Regional development and self-reliance will require the coming together of the nations of a region into the fold of a federation (such as the South Asian Federation) by developing the constitution of the regional federation, to deal with inter-nation (and/or inter-community) collaboration for developments in: agriculture and food production, electrical power and water management, housing and transportation, education and healthcare, industry and trader (outside the region) such a cooperation would help to provide a uniform and high standard of living for the people within the federation.

5.6 Educational program

This model can be implemented as a multi-disciplinary Ph.D program in Community-development engineering (CDE) for functionally-sustainable community development, to help improve the quality of life of rural (and urban slum communities) in developing countries. For this purpose, communities of about 5000 to 10,000 people will be delineated. In each community, the population distributions among the various sectors will be designed (as per the SRC concept) to be:

- 30–40% in the revenue-generating population sector, involved in (for example) agriculture and animal husbandry or pisciculture and floriculture in a rural community, and small scale trades (such as carpentry and shoe-making) for an urban slum community, etc.;
- 30–40% in the community services population sector, involved in civic, educational and health services; and
- 40–30% small business population sector, to be involved in house-building, plumbing and electrical services, banking, legal services, operating shops (or provision stores) and restaurants.

To make the community functionally sustainable, the doctoral students will provide training to these three sectors of the population in:

- trades and commerce (in an urban slum community), high-intensity agriculture and agro-industrial development in a rural community, to generate income;
- community services, to develop and operate municipal services and clinics, road-building and transportation, electrical power and waste disposal systems, schools (including adult education and literacy enhancement) and primary healthcare centers; and
- small-business operation (including finance and marketing).

Additionally, education and training will be imparted in governance, wherein special attention will be given to women's involvement in governance. Specifically, programs will be set up for providing education and training in:

- banking, accounting and trade;
- setting up and operating a local cooperative bank;
- setting up municipal services: electrical supply, water supply and sanitation and waste disposal systems;
- primary healthcare;
- road-building and public transport;
- primary education (including development of curriculum appropriate to rural community functions and environments, and also taking into account women's issues);
- running shops and small businesses.

Essentially, the doctoral students would carry out sustainable econometric analyses and infrastructural development, through the above-mentioned training programs, so as to leave behind a self-sustaining community managed by the residents, at the end of three to four years of doctoral studies.

The Master's degree CDE program curriculum will involve courses in:

- systems engineering organization of community functions, population sectors and their interactive roles;
- econometric analysis and operations research;
- municipal services (renewable energy-based electrical power, drinking and irrigation water, sanitation and sewage treatment, education and healthcare);
- eco-sustainable agricultural development (soil and water, crop and pest, energy and electrical power, production and consumer management);
- small business development and management;
- adult education and literacy enhancement systems (education through folklore, folk songs and drama — training to serve as information disseminators, teachers and health workers);
- women's empowerment (women's role-based school education and involvement in community functions and administration);
- systems analysis of resource development (or revenue generation) sector, community services sector and small business sector;
- econometric analysis of community sectors, so as to determine resource allocation and distribution, and optimize the quality of life.

The above courses will also entail case studies concerning the transformation of urban slums and impoverished rural communities into sustainable communities. Diploma programs could also be offered to train governmental and non-governmental functionaries in the planning and management of community development programs, such as urban slums management and provision of rural community services.

As part of its mandate, the Community development education program can adopt specific communities and help to transform them into model communities by the application of community development engineering. This know-how and experience would then be applied to obtain governmental support to help set up productive FSCs on a large scale, within developing countries. The University sector will coordinate its planning and design, education/training and implementation activities with the Governmental sector, to effect meaningful rural development and urban transformation.

5.7 Societal impact

Community development engineering (CDE) can constitute a scientific approach to poverty eradication, through development of local resources by the local people of communities, to in turn support employment for local inhabitants in the service (for educational, health and utilities and civic services) and small business sectors of the communities. CDE also involves environmental transformation and management, through its community services sector, entailing public health, environmental protection, forest preservation, water and soil management, pollution-free energy, agricultural intensification and diversification as well as producers and consumers management.

Implicit in CDE are education programs for rural women (in developing countries), including adult education and training to enable women to contribute more fulfillingly to their family and community. This program is equally relevant and applicable to both urban and rural communities in both developing and developed countries. Community development engineering is indispensable for those aspiring to work in city and rural planning and administration, as municipal commissioners and government officers. Through it all, it constitutes a solution to Third World development.

Even 50 years after independence, many developing countries are unable to provide, to all its citizens, even basic living necessities (of housing and sanitation, food and drinking water, healthcare and education), particularly to their rural populations. Vast rural areas remain undeveloped due to want of micro-planning. How long can we afford to wait? Even neo-developed countries, that were able to rapidly improve their living standards by full-scale multinational corporatism, are now struggling with a depressed economy and rising unemployment, as a result of migration of the MNCs to cheaper labor-providing countries. In this situation, the CDE program offers the means of developing local indigenous small-scale services-oriented industry, as a solution to unemployment.

Community development engineering can be an innovative program, aimed at developing rural areas (and urban slums) into FSCs. The natural resource, agriculture and industry development, generated by community development engineering can provide the basis for transformation of developing countries. The faculty members and the doctoral students will constitute the task force for rural planning, development and administration. The graduate students will be trained to be the future community planners and governance administrators.

Human beings certainly want happiness,

but they want peace of mind even more.

They want to be able to enjoy the pleasures of nature,

to feel the cool breeze that carries the sweet fragrance of flowering trees.

They do not want to have to keep struggling in their physical plane of living.

They want to go beyond even the psychic plane, to the intuitional plane.

Then, satisfied with their living, they can turn their gaze to the starlit sky and dream,

and live with that pole star emblazoned in their minds.

Their minds will then be infused with noble ideas,

which will make this world an enchanting place to live in.

Human beings will then move into a new dimension of enlightened living.

A school in a slum (in Tilak Nagar, Mysore, India)

Slum children taking exams in the school

Slums behind the school

Ignored by the politicians, the children of the slums are able to get schooling due to the benevolence of the Hilal Welfare Trust. Because more than 40% of Indian adults are still illiterate, it enables illiterate and incompetent (as well as corrupt) politicians to get elected and become ministers. Public spending goals on education, healthcare, sustainable rural development, water-supply and sanitation, electrical power, and infrastructure for agro-industrial development are only political gimmicks.

This situation is compounded by the shunning of politics on the part of the intelligent and honest-minded persons. This is because of the flaws in the current democratic process of governance, in which political parties with no dedication to the community and people's welfare get themselves elected to govern the community. However, our community sector-based electoral and governance system can encourage the young educated concerned citizens and non-resident Indians to obtain professional fulfillment in governance and politicization. This is because in our socio-economic democratic system, all the functional and professional sectors of the community will be directly involved in the governance of the community.

Section II

From Corporatism to Cooperatism, and Power-Politics to Peace-Politics

6

For an Enlightened Human Society

6.1 Progressive human society

The quality of life of a human being is to a large extent fashioned by the society, while society is itself a synergistic collection of human beings. What is implied then is that human beings influence one another. How then can this influence be positive or progressive? This is a fundamental enquiry, which will take us through a panoramic survey of human society, of the different sectors of the society, of how these sectors provide creative and/or fulfilling expressions for its people, and thereby enrich human life.

What is human society? When ancient human beings started to realize that it is in the interests of their self-preservation and welfare to come together, human society started with these first expressions of comradery. Since that auspicious moment, while society has developed considerably in complexity, has it been evolving towards the macrocosm and thereby progressing? In its evolutionary journey, there have been eras when segments of human society in different parts of the world have been very progressive, through their cultural and aesthetic, philosophical and artistic, scientific and engineering expressions. These eras are recorded in history as golden epochs of human civilizations. Unfortunately, these golden epochs have been interspaced by dark periods in which human beings seemed to regress from the ideals of collectivism that made them come together and start to live as members of a community.

Among the human expressions that we consider having a soothing influence (based on our own day to day experience and interactions in society) are kindness and benevolence. Some human beings may have considerable objective knowledge (scientific and/or technical), and their endeavors indirectly help society by making the environment more comfortable for living. Other human beings may be artistic, and may have the capacity to uplift human minds through their works. However, only those aesthetically or intellectually (or even spiritually) endowed persons can benefit society, who have a benevolent nature and extend a helping hand to others to develop and progress, and thereby foster the all-round development of the community. This then brings us to the intrinsic concept of a society: where there is a bigger proportion of such benevolent and enlightened individuals to inspire society members to progress towards their cosmic desideratum, therein only exists the possibility of evolution of a society.

In the days of yore, scholarly and spiritually oriented individuals often inspired young people to study under them as residential scholars. As society developed in complexity, the endeavors of such progressive individuals ranged from philosophy and history, to art and literature, to agriculture and ecology, to sociology and law, to mathematics and physical sciences, to engineering and medicine, to astronomy and cosmology. Then, there evolved the concept of a university, as a place where young scholarly aspirants could study subjects pertaining to the universe as well as for their self-realization, under such enlightened individuals.

The happiness of the members of a society depends upon their being able to develop and express themselves intellectually and/or athletically, scientifically and/or technologically, artistically and/or aesthetically, while being able to have (or afford) the essentials of living: food, clothing, shelter, education, healthcare and chore-reducing amenities. In a progressive phase of a society, people have scope to not only develop intellectually and aesthetically but also supra-aesthetically to nobler realms. The inspirators or at least facilitators of this progress are those enlightened beings who can lift human minds to nobler thinking and endeavors, as well as those in charge of governance who facilitate such a progressive mode of living by enacting favorable public policies. Hereby, we are setting the stage for what makes the society to be evolutionary, for an enlightened societal socio-economic framework, as a template for sustainable peace.

6.2 Collective psychology

Today, human society is in doldrums. It is fragmented by narrow and fissiparous geo-socio sentiments, which result in conflicts between social groups and nations. Materialistic socio-economic theories, inimical to human beings' innate tendency, have caused North and South polarization. Hunger, starvation and auto-immune diseases stalk many Third World countries. Ethnic minority communities have often been persecuted and their cultures suppressed. Religious dogmatism and misinterpreted tenets have led to misguided actions on innocent victims. Behind all this ferment is not only malgovernance but the psychology of benefit-to-self on the part of the self-serving political leaders. Indeed, human society needs to be rescued from this quagmire.

Two types of scenarios exist in the world today. In the countries of the "South", people are struggling to make ends meet and to acquire the basic necessities of life. In the "North", micro-psychic longings for mundane assets have caused psychic diseases, due to the lack of a synthetic philosophy of life. Unfortunately, both the North as well as South countries are under the governing influence of materialistic socio-economic theories, which have failed to solve both the problems of physical destitution and psychic diseases.

"Quo Vadis" is the primary and universal query of human beings. For society to facilitate the journey of one and all to nobler realms, an appropriate collective psychology is needed. This requires, in addition to philosophy, a proper social outlook and an eclectic environment encouraging heightened human expression in all realms of human thought and endeavor.

Human psychology is under the influence of human psycho-physical longings. Generally, human longings are for objects (in one's environment) related to day-to-day living. The impetus for mundane psycho-physical longings (projected as psychic pabula) constitutes the basis of present-day materialistic socio-economic outlook. Since the resources of mundane psycho-physical longings are finite, and since some persons are more skilful in exploiting circumstances, this in turn causes exploitation of some people, some communities and some nations by others.

The perpetration of economic opportunism by one nation on another resulting from misdirected psychology, has often led to cultural imposition as well as suppression of indigenous languages and arts, which has in turn created the psychology of inferiority complex among those who are culturally suppressed. This inferiority complex is difficult to overcome, and results in continued technological and industrial dependence on those very perpetrators of cultural suppression and economic exploitation.

In order to prevent such deleterious complexes, individual psychology must imbibe the realization that the global human society is one and indivisible, that different cultures are but different flowers woven into the garland of the universal human society, that the fortunes and destinies of all persons and all communities and all cultures are interlinked. At the same time, the collective economic psychology needs to cultivate the means by which physical assets are more justly distributed, while the political psychology needs to help facilitate this distributive justice. In this environment, human beings will have the scope for higher aesthetic expressions, which will in turn enhance human civilization.

The collective psychology will hence be for human beings of all social groups and regions to assist one another, so as not to be handicapped by the lack of basic necessities (food, clothing, shelter, healthcare and education), and to develop an eclectic societal framework for individual advancement and collective social progress. From this collective psychology is derived the (regional and global) role of socio-economics to ensure that everyone has the scope to contribute maximally to the society by having fulfilling tasks and employments, and that there is scope for cultivation of higher faculties and for unbarred psycho-aesthetic expression.

A decent quality of life is to be provided for citizens of all parts of the world. However, no nation and region can do it on its own, without interacting with other nations and regions. Hence (as indicated earlier), our recommendation is to form socio-economic blocs and federations, within the framework of a fairer global socio-economic order, based on the premise that the futures of all communities and regions are interwoven. However, in order to develop and maintain such a dynamically stable global socio-economic order, no small community or minority should lag behind culturally, educationally, agriculturally or industrially.

It is but natural for each community in a region to be most concerned about its own problems and welfare, and each community can best address its own socio-economic development. Hence the basis of a stable regional socio-economic order is to have autonomy in planning and governance at the micro-community level. In the interest of progress and peace, nations can effect such a local governance autonomy, in the form of self-reliant communities (FSCs). Within such FSCs, there needs to be appropriate educational and healthcare facilities and scope for fulfilling work opportunities in all fields of human thought and endeavor. Otherwise, the educated and trained youth will emigrate from that community, which will then lag behind.

Today, human society is at a crossroads. Reeling under the onslaught of misguided dogmas and religeosity as well as self-centered psychology and unjust (and even oppressive) socio-economic political systems, it lies tormented and abused, awaiting the soothing touch of benevolence and universalism. "From the mundane to the supra-mundane and the universal" constitutes the ideological journey of human advancement and evolution, prompted by the fundamental query of all human beings. Today's renaissance thinkers and public service officials thus have the sublime responsibility to orient human society on this exalted path.

6.3 Human values and law

Every society has accumulated a set of values from which it derives an ideal representation of human life. This societal culture constitutes a judicious mix of some rational views, a few social norms based on cardinal principles, religious tenets and precepts, and concepts of economic philosophy and political governance system. All of these views and concepts get woven into values, supposedly for harmonious collective living.

Human existence is both individual and collective, and so it has two sets of values: human values and social values based on religious influence and/or socio-cultural geographical setting and to some extent on cardinal principles. It may be possible, in this connection, to distinguish between social values pertaining to a given society and human values. Human values may be characterized by "dharma", which is intrinsic to human existence and distinguishes human beings from other living beings. On the other hand, social values are those values in a society that are selectively produced from life experience and the accompanying conditions. Thus, social values can be influenced by social prejudices and/or mental perversions under the influence of time, space and person. Based on mental perversions, what is virtue in one part of the world or at one point of time can be regarded as a vice in another part of the world or at another point in time.

Social values therefore remain as relative values as seen from the perspective of the total human experience, in spite of their apparent firmness and absoluteness in a society at a certain period of time. Indeed, social values in the form of concepts of virtue and vice, based on irrational and ruthless dictates and injunctions (such as stoning of women in some societies), can be the cause of tremendous exploitation and/or suffering and injustices for human beings. On the other hand, human values are more organically connected with the nature of human beings, to their evolved conscience, to the realization of their intrinsic mission of life. Human values, contribute to human evolution, and therefore transcend time and place. These human values include justice, fraternity, equality, the freedom of unbarred thinking, the attitude of developing our living modes, and even the psychology of mysticism. These values are a product of human beings' insights into human nature and interpersonal relationships, as well as its bearing on their perceived desideratum.

In that context, the fundamental human values are indeed cardinal principles, associated with progression from the intellectual to the supra-intellectual and supra-aesthetic strata of human existence, along the trail of mysticism (the quest of the microcosmic entities for macrocosmic perfection). In this progression, finer human feelings of mercy and sympathy, friendship and love manifest. The starting point of these values marks the differentiation between animality and humanity, whereas a high level of attainment of these values is associated with the confluence of evolved humanity and the blossoming of divinity. Thus, cardinal principles are those human values or principles that promote forward progression of humanity.

At this point, it is appropriate for us to introduce and define "neo-humanism", as a supra-humanistic ideology, that incorporates the most sublime human attributes, that transcends narrow socio-geo-religious sentimentality, that not only promulgates the highest expression of human rights but also respects animal rights and plant ecology, and above all inspires sustained individual and collective progress to the noblest stance. We will hence define an enlightened society to be that which incorporates neo-humanistic ideals in its collective psychology and social outlook in its public policies and governance framework as well as in its judicial and constitutional structures. Verily, it follows from this that those who are entrusted with governance responsibility should be imbibing and demonstrating these neo-humanistic ideals. These human values, based on cardinal principles, can provide the basis for the socio-economic, political governance and judicial-constitutional framework for a progressive society. It is crucial, for collective happiness, that the persons empowered to guide legislation and governance should imbibe such values. This verily constitutes a template for sustainable peace.

From a judicial consideration, that which blocks this forward progression can be deemed to be anti-social and that which facilitates it is considered to be virtuous. If what is considered to be judicially right and wrong is based on human cardinal principles, there will not be cause for variations in interpretations under the influence of time, space and person. Human relationships and judicial frameworks which promote such forward progression can be considered to be beneficial to both individual and collective existence. Thus, primary law should be based on cardinal principles to promote such beneficial relationships and minimize undesirable interactions that both individual and collective forward progression to neo-humanism.

6.4 Constitutional law

Human society goes through social cycles, in which different group psychologies dominate in turn. As a result, many social institutions are formed. The group psychology has resulted in the formation of the state, from which its members expect benefits and protection, without unwanted suppression of their psychic expressions and certain fundamental rights. Hence, it is necessary to constitute principles and rules codifying the conduct of the state, for individual and collective welfare and progress of all its citizens. For this purpose, the constitution has to fulfill certain criteria, as delineated below.

First and foremost, the total environment (namely psycho-social, economic and political environment) must be such as to enable the citizens to fully develop their potentialities and foster progress in all strata of their existence. There should hence be a judicious balance between individual freedom and collective interests, so as to prevent unjust and imbalanced distribution of benefits and opportunities for development.

In order to maintain the solidarity, peace and prosperity of the nation, no one ethnic or geographical group or state should be given privileges over others. The law of the land should treat all equally, while preserving the unity of its diverse socio-cultural groups. For this purpose, in a multi-cultural state with a mixture of ethnic and cultural traditions, it should be possible for all the residents to have equal opportunities for education and societal benefits as well as to participate in the affairs of the state. At the same time, the judicial (civil and criminal, marriage and divorce) codes must be based on cardinal principles, so as to be fair for all ethnic and religious groups.

In any state, all living beings (including animals and plants) must have rights of existence and development. Ecological balance is important for human welfare and the health of this planet. Also, all animals have both utilitarian value as well as the right to living, free from human encroachment. Hence there should be laws safeguarding the environment and the total ecology. Further, in light of human psychology and sentimentality, it is judicious to provide regional autonomy in legislative and governance affairs, while ensuring that cardinal principles are upheld. Then, based on the unifying concept of universal outlook, these autonomous states (or communities) would need to cooperate with one another to help provide the best quality of life for its residents.

Hence, each state of the nation must have the right to self-determination and the responsibility for regional economic development and administration. Each state would be required, by constitution, to be secular in social outlook, to provide for its residents requisite purchasing power to fulfill the basic living needs, opportunities for persons in all walks of life to contribute to the society, and the rights to unbarred noble expressions. An ideal constitution should provide all of its members the opportunity for elevating their human potentialities, and thereby help the society to maintain its forward evolutionary momentum.

6.5 Synergism in society

Synergy in society stands for cooperation and harmony, based on integration and balance of the expressions and attributes of the various sectors of society. Human existence is multifarious, and synergistic living entails a harmonious blend of the various spheres of existence. Thus, if in a society there is emphasis only on culture and aesthetism, and not on science and technology, the standard of living

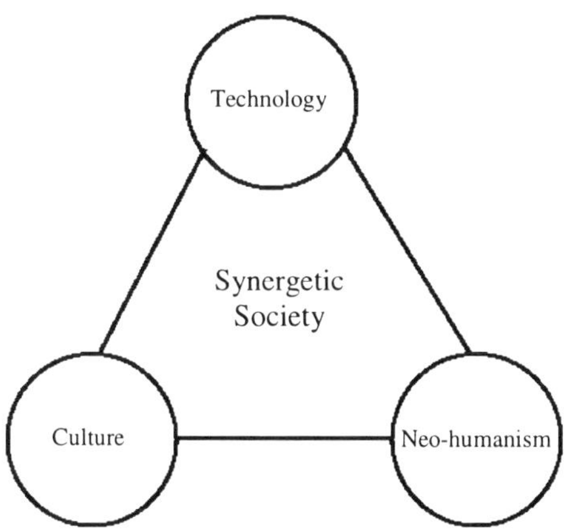

will be low. Conversely, a technocrat society that ignores aesthetic values and erodes culture would not be humanistic. Further, technology should be applied and culture expressed in a neo-humanistic vein, in order to promote a sustainably progressive and enlightened society. Thus, technology, culture and neo-humanism constitute the ingredients (and a balanced triangle) of a synergistic society of an SRC.

What are the synergetic factors needed for economic development of a region? They are agriculture and natural resources, industrial infrastructure and economic culture (i.e. for instance, cooperatives versus owner-based corporations) to convert the raw materials into finished goods.

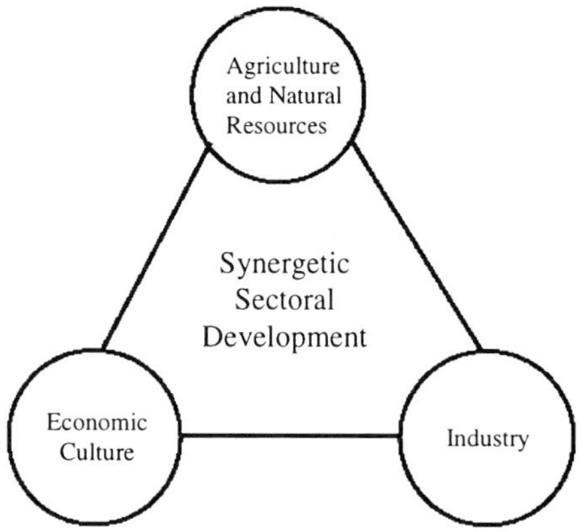

The agricultural sector further needs to have balanced development of primary production, agro (or pre-harvest) and agrico (or post-harvest) industries, and manufacturing industry.

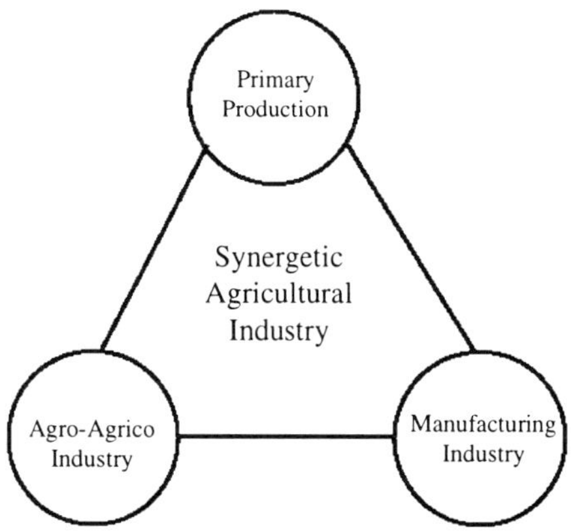

For synergetic development planning, the balanced triangle of synergetic economic policy is to consist of: (1) commodities economy, dealing with production and supply of minimum essentials of life, (2) commercial economy, dealing with monetary and trade policies, for maximum utilization and rational distribution of resources, and (3) knowledge economy, entailing utilization of know-how for economic well-being.

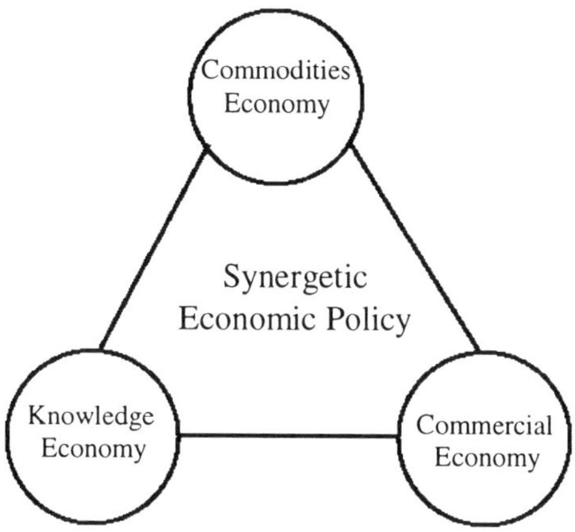

However, there is no way that a single state or nation can have all these factors required for economic development and for providing an enlightened living for its inhabitants. In fact, industrially developed countries depend a lot on developing countries to supply the raw materials for their industrial development and economic growth. Thus, for economic development and well-being, a group of geographically neighboring functionally-sustainable communities need to come together, to share their agricultural, natural and industrial resources, in order to constitute a synergistic socio-economic bloc or region.

In such a synergistic socio-economic bloc, local resources would be utilized maximally through local labor to form an indigenous industrial base. The economic characteristics of such a synergetic socio-economic bloc would be: (1) balanced development of agricultural, manufacturing and service sectors of economy; (2) balance of imported, exported and locally consumed materials and goods, with an emphasis on indigenous conversion of raw materials into manufactured goods; and (3) industrial, ecological and cultural homeostasis.

Finally, these synergetic economic blocs would eventually be part of a regional federation, such as a South American federation. Such an intra-regional cooperation depends upon establishment of economic security and viability at the level of the regional blocs. This, in brief, constitutes the basis of "synergistic regional economic development within a regional federation."

Universities throughout the world need to infuse these ideals in their mission and vision statements, and incorporate them in their curriculum. A synergetic educational program on global harmony and peace (in the context of multi-regional federations) could involve courses and research on the issues of decentralized regional development and utilization of both material and mental resources, sharing of knowledge and promulgation of neo-humanistic ideals, inter-federation trade policy and a common jurisprudence structure.

6.6 For renaissance in society

Science culture: The development of science, catalyzed by the industrial revolution, has imparted a materialistic stance and institutionalization to science — to natural applied and socio-economic sciences. This has resulted in uneven distribution of the material benefits of applied science and in resistance to neo-humanistic principles. While science has helped to develop physical amenities, their fair distribution was not made possible in the prevalent global socio-economic order. On the other hand, science culture has promoted the analytical faculty of mind, but is only now starting to probe the faculty of consciousness and cognition. Psychic interactions cause mental stress, which needs to be dissipated by mind elevation (or transcendence) to higher planes. This science of acquiring enhanced consciousness now needs to be developed, to prevent psychic ailments (impart a new dimension to psychiatry) and to inspire progress to neo-humanism.

Hence today, human society stands at crossroads. One avenue is the present culture, with so many people unable to express their supra-mental potentials, while being burdened by economic hardships and/or mental distress. Science was expected to move into this realm, of transcendence of the physical realm to deal with intuitive and cognitive states. As a result, a big segment of society (those who dissociate humanities and social sciences from natural and applied sciences) is now unable to feel an affinity with contemporary science culture. The alternative is for science to address both material needs and cognitive states of human beings, and to provide for both material and psychic fulfillment. At the same time, availability of the means for developing and qualifying higher faculties of mind would lift society above materialism, enable people to experience transcendal states of the mind, and prevent psychological conflicts and drug abuse. Further, a universal social outlook would make it possible for all people to live synergetically.

Social outlook: Human beings have two roles of existence — individual and collective, which are in a way complimentary. As an individual, it is the intrinsic nature of a human being to seek fulfillment in undisturbed peace. On the other hand, the collective role of a human being is in fact to help to create such an environment for people to live in, so that their energy is not entirely spent in the struggles for physical existence and fulfillment of micro-psychic longings, as well as in dealing with mental ailments. Thereby, their attention can be turned to liberation-of-intellect and to self-realization. Concomitantly, the role of education is also to help to inculcate and to teach the means to satisfy these needs.

All human beings have a common heritage and a common destiny. Yet, the conflicts and struggles in different parts of the world today can be linked to the lack of realization that human society is one and indivisible as well as of the cosmic desideratum of human beings. This has led to suppression of the cultural and psychic expressions, socio-economic exploitations within and among nations, and an outlook of mundane exsistence. Hence, it is important for human welfare, to develop a neo-humanistic social outlook (free from the narrow confines of all sorts of groupisms, racism, regionalism and even nationalism) as well as psychology. This outlook also emphasizes that the welfare of all living beings is interlinked. All living beings, including plants and animals, have both utilitarian value as well as existential value. Hence, a balanced ecological environment is necessary for all of them to develop their full potential.

Indigenous development and synergetic economics: Economics as taught today is firstly somewhat empirical. Secondly, it subtlely promotes the psychology of economic exploitation and monopoly, which has polarized human society and failed to fulfill the basic living needs for all the people. In the realm of both micro and macro economics, the concepts of competitive strategy need to be revised, so that the players in any particular market can operate at an optimal price and profit value for business sustainance. Thirdly, as per the psychology of economics-in-practice, it needs to be recognized that for regional economic development: (1) people will work better if they have a stake in the accruing economic returns, through structuring of corporatives, and (2) it is necessary to cater to the welfare of the local people by maximizing the socio-economic potentiality of the local community by the local people themselves.

The local residents are to be empowered, in order to ensure maximum development of local resources, by ensuring local conversion of locally available raw materials and produces into manufacturing and processed goods. In cooperatively structured industries, the production would not be primarily profit-oriented, but also based on sustainable consumer demand. Most importantly, the capital generated locally ought to be utilized for local development. In this way, by facilitating availability of basic needs, arranging for full employment, keeping prices at sustainable demand, augmenting the economic development of the region through technology and know-how transfer from universities, the purchasing capacity of the people and hence their living standards would be continually raised.

Finally (as indicated above), the premise of competitive strategy (intrinsic to micro and even macro economics) needs to be altered, from the psychology of anihilating competition to imbibing the spirit of synergy, in the arena of international trade and economics. By adroit application of game theory, we need to work out how the various nations and communities in a region can cooperate (in astutely structuring the export and import of commodities and know-how), so that all the nations can provide their inhabitants with a uniformly high quality of life.

We cannot afford to let academic economics be a theoretical extravaganza, while real-life economics continues to be like the monopoly board game, where each party is intent on liquidating the others. Economics theory need not be built on the psychology of competition, but instead on the psychology of cooperation. Further, it is possible to develop micro and macro economic simulation models, to determine the optimal parameters of pricing and profit for a multi-player business market. Academic economics could contribute to innovations in indigenous development, by developing the cooperative economics of local development (i.e. for collective capitalism) to benefit the residents of a cooperatively structured SRC. This cooperative economics (of collective capitalism) would provide the means not only for Third World development but also for warding off economic recessions.

Human rights: Violation of a legal code is known as crime, whereas violation of cardinal values is termed as sin. While cardinal values remain unchangeable, conceptions of crime undergo transformation with time and society. In a progressive society, the difference between crime and sin will become less and less — and where does law fit in? Jurisprudence is to ensure that the society can stay progressive. The human rights of individuals to dignified living and minimal necessities of living are to be guaranteed. However, we cannot stop here! We need to also guarantee the fulfillment of the intrinsic nature of human beings for unbarred expansion and expression of the mind.

Responsibility of educators and governance policy enactors: Today, human society is in anguish, bleeding from its being subdivided and vivisected, deprived and stifled by dogmatic injunctions. In its dark night of despair and convulsions, who will come forward to give it a healing touch? Only neo-humanistic educators and thinkers (not self-interest promoting politicians) have the unique opportunity and the capability to administer to society the life-generating amrit, for enabling all its entities to live in dignity, to develop all of their potentialities, and to facilitate the exalted progress of one another. They alone should be elected as socio-political legislators or governance executives.

The emphasis on human values will help guarantee appropriate use of science and technology, economics and political science for human benefit. Inculcating a universal outlook will ensure the cultivation of such public policies that no community segment in any part of the world lags behind physically and psychically. Further, education should also provide liberation of intellect (from narrowness) and enable mind transcendence, so as to help conceive nobler ideas and ideals. The following triangle of synergistic education summarizes the balanced factors of real education — education for collective welfare and individual enlightenment.

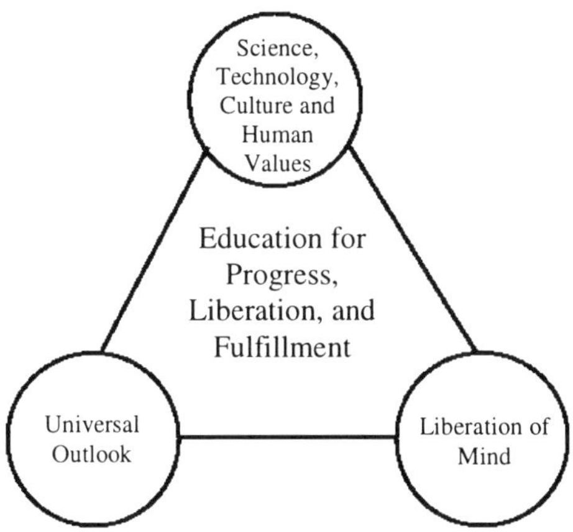

An enlightened human society can come into being from noble ideas,

Conceived when the mind gets cosmically lit up.

An illuminated mind is like a radar,

Guiding its ship along a safe course to its home shores.

Children scavenging recycle near smoky mountain in Tondo, Manila (Philippines)

Scavenger's houses near smoky mountain Tondo, Manila (Philippines)

Why should some children be scavengers, while others attend school and get a good education? Is it because there are no schools in their neighborhood or because they cannot afford to attend school as they are engaged in scavenging for survival. Every child has a right to education and every family has a right to the minimal necessities of life, as part of our charter of human rights. So then, who is responsible for this deprivation of civilian rights?

Obviously, it is the elite governance society of political parties' politicians! Without knowledge of the various sectors of the community, how can they administer these sectors. Does it not make sense for these community sectors to be directly involved in their own governance, through their elected legislators? This is why we need to have a civilian democratic governance system with people-centric constitution and politicization, for renaissance in society.

7 Corporate Capitalism to Cooperative Capitalism and Social Democracy

From the enslaved girl-maids to women-beggars (in *purdah*), from homeless HIV-infected mothers and their children to the destitute street-dwellers and blind beggars standing all day to beg, from societally ostracized lower-caste women and men to imported laborers who (conned into taking impayable loans to land well-paying jobs in affluent countries) are relegated to working (for the entire life away from their families) in subhuman conditions, goes on and on endlessly the poignant tale of the grim struggle for survival. Who has been responsible for this stark misery?

7.1 Our disabled human society needs rehabilization

Human society has been cheated and polluted all along and even in the last century by many groups of people:

- communist dictators, by crushing human spirit and creating a terror-prone and merciless society, totally devoid of human expression and compassion;
- the capitalists, by using their capital to support the election campaigns of undeserving political leaders in return for favorable public policies (such as the cases of the tobacco and armaments industry's protectionist measures), by inducing people (in the garb of democracy and free enterprise for providing unbarred opportunities to become rich) to bankruptcy through investments in unethically maneuvered over-inflated corporate stocks;
- dogmatic clerics, by keeping a vast majority of people subscribing to archaic dogmatic beliefs and practices (associated with millenniums old sociology) that thwart supra-aesthetic development, and by dehumanizing women and preventing them equal opportunity in societal affairs;
- political leaders, by infusing narrow sentimentality among people so as to maintain their popularity, and by misusing people's trust to promote their self-interests.

This is why, for societal rehabilitation and renaissance, we are advocating:

- economic empowerment of the people in the form of collective capitalism, socio-economic democracy and distributive justice;
- governance autonomy for the regions and states (or FSCs) of a nation, to shape their own destinies;
- political party-less enlightened governance of micro-communities, by competent and moralistic persons elected by members of professional societies representing various sectors of the community;
- cooperative organization of all collective human activities, involving both work livelihood (so that all human beings can live in dignity and be partners in a fair sharing of revenue, commensurate to their input in business development and/or revenue generation);
- enlightened living, to be provided by societal framework and public policies conductive to constitutionally legislated human rights, so that all people have equal opportunities to share the glory of contributing to societal progress.

7.2 Replacement of problematic economic-political systems

What is the justification for a new economic-political system? What have been the drawbacks of this last century's systems? If we need a new system, what is it to be based on — the inherent basis, tendencies and needs of the persons? The answers to these queries and issues are provided in this chapter.

As regards corporate capitalism (involving subjugative cooperation), there is something inherently wrong and unethical about a system that promulgates a mundane materialist psychology to get richer and richer, by competing for a living, by promoting strategies of annihilating competitions, and in which:

- there is an incessant drive to over-promote products to create a deceptive consumer psychology of grossly inflated demand for products, to thereby augment staffing to cope with the heightened market demand, and then carry out massive retrenching when the consumer demand falls to realistic levels;
- bigger and bigger profits constitute a measure of performance and standing;
- big profits are faked by CEOs of corporations to induce people to buy their over-inflated shares, and risk getting bankrupted when the shares plummet to reflect the real worth of the corporation;
- real-estate prices are allowed to escalate far beyond the real value, and force people to generations of debt;

- manufacturing companies move from one country to another, to unabashedly take advantage of the cheaper labor force;
- gimmicks like globalization are conceived to enter and capture new markets of Third World countries;
- recessions and depressions are intrinsic to its economy dynamics;
- corporations can file for bankruptcy to avoid paying pensions to retired employees; and
- hegemonism is inevitable.

This definitely does not reflect a noble-minded civilization. Today's international-capitalism is riddled with cronyism and stock (and currency) manipulation, while being the prime financial supporter of political parties and beneficiary of public policies. Is there no alternative for a developing country but to adopt the "herd instinct" and align itself with political and economic hegemonism for its survival, to implement the capitalistic corporational route for economic development, and accept the debilitating formulas to misnomered international development (loans-providing) agencies to:

- stop start-up fundings for indigenous enterprises, and open their markets to outside products (at the risk of damping indigenous initiatives);
- essentially become an economic colony of the powerful industrialized nations, or face international isolation and even economic sanctions.

Of course, we are absolutely ruling out communism as an alternative. Fifty years of communism, associated with physically and psychologically stifling and repressive regimentation, has once and for all convinced people of its pseudo altruistic attributes as a cover-up for its ideological fanaticism and repressive governance system, with its ruthless and megalomaniac politicians making the people live in terror of being imprisoned or executed for not being adequately ideological. We are also ruling out the dictatorial system of governance. As regards dictatorial regimes, although in rare cases the dictators could be competent and moralistic (and even benevolent), yet in most cases they have tended to be perpetrators of terror, repression and mass-killings.*

Developing countries need to come out of this depressing spiral of "third world" label, and collectively operate and trade as regional economic blocs. We

*Adolf Hitler (Germany), Joseph Stalin (Soviet Union), Mao Zedong (China), Idi Amin (Uganda), Pol Pot (Cambodia), Saddam Hussein (Iraq), Augusto Pinochet (Chile), Slobodan Milosevic (Serbia), Théonaste Bagosara (Rwanda) are only a few among hundreds of brutal terrorist dictators who have caused genocides and democides of their own people. Unless their crimes against humanity are addressed, it is impossible to tackle the phenomenon of terrorism because they (with the acquiescence of the heads of so-called civilized nations) are the original terrorists and founders of terrorism.

want to discard not only communism but also the political party-based democratic (governance and electoral) infrastructure and machinery, in which:

- aspiring politicians are not interested in providing good governance for societal advancement, but to merely get re-elected at any cost;
- incompetent and incapable, ignorant and insolent, unscrupulous and incorrigible people get to be in charge of governance portfolios.

This is why, our proposed people's participatory economic system (PPES, in which corporations are structured as cooperatives) and socio-economic democracy (SED) and civilian professional governance (CPG) system, entailing:

(i) collective capitalism,
(ii) democracy sans political parties and their self-interests (above people's welfare),
(iii) civilian governance by the most qualified people in their respective fields (in place of loyal incompetent party members being given governance of various portfolios), and
(iv) political structuring of economic blocs and federations (to provide economic buffer and parity to the G-6 or G-8 nations),

constitutes the only viable way for Third World countries to develop and function with dignity, while inculcating a universal outlook and a spirit of one for all and all for one.

7.3 Indigenous people's empowerment

The primary lesson for the economic development of Third World communities is to never allow your natural resources and industries (such as oil, electric power, minerals and forest resources) to be privatized, because this is verily the shortcut to economic bankruptcy of the country. The second lesson is to resist being forced to privatize your natural resources or concentrate on a single export crop or product, when forced to take loans from (so-called) international agencies who are themselves friends of capitalist cartels (such as the Enrons of the world). It must be born in mind that pressure for privatization is a backdoor attempt at piracy of resource-rich developing countries by capitalist cartels, which can plunge the country into bigger debt.

The third lesson is recognition of the primary rights of the native people of the land to ownership of their land resources. If these resources have to be cultivated and developed, then the community (FSC) governance should form cooperative industries in which the native people can be employed. If financial assistance is sought from outside the community (in the form of bank loans and/or investment), then the native people should be also considered for renumeration, instead of being deprived of their land and then left to live in poverty. For maximum benefit to the indigenous people, all natural resources should be converted into industrial products locally, and then only exported out of the community.

The native people should realize their own rights and power. The big power base at the community level belongs to the people of the soil. It is they who own the natural resources, and only they can decide how to convert these resources to economic wealth, to upgrade their living standards. When this is negotiated, they should be the primary beneficiaries. When the raw material is converted into products, ranging from foodstuffs to commodities, the community people should be involved, so as to receive their fair share of renumeration. Further, before exporting, the local need should be satisfied and thereafter the surplus can be exported. The basic need and concept of Third World development is not just sustainable development but grassroots development by and for the local people.

The FSCs could also initially protect their agricultural and manufacturing cooperatives, by giving them time to develop and become regionally and globally competitive, by initially only importing what is not locally available or produced. Free trade does not imply mandating the developing nations to kill their embryonic indigenous industry and trade. Of course, in the spirit of free trade, levies need not be put on imports of items and commodities that are needed but not locally available. This benefits the consumers by their not having to pay bigger price for the commodities as well as the exporters by a bigger consumption of their products.

Finally, it needs to be recognized that the high standard of living enjoyed by a small fraction of the world population is because of (1) cheap labor being employed in industry and construction (e.g. in building industry and manufacturing industry, in oil and mining industry), and (2) pirating of the land of indigenous people without having to pay for the resources of land. If this poorly paid labor force was paid better and more respectable salaries commensurate to their labor, then the salaries of the managerial staff would diminish, and the profits shared among the corporation shareholders as well as the CEOs and CFOs would also diminish, with consequential reduction in their living standards.

7.4 Self-dismantling of corporate capitalism

Deceit and greed combined with know-how for fictitious performance projection has become the characteristic of many big-time companies. Their CEOs and CFOs have been jettisoned into public glare by virtue of their scandalous business practices, ranging from:

- CEOs being paid unjustifiably bloated multimillion dollar salaries and bonuses, bearing no correlation to their acumen and performance;
- CEOs continuing to pay themselves immorally high salaries even as their firms bleed heavily;
- accounts fabrication and designing of false profits, under the direction of CEOs, so as to artificially get the company stock prices to go up;
- CEOs covertly buying the companies stocks in expectancy of the scaling up of the prices of their fictiously boosted stocks (based on false profits generation and announcements);
- public exposure of these companies scandalous practices, causing their stocks to crash and bankruptcy of the innocent stockholders.

Today's companies are hiring more business administrative experts (as glorified financial manipulators), instead of honest to goodness people with expertise in the company's products and technology. There is an over-stocking of MBAs in companies, relative to people with technological expertise. The exponential expansion in MBA degrees offered by each and every university from north to south and east to west is an indication of the fictitiously over-inflated market demand for MBAs. What do those superfluous MBAs do in a company? Well they can help develop virtual and productless companies to become middle-brokers and wheelers and dealers, without having their own primary products.

CEO salary boom started spiralling from mid-1980s onwards and reached scandalous proportions by 2001, until the Enron scandal created headlines. Most of this rise in CEO renumeration package was tied to their companies climbing the stock exchange ladder and the spiralling of stock-exchange indices (another pseudo index of economy). In other words, the basis of this extraordinary salary scale was tied not to the enhancement of the company's products and services, but to the company's induction into new markets and the glitter of being displayed on stock exchange billboards. Although micro-economics is structured to deal with companies financial (pricing and profits) dynamics, instead of with the science of cost-effective product development, yet there is nothing even in this capitalist-biased micro-economics structure ("theory" would be a misnomer) to justify this absurd phenomenon of CEOs' financial packages being of the order of 100 times the average employee's salary.

However, this is not all. Essentially, corporations have become living entities with all their privileges, without the associated responsibilities. They cannot be persecuted for their crimes of robbing people. Corporate welfare is of greater interest to capitalist-democratic political leaders than common people's welfare, because corporations contribute substantially to election campaigns. The corporate profile is further enhanced by the incongruity in (1) taxes paid by them (compared to that paid by common people) relative to their earnings, and (2) the disproportionate publicity given by the media to politicians and corporations, instead of to the common people's day-to-day problems and ways of solving them. This is because big corporations in super-capitalist countries control the media.

Today, the corporate world is rife with corruption. In developing countries, corruption was invented by (and became synonymous with) politicians and government officers. However, the amount of pilferage by the corporate bosses is of an altogether different order of magnitude, and could well exceed the GDP of some developing countries. The practice of providing share options to them has made the problem even more acute. Unless one's morality is founded in spirituality, one would be hard put to resist getting the accounts maneuvered, in order to show fictitious profits. Then as the company's stock goes up, these corporate bosses sell their company's shares and make big fortunes. The sad part of this story of greed and corruption is that the corporation boards have felt justified to provide such morally unjustifiable incentives to their top administrative and financial managers, in order to motivate them to get the company stock to go up by hook or by crook, so as to benefit themselves.

An even sadder aspect of this ugly face of corporate capitalism is that it constitutes the basis and sustenance of today's (political party-based) democracy. From the wealthy democratic nations to the impoverished democratic nations, all election campaign funds and political parties' funds come from these very corporate houses and their bosses. Hence, public institutions and government structures have also been infected with this virus of greedy self-centered corporate egoism. Today sadly, we live under corporate capitalism or corporatism. Corporations are engineered to squash competition and convert the society to monopolistic capitalism. Today, we have politician's and corporate sovereignty instead of people's (or civilian) sovereignty.

We are proposing an alternative public-centric humanistic corporate structure, wherein the drive is not to maximize the profits at all cost, but to provide value-laden and demand-based reasonably priced products to the consumers. We have also formulated a grassroots-based governance (electoral and management) structure, that will only permit highly qualified and moralistic role-model FSC citizens to be inducted into societal governance network (from SRC to world government). We have also spelled out the mechanism by which transformation to this neo-political governance framework can come about, but how soon? The answer is that, this insatiable drive for the creation of virtual wealth rather than actual wealth is hastening this immorally monoistic corporate capitalism to the same fate as at that of ruthlessly inhuman communism. This phenomenon of greedy cancer-stricken capitalism will in fact help to bring in our neo-economic-political framework, as a natural and inevitable course of events.

7.5 Reforming the corporation's management culture

It can be said that a shady business structure never makes a sunny ambience for that company. Company managers should learn some ethics of respecting their employees (who give their all to the company), instead of treating them as mere digits. Aside from the disgraceful aspect of managerial greedy toadyism (as it stands exposed today), is this psychology of corporate culture (and the MBA program culture) as to how to think strategically to:

- act smart, pretend to be knowledgeable and having the adroit acumen representing the knowledge resource of the company;
- inspire confidence in investors, even when your firm is cheating and sinking.

So then, today marks only some initial steps in the transformation of the corporate capitalist industrial empire. Genuine knowledge is to be considered important in the corporational arena, in order to innovate know-how(s) and technologies (and not to merely artificially and unethically hike up a company's image performance and stock). Talent in the workplace must include an adroit combination of intelligence, ethics and emotional quotients. The template for the corporation of the future is to be as follows:

- the corporation should be structured as a cooperative;
- the mission of the corporation should be to develop real value products, priced at a level whereby the company can continue to operate in financial security without opulence;
- the strategy for the mission should be to develop high-value products, using appropriate technology;
- to not make profit-only its monoistic deity, but to incorporate its product value and its employee welfare as corporate icons; and
- to cooperate with other competing corporations to strategically share the market.

In the framework of economics embedded in real knowledge guided by neo-humanistic conscience, a role model corporate manager (CEO, CTO and CFO) should:

- advocate real product value;
- ensure cost-effective products, of benefit to the company as well to the consumer's pockets;
- make the corporate culture icons to be "knowledge and acumen combined with honesty and integrity", in order to enhance the above two ideals;

- make the employees feel that they constitute the real assets of the company, by economically rewarding them appropriately;
- recognize the historical perspective that only real-value companies can be respected well enough to last, while those companies aiming to get rich by hook or by crook will die due to their insular mind-set and business culture.

Guidelines for a respectable corporate culture: Forming the basis of corporate culture is management psychology and ethics, which in turn are governed by corporate economics and management. Hence, to start with, it is about time that the discipline of economics and the values of the MBA program are revised to:

- develop a hard core science of product pricing and corporate operational efficiency, to ensure respectable financial revenues, so as to be able to support the corporation's staff and new product development;
- incorporate human behavioral science in the MBA curriculum, so as not to make its executives street-smart but rather more humanistic;
- treat a company's hard core workers as prime resource and social capital;
- employ banks to borrow money and not use non-employee shareholders to raise money;
- develop new corporational performance indices: technological index (CTI), performance index (PFI) in terms of sales and earned revenue, optimal product pricing (OPP) for ethical profit-making — expressed as a profit index (or PTI), resource-index (RSI) in terms of equipment and salary costs, and cost-effectiveness index (CEI) equal to PFI/CEI;
- develop new corporational social responsibility index (SRI): of employee welfare, consumer satisfaction and social accountability;
- so as to optimize the corporation's operations, by maximizing CEI or to strike a balance between CEI and PTI.

What sort of corporatist culture will restore respectability and help develop true economy and not a bubble economy? The template for this neo-corporatism will include:

- combining knowledge with integrity to develop high-value products;
- corporational mission to do maximal good to and for the consumers;
- treating all the members of the corporation not as employees and digital numbers but as members of one family;
- providing encouragement to the corporation members to continually enhance their knowledge and skills, by supporting their continuing education;
- sharing revenue and profits among the corporation staff;
- respecting people within and outside the corporation, by carrying out the above mission statement.

- making the corporation to be part and parcel of the local and regional community, by providing technological assistance to its educational institutions and by enhancing the ecological ambience of the community;
- obligation and commitment to return to the community at least as much as is taken from the community;
- making the corporation (1) a storehouse of intellectual and technological knowledge in its specialized field and (2) harborage of social values, so as to (3) enrich the community with this type of eclectic corporate culture.

7.6 Capitalistic democracy versus socio-economic democracy

In the current company corporate-governance culture, corporate managers essentially act in their self-interests, in the guise of acting in the corporation's best interests. By deliberately showing fictitious profits, they make the stock prices go higher. With this *a priori* knowledge, they buy their company stocks before they go high, and then sell them straightaway, before exposure of their "accounting error" downsizes the stocks. The unsuspecting stock players and naïve investors note the stock price going up. Unsuspectingly, they hope to catch the upward trend, but end up bankrupt when the fictitiously over-inflated stock crashes.

In the present day government corporate culture, similar malpractices prevail. The managers (namely the ministers) are engaged in manipulating information to be provided to the public, so as to boost their image and downsize the opposition parties and to even wage wars; they have no time to attend to reforms or policies promoting public welfare. They do not feel the need to consult their electoral precincts before making decisions, even when commiting their nation to war. Rather, they first make decisions, and then concoct data to get public support. Infact, important decisions concerning both home and foreign policies are made by the ruling political party to suit its election chances. As a result, it can happen that a country A's ruling party stays adverserial to country B for two years because of its racial prejudices. Then, in view of the coming elections, it makes an about-turn and negotiates peace with country B, oblivious of the tramma caused to the people by its earlier policy. This is the sad story of India and Pakistan.

The most vagrant violation of democracy and public representativeness is their autocratic policy-making decisions. The current democratic electoral system is, in any case, too unwieldy and costly for them to go back to the public to determine their opinion on policy matters. On the other hand, in our sectorial-electoral system, it will behoov of the legislators to consult their electoral agencies and recommendations, because the legislators will be beholden and responsible to their community sectors' agencies. Furthermore, in our proposed system it would be quite convenient for legislators to have continual parleys with their electoral agencies.

One of the most stringent cases against the political party democratic system of governance is the party protectionism to its wayward members. In the vast majority of cases, these legislators (as national heads or as ministers and/or heads of states governance):

- do not have the qualifications to be governance executives;
- totally ignore their public service role, by being full time involved in ensuring their party dominance at all levels of local elections, and spend public funds as well as coerce or extort funding from companies for their election campaigns in return for their political favors;
- are primarily responsible for the parallel black economy by virtue of elicited unaccounted for donations to their parties;
- arrange for big government contracts to be given to their corporate supporters as payback for funding their election and publicity campaigns;
- contemptuously violate human rights and UNICEF charter, abrogating (with impunity) the state responsibility for supporting primary and higher education;
- commit crimes against humanity by encouraging ethnic riots and killings (through their backdoor agents), and then capitalize on stirred-up public racial emotions to win more elections;
- choose to wage war against neighboring and/or weaker nations in the guise of national security (in order to garner public support for their aggressive policy), while providing backdoor defense contracts to their cronies' companies.

A prime objection to the present system of capitalist democracy is the tactic of playing up to people's emotions (on the contentious issues of national security and defense, religion and economy) so as to maintain public support. On the other hand, in our proposed **socio-economic-democratic professional-governance (SED & PRG)** system, the elected governance official will conscientiously administer specific portfolios commensurate to their expertise and competency, like any other person working in a public (or private) institution or agency. The legislators will have the same privileges as the civilians, and will also be accountable to the people for malgovernance.

A prime disadvantage of the political party system of democracy is that the elected ministers are not experts in their portfolios. It is said that the real governance administrators are the civil servants. However, even the civil servants are not experts: they are generalists, who are used to doing routine "maintenance" work. The civil servants are not thinkers, and yet they are the advisors to the ministers in policy-making. Hence, in this "party system of democracy" (PSOD) or in this pseudo democratic system, there are no experts involved in decision-making — it is only the "generalists advising the ignorants".

The below Table is an attempt to delineate the qualities of a legislator or minister.

Index for Suitability of Politicians for Public Office (ISPO)

Parameter (Pmi)	**Qualities (Q) (Range: Minimum 0–Maximum 10)**	**Liabilities (L) (Range: Minimum 0–Maximum 10)**	**Parameter Score (S_i) = Q – L (Range: –10 to +10)**
Pm1	INQ: Intelligence Quotient	STO: Stupidity Quotient	
Pm2	EMQ: Emotional Quotient	AMQ: Amicability Quotient	
Pm3	EDQ: Educational Quotient	ILQ: Illiteracy Quotient	
Pm4	KNO: Knowledge Quotient	IGQ: Ignorance Quotient	
Pm5	HOQ: Honesty Quotient	COQ: Corruption Quotient	
Pm6	MOQ: Character Quotient	DVQ: Immorality Quotient	
Pm7	IHMQ: Honest Earnings Quotient	MAQ: Devious Earnings Quotient	
Pm8	HUQ: Humanistic Quotient	SFQ: Selfishness Quotient	
Pm9	SQQ: Secularity Quotient	BGQ: Bigotry Quotient	
Pm10	CHQ: Human Rights Quotient	DPQ: Irreliability Quotient	
Pm11	COQ: Compassion Quotient	MNQ: Meanness Quotient	
Pm12	SPQ: Neo-humanistic Quotient	CRQ: Crudity/Fraudulence Quotient	

$$\text{ISPO} = \left(\sum_{i=1}^{12} S_i + 120 \right) (100/240)$$

The range of ISPO would be from 0 to 100. A score of over 85% would be termed as an A grade, 70–85% as B, 60–70% as C, 50–60% as D, and <50% as F.

It is seen that this ISPO can have a wide range of values from 0 to 100. For the present day system and politician, it would be useful to implement this template. Because of the poor quality of current politicians, even if a politician can obtain an ISPO grade C, it would be acceptable. The chances are that most current national heads (prime ministers and presidents) will get ISPO grade F (score of less than 50%).

7.7 Educational qualifications for politicians, civil and governance services

In our proposed socio-economic-democratic professional-governance **(SED & PRG)** system, as opposed to the present day PSOD system, the elected ministers would themselves be experts, capable of invoking and bringing to bear considerable state-of-the-art knowledge to their portfolios. Working under these experts, the "civil servants" would also become well versed in the affairs of various community sectors. Still, we will be instituting a graduate (masters) degree program in Community administrative science (CAS). The curriculum of this CAS program will consist of subjects related to the functions of all the sectors of the community as for instance: healthcare, education, water supply, sanitation, electrical power, railways, airways, seaways (generation and distribution), roads and public transport, small business and entrepreneurship development, big business and commodities, production, agriculture, law and jurisprudence, civil and social security, home and external affairs. This degree will be the minimum qualification requirement for anyone to be in administrative and governance services.

Additionally, those CAS officers who want to be involved in policy- and decision-making (and hence wish to serve as heads of the above-mentioned government departments) would be required to do their doctorate degree in CAS. The research and dissertation component of this CAS-PhD degree program will require them to do in-depth research in any two sectional areas of the community, such as in rail and air transportation, water supply and sanitation, primary and tertiary education, agriculture and dairy farming, primary and tertiary healthcare, forestry and ecology, finance and banking, trade and commerce, corporate and constitutional law.

This SED & PRG system will help to bring to bear a high level of competence to the governance system, in addition to integrity and transparency, dedication and commitment. Further, they will also have to be periodically reviewed for their governance competency. The legislator's performance will be periodically reviewed by their electoral constituencies, while the CAS officers performance will be assessed by the ministers. Finally, both the legislators and the CAS officers will be held accountable to the community who they govern.

7.8 Synergy of science, education and socio-economic order

In a society,

- the role of engineering and science is to provide the means for both physical (objective) and psychic (subjective) fulfillment;
- the role of societal (socio-economic) order is to enable the means to be available to all people;
- the role of university education is to develop the ideals of a progressive society, by appropriate formulation of the curricula of the diverse subjects of human thought and endeavor.

The synergistic balance of science, education and socio-economic order will contribute to a progressive society, as graphically delineated in Fig. 7.1.

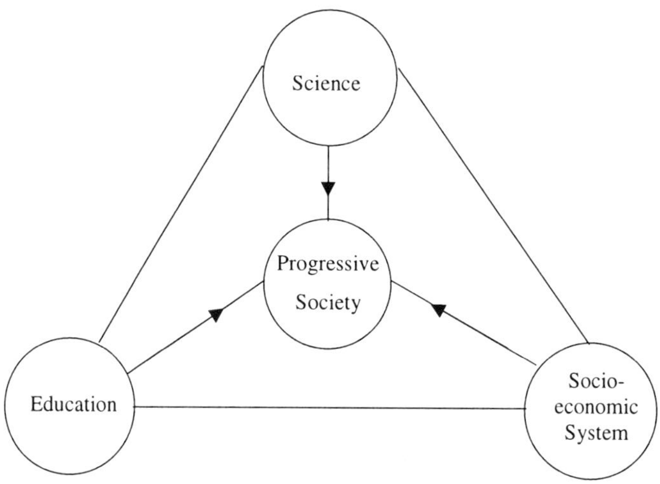

Fig. 7.1 Synergistic balance of science, education and socio-economic system for a progressive human society.

It is more dignified (and akin to natural phenomena) for human beings to live and work in coordinated cooperation than in competition. Our economic system of work and living cooperatives will elevate both work and living conditions.

The concept of having a salaried job in a corporation (as practised under today's capitalism) is not as satisfying and dignified as working in a cooperatively organized corporation, and being remunerated for the level and importance of one's services under our proposed collective capitalism system. In such a work setup, the welfare of all is interlinked.

They are smart persons who can corner and accumulate a lot of capital. However, wiser persons can accumulate a lot of friends and goodwill by practicing "collective capitalism," which is the basis of economic democracy. Then, sectorial representation in the legislative assembly leads to civilian governance and democratic politics.

Neo-humanists will even go a step further while walking on the road to a progressive society. They will in fact stay to give a helping hand to those in distress, wait for them to recover, and only then move forward collectively. This moving forward in unison constitutes the spirit of an enlightened society.

It is good for people and nations to be engaged in business, but more elevating to be engaged in providing services to one another. In fact, trading services and know-how can also be financially remunerative, but in a more dignified way. Hence, it will augur for better harmony among people and nations to be engaged in services-providing interactions. In this spirit of concern for mutual welfare, all the nations and regions of the world can constitute one global cooperative!

People in slums next to skyscrapers at Nariman point (Business Headquarters, Mumbai, India)

Two girls carrying water pot on their heads in this slum area, Bombay, India

Alongside the high-rise buildings (housing big businesses) are these slum dwellings in Mumbai, the financial capital of India. Indians abroad (and particularly in the US) are excelling themselves as educators and academics, as engineers and information-technologists, as doctors and pharmacists. However, in India (the world's biggest democracy), so many have no opportunity to progress. What kind of democracy is that? Why is it that the so-called political leaders (from political parties) are unmoved by these sordid dwellings?

We need a paradigm shift from corporate capitalism to cooperative capitalism with civilian community sector's involvement in community governance. Definitely, our Civilian democratic governance system will be more responsive to civilian needs and sufferings. We need to educate these sweet smiling children, and enable them to be a part of economic development and governance.

8

State and Group Terrorism, Justice and Reparation

8.1 Trails of terrorism

By definition, terrorism is an act carried out by a group to instill terror among the adversaries. Does terrorism have a conscience? Can we say that its roots are traceable to the times (66 to 73 AD) in the Middle East, when the zealots were killing people in the streets by way of terrorizing the Roman occupants of Palestine. No, because the Romans inflicted more terror on the citizens. It has always been this way. State terrorism against its own people (e.g. by communist and apartheid regimes) is not regarded as terrorism, but the desperate people's violent protests is regarded as terrorism.

8.1.1 Hypocritic sociology of terrorism

Colonization and systematic looting of colonies, repression of people by despotic regimes, as well as large scale extermination of the native an certain ethnic populations of countries have not been regarded as terrorism. However, retaliatory terror bombings of governmental civilian targets and assassinations of politicians and agents of repression by the so-called "civilian rebels" have been termed as terrorism! So then, how should history regard the Irish and French revolutionaries?

While condemning terrorism by protest and rebel groups on civilian populations, what needs to be recognized is that behind many so-called "protest or rebel terrorism movements" have often been ruthless state-terrorisms: how else can one describe the terror blitzed by the extremist communist regimes on their own people? These state-terrorism activities have been in the form of suppression of civic liberties, imposed norms of ideological psychology, along with persecution of dissidents and protestors. In the citadels of communism in Soviet Union and China, a reign of terror prevailed during the middle of the last century; further in both the countries, the imposed agricultural policies of the regimes proved disastrous for the farmers and the economy.

State terrorism has resulted in mass murders or democides. The terrible purges meted out by Joseph Stalin from 1924 to 1953 resulted in democides of some

20 million citizens. This brutality is matched in numbers by what Mao Zedong did to the people of China, but surpassed in terror by what Hitler did to the Jews. The world has largely ignored state terrorism, and chosen to focus on people's terrorism movements. So, what can be said is that all forms of "terrorism of innocent people" are unjustifiable and condemnable.

An analysis of vehement protest and terrorism phenomena through the ages will reveal one common thread in the international terrorism fabric — that terrorism springs from acute feeling of discontent and anger by the supposed victimized people against perceived and/or blatant injustice associated with (i) repression and deprivation of basic necessities of living by their government regimes, or (ii) with covert and/or overt domination of their lands and influence on their culture by outside powers and/or dictatorial regimes. Initially, persuasive approaches on their part fail to remove this covert injustice and/or overt subjugation and occupation of their lands. Then, a deep feeling of helplessness sets in, which turns into antagonism and seething anger, ultimately resulting in a noble cause for freedom through terrorism.

8.1.2 State terrorism and democides of entire communities

People have not forgotten how it used to be during the terror-filled hey days of the communist empires. No one felt secure, as everyone was being spied upon, and could at any time be taken away to far off hard labor camps, from where they generally never returned. Millions lost lives in this ruthless state terrorism. Indeed, the cruelest terrorism movements have been these state terrorisms by their secret service agencies. Among state terrorisms against entire communities, the Holocaust (mass killing of Jews, under Nazisn, before and after the Second World War) is a grim reminder that human beings are not yet civilized and are capable of committing genocide.

Mass terrorism against the native inhabitants of the so-called re-discovered lands has gone relatively unnoticed. It is well known that millions of Indians on the Western side of the world were killed in a blood bath of epic proportions. During the hellish apartheid period, everyday was terror-filled. Yet none of the present day nation-champions of the fight against terrorism did anything about it. In fact, they merrily traded with the resource rich apartheid nations. Could the present day level of terrorism be comparable to the state terrorism inflicted on these innocent native people of South Africa? It is to their credit that, after their freedom (following the dismantling of apartheid), they did not resort to conducting a "vendetta-war on terror". So who can be pronounced as moralistic, the state terrorists and their allies or the native people of the soil, whose only criterion for being discriminated and disqualified (by their civilized state regime and its allies) was the color of their skin (over which they had no control).

The history of so many communities that have gained independence from their oppressive regimes is soiled by the blood of their martyrs, who were then labeled as insurgents. During their freedom struggles, they rarely got international support from other countries. This is the problem with all political regimes that are products of present-day forms of political systems; they all have their own vested interests to protect, and moral conscience has little to do with their policies. This is why the one and only Nelson Mendela declared on 30 June 2003 in Galway (Ireland), where he received an honorary doctorate in law from the National University of Ireland, that he appreciated Irish support for the South African people's struggle to end the apartheid racial rule at a time when it was not fashionable to do so.

8.2 Freedom struggles from perpetrated injustices

History bears evidence that military means may not be able to curb even misguided (let alone popular) rebellious movements. When rebellion and insurgency are borne out of a mass perception of injustice and suppression, punitive action alone cannot eradicate it, especially when the imposition is levied by regimes perceived to be the cause of perpetrated injustice and suffering. In 1975, the now independent East Timor was invaded and subjugated by Indonesia, a US ally at that time. Then followed a period marked by excessive human rights abuses in response to the freedom demand and struggle by East Timorians. In August 1999, the people of East Timor voted to begin a process towards independence. Angered by this provocative development, the Indonesian military moved in to clamp down on the traitorous independence movement and, in that process, committed immense atrocities on the people of East Timor. In October 1999, a UN transitional administration was set up to administer the Territory, and on 20 May, East Timor finally became independent.

Let us take another situation of the now independent country of Eritrea, whose annexation by Ethiopia as a province in 1962 sparked a 30-year struggle for independence by Eritrean rebels. In 1993, independence was overwhelmingly approved in a referendum. However, this did not end Eritrea's woes. The May 2000 Ethiopian offensive into the northern portion of Eritrea caused severe damage to its agricultural capacity and economy. While the UN peacekeeping force was set up in December 2000 to monitor the border region, Eritrea has yet to solve its internal problems of illiteracy, dependence on Ethiopian trade for its ports, and an economy based on subsistence farming and herding and that too in a semi-arid climatic region, and low level of skills for industrialization. This emphasizes the need for cooperation (based on neo-humanism) by neighboring countries of a region to form a self-reliant economic bloc, in order to support the maturation process of a newly independent state in the region.

Like East Timor, there are many other provinces within countries, for which strong cases can be made for independence, based on their cultural and psychological alienation and/or marginalization from their parent countries. In all such cases, there has unfortunately been ruthless suppression by the parent countries of these communities' demand for governance autonomy and self-rule. Why does it have to be this way, why do the political regimes of big countries (whose certain provinces have markedly different ethnic populations from their other provinces) have to suppress their communities that no longer feel affinity with them? Why do people of these autonomy demanding provinces have to become martyrs in order to gain freedom to live in dignity? The question in our mind is that why could not the international community solve the Palestinian problem in the same way as the East Timor problem. In the case of Palestinian people's struggle, it would have been so straightforward for the UN security council to position UN peacekeeping troops to maintain peace between the two communities, and work out the blueprint of an independent Palestinian nation. If this was done for East Timor, why not for Palestine and Chechnya?

Why do the political leaders of other countries refuse to turn a blind eye to the oppressed provinces and communities' freedom causes and struggles, for fear of displeasing the political regime of the "parent" country? Why do the political heads of big countries form unholy alliances to support one another's suppressive policies and crimes against humanity? Take the case of the Republic of Chechnya. On 30 May 2003, against the backdrop of the St Petersburg festival associated with the EU-Russia summit hosted by the Russian President, the director of Human Rights Watch's European and Central Division declared that the EU and US leaders should look beyond the festivities to Russian's appalling human rights record in Chechnya. The extravaganza of the St Petersburg festival could not eclipse the big number of murders, forced disappearances and tortures committed in Chechnya, as the Chechen struggle for independence enters its fourth year, making the Republic one of the most dangerous places on earth.

It is because of this immoral alliance-of-convenience among the political-party heads of powerful countries of the world that the people of freedom-starved and culturally-suppressed provinces (like Chechnya and Tibet), that are culturally isolated and suppressed within their imperialist empire-countries, have to undergo immense suffering. If East Timor's case merited independence, there is even more justification for Tibet to at least have governance and political autonomy, for similar reasons. From a moralistic viewpoint, when a province cannot identify itself with the country's politics, is mistreated and is culturally (and ethnically) at odds with the central government of the country and demands governance autonomy, it is pointless and immoral for the country's political regime to forcibly impose its governance over it. In the interest of peace, let the people of that province (or state) decide how they want to live and if they want governance autonomy. This could apply for instance, to Kashmir and Tamil Eelam.

Further, it is quite possible that this new autonomously governed state would not have the resources for sustainable functionality. Hence, it is the moral duty of the neighboring countries to assist this state in its development. For instance, Eritrea cannot maintain itself. Hence, it needs to form a socio-economic trading bloc with some culturally compatible neighboring countries, such as Kenya, Somalia and Sudan. As regards, East Timor, there is a possibility of finding some deep-sea oil resources off its shores. Even then, it is the moral duty of its neighboring countries to assist its all-round development in education and human capacity as well as in agriculture and industrialization.

Today, there are some regions that have had long-standing inter-religious acrimony between two primary religious communities, or were partitioned into separate ethnic and/or religious communities by their colonial occupiers at the time of independence. In these regions, the peoples' suffrage has continued and in fact escalated. In this context, take the case of a nation B whose old-time inhabitants A were displaced from their lands by the new immigrant community B and pushed into living in certain restricted zones. Now, after years of status-less living within nation B, the inhabitants A of these zones demand that it is only fair that their habitats be recognized as a seperate nation A. After decades of this unmet demand, some groups among these state-less inhabitants A become militant, and out of helplessness resort to suicide-bombings. This prompts the nation B to have its military forces repeatedly bomb the territory of people A, in order to root out terrorism. Then, ignoring the root cause of terrorism, the nation B declares that there could be no negotiation, and the occuption forces B would remain in the territory of population A, unless the protesters of community A started acting in a civilized way. But how can people of community A stop protesting when their homes are being destroyed, their lands are being invaded by the B forces, and they have been living status-less for years? It is often this feeling of helplessness and hopelessness that cultivates terrorism!

8.2.1 Social rebels or freedom fighters?

"Terrorism for the cause of justice" figures in the history of most nations. Today, etched in the annals of history, are the so-called treasonists and terrorists of their times, who were persecuted for defying state terrorism. Today's role model social liberator, the icon for freedom and dignified living, Nelson Mandela was charged with treason and imprisoned, for challenging the racist political system of apartheid in South Africa, for 27 years of hard labor. Then, there is Mzee Tomo Kenyatta (1889–1978) who, before becoming the prime minister of a free Kenya in December 1963, was imprisoned for seven years of hard labor for causing "disturbance of peace".

Why has folklore popularized Latin-American hero Dr. Che (Ernesto) Guevara for fighting for the rights of peasants against dictatorial regimes, and Robin Hood for robbing the rich to help the poor by defying the dreaded forest law (retaining vast lands as preserves for the king and his officers)? Then, there is that song about Kevin Barry, about how he lived to free Ireland. Even though he was dubbed as a traitor by the colonial regime and hung in 1921, according to the Irish he still lives in the hearts of all free men.

Let us journey to Ireland in the late 18th century. Inspired by the American War of Independence and by the democratic ideals of the French Revolution, the Irishmen exercised their right to gain their liberty by the use of arms. Continued ruthless suppression of this struggle for independence led to the formation of the Irish Republican Army (IRA) and its declaration (in 1916) of the independent Republic of Ireland. By 1919, a widespread guerilla warfare had begun. The terrorist activities of IRA became examples of guerilla warfare, for future anti-colonial struggles throughout the world. So many IRA liberators or terrorists (depending on which side they are perceived) became martyrs, while the IRA chief-of-staff Sean MacBride in the 1930s was awarded the Nobel Peace Prize as well as the Lenin Peace Prize.

In fact, in every continent, there have been rebel movements and terrorist activities against directly or distantly ruling regimes. Depending on the side from which these movements are perceived, the people engaged in these movements have either been labeled as political activists or freedom-fighters or rebels or terrorists. So, there is a global divide in the perception of these activities as rebellions or freedom struggles or terrorist movements. Such are the trials and tribulations of even genuine freedom fighters that to their victimized people, they are heroes. However, to the establishment, they are perceived as treasonists.

According to the leader of the Liberation Tigers of Tamil Eelam or LTTE, when the non-violent democratic struggles of the Tamil people of Sri Lanka (to determine their own political and economic life, to solve their basic problems) were met with military repression, he felt that armed struggle was the only alternative, while being fully aware that the liberation movement would be outlawed. So, is the LTTE movement to be regarded as an outlawed terrorist movement or a separatist movement for self-government? One wonders why the supposed International Anti-terrorism movement has not included terrorism activities in Northern

Ireland, Chechnya, Sri Lanka, Kashmir and many other hot-beds of terrorism in its sphere of operation? The reason is that the so-called big powers are divided in the labeling of these activities, depending on who their allies are. Also, it is in the covert interest of nations (in their gambits for enhancing their own spheres of influence) to thus have the power of other rival nations diminished by this internal turmoil.

8.2.2 "Religion for virtuosity" or "terrorism for religiosity"?

There is today yet another stimulation for terrorism, namely religiosity. Could we regard the massacre of Jerusalem by the crusaders in 1099 as terrorism or holy war? Almost four centuries earlier occurred the invasion and arabization blatant of Persia, involving large scale killing and virtual extermination of zorastrians — could that be regarded as invasion or *jihad*? Indeed, religiosity has all along been a stimulus to wars and invasions. What characterizes terrorism emotionalized by religiosity (or "holy terror") from supposed secular terrorism is its aura of conferred legitimization. From time immemorial, religionistic terrorism has all along been given a moral adjudication.

It is not just a present-day phenomenon of zealotism and religionism. Nevertheless, even for obtaining freedom from terrorism, fueled by religiosity, one needs to study the terrorism trials. Is there no historical evidence that terrorism and militancy have germinated in the face of perceived psycho-religious and oppression by unsympathetic regimes? Further, have not suppression of these movements exacerbated these problems instead of solving them by rationality?

In all forms of violence (terrorism and war), these are persons of words who stir up the persons of action. In the case of religious radicalization, the inspirationists decree that violence and death in the case of religion is virtuous. In the case of war (declared to supposedly protect the people of the land), the chief politicians make public speeches and visit battle zones in fake combat uniforms, to try and act heroic, and impress patriotic fervor within the soldiers (that they are fighting in the cause of nationhood safety and freedom).

Indeed, what constitutes virtuosity needs to be carefully considered in order to avoid mental colonization by dogmatic paragons of virtue, especially because some religious dictates could well be specific to the then prevalent culture of the place of origin of the religion. It would indeed be a human rights tragedy if the dedication to religiosity be further carried forward to help create theocratic states, wherein jurisprudence is based on interpretation of religious tenets and laws (handed down from the still prevalent but irrelevant ancient social customs) than on cardinal principles?

8.3 Freedom from terrorism

8.3.1 Extermination by elimination or elimination by assimilation?

To date, a prime cause of terrorism in various parts of the world (including Palestinian territory, Northern Ireland, Chechnya, Kashmir and Tamil Eelam) is that the communities involved want self-governance, so as to be able to express themselves more intrinsically in different facets of living. This requirement is so basic that it should not pose a dilemma, except to political leaders who cannot accept their nation's territory to be diminished. Another major cause for international terrorist movements is anger over their nations being ideologically dominated and neo-colonized by the powerful nations. Would it not be possible for these militarily powerful nations to understand this feeling of humiliation caused by the presence of foreign military forces on their lands?

What is not tolerable is some perceived notion of a religious empire comprising of several religious nations, culminating in international religious terrorism. So then how to diffuse and dismantle terrorism: should we exterminate terrorism by simply eliminating the terrorists, or should we eliminate terrorism by bringing would-be terrorists into the mainstream of society, and how? Does present day terrorism require a coalitional militant response to all the diffused pockets of terrorism throughout the world and/or some kind of an international forum to investigate and diffuse the perceived inequities of our times?

Another potential brewing of discontent has been stemming from an enhanced consciousness of resource channeling from resource-rich Third World nations to industrially developed as well as militarily powerful countries. This could be compounded by the call for globalization and free trade by these powerful nations. However, even in these industrialized nations, politically conscious segments of population share the opinion of Third World nations that globalization and free trade are neo-attempts by the "successful countries" to further deplete and cause large scale unemployment within the "lagging countries".

By trekking the trails of discontent and terrorism, we can obtain some idea of the diverse psychological terrain of terrorism. Within this psychology, dogmatic religionism can be overcome by rationality, education and spiritualism (by uplifting of the mind). Aside from this psychology, there is this prevalent feeling of threat (among many people of the developing regions) of further erosion of their means of livehood and culture by the prospect of forced globalization. Embedded in this psychology is yet another potential breeding ground of terrorism.

Hence, in order to mitigate this growing perception of injustice (and the brewing of terrorism),we need to develop a neo-socio-economic political order, which will result in: (1) a more just and equitable distribution of resources and privileges, (2) opportunities to acquire better living standards by the big majority of (the poor) people in the world, (3) a better quality of life for everyone, (4) diffusion of the causes for perceived injustice, (5) assimilation of potential terrorists into the mainstreams of society (by also reforming it), and hence (6) sustainable peace.

This requirement is satisfied by our proposed socio-economic-political framework of:

- cooperative and more democratic capitalism, within a professionally governed socio-economic democracy;
- of grassroots sustainable communities (FSCs) within each economically self-reliant bloc, with a cooperative psychology and setup to assist one another to enhance their respective living standards;
- self-reliant zones, cooperating as regional federations under the aegis of a non-hegemonic world government system, providing equal empowerment to all nations; and
- having a comprehensive constitutionally incorporated charter of human rights.

Such a composite neo-humanistic (socio-economic political) system can provide the means of preventive cure from terrorism, how?

8.3.2 The causes and symptoms of terrorism

There are basically three ideological forms of terrorism movements. One forum constitutes a concentrated movement for right of self-governance by communities within nations. The second is a movement of diffused terrorist groups, unified by a common cause of freedom from threats to the fundamentalism of their religious culture. These groups also feel threatened by prospects of economic globalization. They also find the presence of foreign troops and military bases on their lands to be intolerable. The third type is a movement by victimized people, marginalized from society because of their ethnicity (such as the native people of Australia) and caste (such as the Dalits in India) and/or by persisting and seemingly incorrigible situations that keep them impoverished.

This last-mentioned forum and group can be satisfied by our system of: (1) work-based and residential cooperatives, and (2) recognition of the rights of the people of the soil in having a prime role in the development of natural resources and in converting them into in-demand products. The psychology of work and living cooperatives will be to live and work cooperatively, to assist one another to develop all their potentialities, to be able to earn adequately for a decent living, while also having social security provision for one's old age. Further, in our enlightened societal structure, it would be awkward for anyone to be caste conscious. In any case, the poor and socially ostracized people (hitherto forced to live outside the townships) could also be organized into cooperatively structured micro communities, with governmental funding (from their economic bloc) to develop their work and living modalities.

The second-mentioned movement is based on the group's perception that globalization will result in cultural colonization, and hence could dent their religious values. There is also heightened concern and antagonism against the growing superpower-militarism of their lands, perceived by them as an alternative mode of colonization. Our system can also provide a solution to this issue, by means of our:

- neo-concept of "economic democratic and equitable globalization," which will (1) provide equivalent renumerations for equivalent work services, thereby paving for convergence to economic parity, and (2) grant FSC status to big religious cultural groups or communities, with autonomy in governance as long as their laws are based on secularism and not on ancient outmoded regulations and religionism;
- world government system, in which there will be no scope for belligerent adventurism on the part of any nation and also no provision for any (micro or super power) nation to station troops and military bases in other lands.

Now, with regards to the first-mentioned terrorism movement for the right to self-governance, there is a distinct scope in our socio-economic political structure for communities that are dissatisfied with the treatment and biases of their governments, to be granted FSC status. This also applies to displaced and homeless communities. All of these maginalized, displaced or alienated communities could live more peacefully and govern themselves in their own states. They would then be able to chart out their own destiny and constitution. This provision does not mean that these newly emerging FSCs could also impose religionary (civil and criminal) judicial codes. In fact, under the world governmental system, there would be secularism and jurisprudence based on cardinal and neo-humanistic virtues (of benevolence, prudence, temperance and fortitude).

8.4 Premises for peace

Today, there are many instances of communities and provinces that are unhappy with their national governments, and are sites of terrorism. They feel politically neglected by the national government and alienated from the mainstream national culture, and want to become independent or at least have governance autonomy. So for a community or a province that is grossly dissatisfied and discontented with the way it is treated by the country's government, and also does not share a common identity with it, the first premise for peace is that it be given autonomy in governance.

Even the more difficult problem of a cultural desecration cause-related diffused terrorism, by members of a community P, can be solved by recognizing that the prime cause for terrorism is the widespread antagonism against encroachment over their lands, and destruction of their habitat with concomitant cultural denigration. For instance, the solution of the Israel-Palestine problem could have been carried out years back, by according nationhood status to Palestinian lands, so as to enable people of both sides to live peacefully. Way back in 1967, General Yitzhak Rabin should have insisted that Israel return the Arab territories that it had won, in exchange for peace. Often, it takes a visionary general to recognize the imperils of war and exchange annexed territories for peace. Unfortunately, it is the virtual generals, in the garb of ministers or secretaries of defense (who would be dead scared of being in a battle environment, except on television), who are generally the biggest advocates of war and hard-line approach. Often and unfortunately, the politics turns out to be these war-mongering defense ministers (or secretaries) versus embattled generals for peace.

Two generations of Palestinians have been living as displaced people. After years of living without national identity, is it not justified for at least their habitats' territories to be given the status of nation? In fact, the morality-preaching righteous countries should have seen to that long before some Palestinian groups became militant after years of desperation. Over the past turbulent years, the UN has allowed the indiscriminate killing of Palestinian civilians as well as rampant destruction of their homes, causing distressed Palestinians to carry out suicide bombings in civic zones of Israel and death of Israeli civilians. Could not the UN have averted this decade-old bilateral tragedy by placing a peacekeeping force to monitor the border (as was done for Eritrea), while the Palestinian nationhood procedures would have been finalized? Likewise, the Chechnyan problem could also have been similarly resolved. The tragedy is that the UN can only act and intervene at the consent of the major powers.

The reason for this contrived prolongation of the sufferings of the Palestinian and Chechnyan people is because in both cases the interests of the political leaders of some permanent members of the security council have been involved; they have formed a nexus to protect their interests. The international handling of these struggles depends on the political interests of the heads of governing political parties, who impose their political will and decisions (contrary to the peaceful desires of their people) by sentimentalizing the people to suit their political and financial interests. They, thereby, manipulate people's support of their anti-peace designs antipathic to civilian interests. This is a prime reason for us to end this oligarchy of political parties and usher in civilian democracy (devoid of political parties).

This granting of governance autonomy to discontented communities, perceiving themselves to be disadvantaged or suppressed (as in the case of Tibet, Chechnya and Tamil Eelam in Sri Lanka), need not be regarded as a sign of weakness on the part of the nation's political regime. Rather, it should be regarded as a decision in the best interests of all concerned, and a step towards peace. However, the current centralized and political party-based (so-called) governance of a country makes it very difficult to address the needs of neglected states and provinces that are geographically and/or culturally distant from the nation's capital. Very often, distant and border provinces of big empire-nations (such as China and Russia) are also culturally quite different from the mainstream population within the nation. Yet the decision to grant governance autonomy would be deemed to be a sign of weakness on the part of the political governance party, and would generally be counter to the sentiment of the majority of the people.

Since in the current political party system of democracy (PSOD), the overriding factor is for the party in power to hold on to it at any cost, the political system mitigates awarding of governance autonomy to disenchanted and alienated provinces. However, in our proposed socio-economic democracy and professional governance (SED & PRG) system, the legislators would be independent of party pressures and interests, be only concerned with collective welfare, and recognize that the granting of FSC status is a step to alleviate antagonism and bring about peace. If FSC status were to be given to many disenchanted communities, it would go a long way to bringing about a peaceful atmosphere, globally.

The second premise is that, within an FSC, the rights of the people of the soil need to be recognized in projects for the development of natural resources in their lands. Powerful nations should not even be indirectly involved in attempting to have influence on a newly formed state or FSC, so as to gain control over its natural resources. The third guideline is that these newly formed autonomously governed states or FSCs be assisted by other neighboring states to develop agro-industrial infrastructure and community services (with an emphasis on education). This could consist of assistance with developing natural resources and their conversion into products, educational and healthcare institutions, water supply and sanitation services, electrical power supply and industry.

In other words, this new community needs to be integrated into the regional economic bloc. For this purpose, discussions need to be held between this newly formed autonomously governed community and the neighboring FSCs or nations, as to what items can be exported by this community to its neighbors and what items need to be imported, so that:

- the community population's living needs are catered to, and
- there is balance of imports and exports, so as to gradually transform this new community into a functionally-sustainable community.

Throughout the history of human civilization and even today, the vast majority of the people have been poor while their rulers have been prosperous. Is that fair? Now, with so much rhetoric on "security from terrorism" by the political leaders, the plight of millions of poor people has taken a backseat. In gearing developing countries to support their campaign against terror, the political leaders of Western countries have been issuing the slogan: without security, there cannot be prosperity. However, the viewpoint of the neglected poor is: without prosperity, how can we have security!

8.5 Reparation programs

8.5.1 Reparation for state terrorism and crimes against humanity

Recently, a Reparations Coordinating Committee (RCC) was formed by a powerhouse team of Afro-American lawyers and academics to sue corporations (with a history of association with slavery) that dealt in slave trade (purchase and auction), slave indenture, slave labor (of mining, oil and railroad companies) and slave insurance. It is the contention of RCC that because these corporations made and possessed wealth that was created by slaves, it is time for the descendents of those slaves to reclaim that wealth and use it for upliftment (for education, healthcare and neighborhood rejuvenation) of the present day descendents of the slaves.

Similar reparation justification arrangements can hold good in the case of nations that have been involved in state racism and terrorism (apartheid), and/or have systematically carried out "ethnic cleansing" by mass killings and/or driving out the "other racial groups" to make them refugee communities. It can also be contended that the present day gap and divide between the First World countries and Third World nations is partly because of two to three centuries of colonization by many of the present day First World countries. These colonial powers systematically looted and depleted the resources of their colonies, repressed their people and deprived them of their fundamental rights as children of the soil. They persecuted those who dared to demand (let alone fight for) independence (and freedom), branded them as terrorists, and prosecuted them for treason.

These eras of entire native communities (of, for instance, the American continent) of slavery, colonization and apartheid (spanning over the not too distant past) violated all norms of human decency, and caused tremendous physical and psychic trauma to the victims of ethnic massacres, slavery, colonization and apartheid. Not only that, the perpetrators of slavery and apartheid as well as the colonial nations carried out untold crimes against humanity. Today, years after these eras have ended, their victims and their progeny still bear the economic and/or psychic scars of the tortures meted out to their forefathers.

In India, the colonial rulers levied a tax on farmers, by virtue of which they had to give a portion of their produce to the local ruling authorities. Could not this tax be regarded as a torture? Farmers provide food, doctors provide healing, while teachers provide knowledge and inculcate values. They all merit the community's respect and gratitude. Particularly, in developing countries, farmers borrow and toil to till the soil, but are at the mercy of the rains to raise the crops to feed the people and to maintain themselves. They live and die in poverty and debt. It is hence unethical to tax farmers, in terms of a portion of their crop produce. Hence, such taxation levied on these poor farmers by the colonial rulers constituted a most inhuman act. However, while these poor farmers died toiling, others died for expressing that their lands be free.

8.5.2 Conscience-clearing reparation programs

It is now time for these perpetrators of crimes against humanity to apologize, and provide compensation damages, as a matter of principle. While this will not right the wrong, the attitude of these communities and nations whose ancestors treated fellow human beings so inhumanely will go a long way towards soothing their conscience and creating goodwill towards them from the aggrieved and victimized communities. For instance, if the former colonies and communities whose people were abducted to serve as slaves were compensated and their stolen heirloom returned, this amount could be utilized for their community development programs — to develop the agro-industrial base as well as the municipal, educational and healthcare services. As a result, it could be possible for these Third World countries to at least become Second World, thus serving as more effective trading partners for these First World countries. This will bring to bear some decency in ameliorating the present day ever-widening gap between the former colonial nations and the colonies, to serve as a starting point of globalization.

As a first step, all of these former politically colonized nations, communities of people whose ancestors were enslaved and victims of ethnic cleansing, as well as former communities that were colonized by and persecuted under communist regimes (by those nations that controlled and exported communism) should organize reparation committees, investigate the history, develop detailed documentation of crimes against humanity, and study the legal avenues of seeking reparation from the crimes' perpetrators. If these reparation groups lend solidarity to one another, it could become an international group movement.

The reparation could take various forms. In the case of discriminated and/or formerly enslaved communities and/or exterminated native communities, the reparation would have to be by the governments of these countries as well as by the institutions and corporations responsible for the inhuman treatments (such as, for example, temples and churches, specific mining and farming corporations, as well as insurance companies and banks). The reparation could be in the form of neighborhood upliftment for better living conditions and jobs creation, augmented educational and healthcare facilities, better purchasing capacity and social security.

In the case of former political colonies, the reparation could be in the form of rural development and urban upliftment programs, improved healthcare delivery, agricultural and industrial technological assistance, and extensive higher educational opportunities in their former ruling nations. Instead of financial compensation to the governments of these former colonies (which could run the risk of misutilization and of augmenting the assets and furbishing the homes of their politicians), itwould be better for these former colonial nations to be directly involved in community development projects in order to ensure proper utilization of these compensatory schemes. In fact, the people of these former colonies would also prefer and welcome the direct involvement of the former ruling nations in these community development projects, because of their distrust of their own politicians.

In the case of communities that have become generations of refugees in foreign nations, the reparation would have to entail making provision for them to return to and be settled in their homelands, along with schemes for living and occupational rehabilitation as well as educational and healthcare facilities. These resettlement procedures should be immediately carried out, as a just solution for people driven out of their homelands. Further, the homeland on which these displaced native people have been living should be accorded the status of nationhood, and the two contentious parties should be separated by political and physical boundary. The contention of "no negotiation unless violence stops", by the occupant nation against the native people, is untenable on two grounds. Firstly, the sooner the nationhood is granted, the better it would be for peace and security of the region. Secondly, on ethical grounds, the former inhabitants of the region should have nationhood granted at least on the small land to which they have been relegated to living.

8.6 Global movements

As to who or which agency should be given responsibility to enact these reparation procedures and rehabilitative programs (at least until the neo-political structural reorganization takes place), the International Court at Hague could undertake that responsibility, and direct the United Nations to implement their decisions. Thus, the various reparation committees could make representations to the International Court at Hague. Who can and would be able to devote time to this noble cause? In this endeavor, it is necessary for the Third and Fourth World group leaders to come together and coordinate their efforts. Academics at Universities (the professors of history, political science and law) could also be involved in this movement through courses and supervision of doctoral research and theses. In fact, a global reparation and rehabilitation movement (GRRM) could thus be launched, in order to bring awareness to the unbearable torturing and persecution of certain castes and races, ethnic and indegenous populations by governments, political leaders and powerful social groups.

Let us, however, keep in mind that reparation and justice are not an end but only the means to bring about awareness of our past mistakes. From now onwards, we need to adopt a philosophy of life, linking us all by one fragrant garland of goodwill, so that we start living altruistically. Cooperating to promote the welfare of one and all, let us initiate a global movement to bring about sustained peace on our earth.

Let us elevate our minds to a higher level of consciousness, so that we can then ascribe our ignominious history to our pre-evolutionary state.

Let us develop a lofty philosophy of ideation and living, so that we can help one another to progress to a nobler dimension of living.

Let us populate our democratic governance system with enlightened colleagues,
so that we can usher a new era of cooperative living.

Imbibing the lofty ideas of neo-humanism, we can rise above narrow sentimentality,
so that we can live as a universal family.

Flooding our minds with these ideals, let us move in unison along the ethereal avenues,
to live among loftier civilizations in the cosmos.

A Palestinian woman reacts as she looks at her demolished house in the Brazil neighborhood of the southern Gaza Strip town of Rafah 23 May 2004. Intense gun-battles broke out on the streets of Rafah, as Israeli tanks and bulldozers backed by helicopter gunships demolished buildings. On day 6 of Operation Rainbow (the Israeli army's biggest-ever operation in the Gaza Strip) which left 43 Palestinians dead in less than a week, after 13 Israeli soldiers were killed in the Gaza Strip in four days in the previous week. This bilateral ongoing tragedy could have ended long ago if the UN had been independent to authorize UN forces along the Israeli-Palestinian border and pass a mandate for an independent Palestinian state.

No one is caring for this on-going human tragedy. In our uncivilized world, state governments operate as short-term contractors, to somehow get elected to manage the resources and control the policies of states (in the guise of state governance). They cannot be relied upon or expected to care for and solve human tragedies that do not impact their contract renewals (through elections) for another term of governance. It is the immediate neighbors of Palestinians and Israelis who have lacked the will and moral courage to solve this problem.

A separate Palestine state should have been established, by UN mandate, long time back. Hence, it is unrealistic to keep waiting for the US and the other permanent members of the UN Security Council to take up this issue in the UN, unless economically and politically pressurized by the united front of Arabic countries. For this purpose, the Middle-Eastern countries should form a powerful economic-political bloc, which can exercise the requisite pressure on the UN "law makers".

9

Ethics of Politics: Politician versus People Sovereignty

9.1 The powerful weaponry trade

Weaponry is probably the biggest industry and trade in the world, followed perhaps by trade in drug and endangered species. This is a shame on the level of civilization on our Planet Earth. Even chemical weapons as well as weapons of mass-destruction have been extensively used on human populations, and that too by the most powerful nations who in turn hypocritically impose economic sanctions and even launch military campaigns against weaker nations suspected of developing nuclear arsenals. Ignoring protests of human rights groups, some of these nations have even carried out testing of their nuclear weaponry in international areas and waters, thereby endangering the lives of human settlements in that region. Then, it seems hypocritical for them to adopt the stance of morality, to denounce smaller countries aspiring to develop their nuclear arsenals, and even pass United Nations (UN) legislations against the development of weapons of mass destruction.

It is, hence, morally and ethically appropriate that no country should have weapons of mass-destruction. However, weaponry trade constitutes a huge income to the militarily powerful nations, whose powerful weaponry industry (providing major financial support to their democratic/political elections) would not permit such an ethics-ridden legislation. Also, who is to decide and impose this legislation on this powerful league of destructive weapons-owning nations. The UN is inept, crippled and dictated by those very countries. The smaller nuclear club membership-aspiring countries would also not want to be thrown out of the global trade network. So no one dares to say anything, except meekly allow themselves to be dictated (concerning their behavior and policies) on the international political stage, or face dire consequences of economic blockade or even invasion (especially if an ambitious small nation is sitting on rich natural resources).

The moral solution is for no country to have weapons of mass destruction. But who will dare to pass this legislation, when the UN Security council is only concerned with the interests of its permanent members. Besides, with the UN's past record, will countries (especially smaller nations) trust that the UN will provide them protection in the case of attack from other countries. This is why such a resolution may not be feasible unless we can develop such a global socio-economic political order that mitigates the need for nations to protectively arm themselves. That is why we propose a total transformation of the global political structure of nations, in favor of the system of culturally homogeneous economic blocks under a world government. In this neo-global political structure, devoid of political parties and professional politicians, the primary cause to be served by the elected governance officers would be the sovereignty of the people and not of the political parties. Further, the world government charter would make it implicit that all governance and legislative members (of communities, blocs and zones) are expected to work for the welfare of the people, of all people — local, regional and global.

9.2 Ethics of democracy

The 2002 UN Report on Human Development asserts that democratic governance is fundamental for human development, because of the premise that democracy provides equal opportunities for all people to live equally. However, analysis of the richest and poorest democratic countries can reveal that the characteristic feature of their societies is gross inequality, in:

- the salaries of people working in the same organization;
- the wealth of people, with the acceptance that all is fair in money-making endeavors, unmindful of who gets short-changed;
- the ratio of income tax payments to the wealth of the payers;
- the wealth of politicians compared to that of people working in government organizations;
- perception and realism of democracy; and
- learning, dedication and morality of politicians and academics.

This indicates that the so-called democracy-in-practice is all talk and no substance. The most concessation that capitalist political scientists can conceive of is to make capitalism more democratic, by democratizing financial institutions into providing insurance to home-owners to protect themselves against their home losing value. However, they fail to perceive the non-democratic nature of the electoral process based on the financial strength of the political candidates and on the financial support to their election campaign by big corporations. They also fail to note the dictatorial ways of the political heads of (i) so many developing countries, in being apathetic to their people's struggle for living, and (ii) powerful nations in making crucial decisions affecting peoples' lives and global peace. Even then, the capitalist democratic governance is deemed to be the preferred governance system for all nations.

Today, throughout the world, the only voices heard are those of political leaders; their pompous lifestyles and their doings make headlines, while social scientists and intellectuals waste their time discussing them. These political-party heads do not represent the moral conscience of the people. Rather, they play on the narrow sentiments of the people to gain their support. Further, these political leaders (or hijackers of democracy) collude with one another to support their adventures in controlling weaker developing nations. Unfortunately, the developing nations also do not have moral and courageous leaderships, to form non-aligned nation-blocs to help one another to together constitute economically sustainable and politically independent nation-blocs. All they are capable of doing is approaching the leaders of powerful nations with begging bowls, in return for supporting their foreign policies or for giving them military bases. This is why the polarization of the world continues today.

This is not democracy of any form. Democracy implies that the people are in the forefront. Their voices, their needs and feelings, their despair and ideas are heard and implemented by an eclectic legislature. At the World Economic Forum held in Jordan from 21–23 June 2003, in a special meeting organized by the British Broadcasting Corporation on Democracy in the Arab world, some of the democracy attributes mentioned by the panelists and the participants were that democracy entailed government accountable to the people, opening up of political space, listening to the voices of extremism, civilian society designing local agendas and governmental institutions, government involving the civil society as a partner in dialogue towards a more responsive governance.

Unfortunately in today's politics, based on the loyalty norms of functioning of political parties, all the credit for policies has to be attributed to the heads of states, from economic strategy to peace plan. Can Reaganomics be regarded as an innovative economic policy, conceived by former president Ronald Reagan? Likewise, can the Road map to Peace and creation of a Palestinian state be attributed to George Bush, when something so basic and rational has been promulgated for decades and even though he has denied the right of Palestinian refugees to return to their homelands. Indeed, politicians get themselves exempted from many crimes that civilians get indicted for; one of them is plagiarism. Another common ailment that most politicians suffer from is megalomania. For instance, China's constitution had to amend to incorporate Jiang Zemin's Three-represents Theory, allowing capitalists to join the communist party — a contradiction to communism! In most cases, the heads of states (i.e., of the ruling political parties) have neither original ideas nor intellectual capacity, and neither vision nor conscience to enact people-centric policies.

In all present-day political systems, the process by which politicians become CEOs of governments makes it inevitable that most heads of nations (from the most advanced to the most under-developed) are blissfully ignorant of governance matters and incompetent to frame policies. They mostly rely on their aides and cabinet members, who (as prices of loyalty) are expected to bequeath all the credit to their bosses. So, why not have a democracy wherein the experts themselves are governance executives (representing their community sectors), and involve them directly in the framing of public policies with the support of their respective societal sectors. Indeed, our proposed socio-economic democracy (with its professional governance system) can bring about people's sovereignty, and provide an avenue for the development of lagging nations.

9.3 Safeguarding people from malevolent regimes and outside interventions

In today's global politics, non-democratic regimes of militarily powerful empire-nations (such as China and Russia) and of oil-rich monarchist nations (of the Middle-East), with big markets for consumer products, are respectfully solicited by the so-called global forum of democratic nations (GFDN). On the other hand, small nations perceived to be stepping out of the democratic line are punished and suspended from membership in various leagues of nations. Yet, monarchy regimes of oil-rich nations and even repressively dictatorial communist regimes of nuclear-league countries, with notorious human-rights records, are in fact courted by this democratic nations forum. However, it has been shown that this political-party system of capitalist democracy (PPCD) is corrupt inside-out. Hence, it may not necessarily be the best system for a country with a low level of political morality consciousness as well as a low literacy rate. If in such a country, an ethical military head takes over the governance, then thousands of corrupt politicians and their party people are put out of their shady businesses. All of this can immensely help the average person, who has to contend with having to grease the hands of government staff to get even the smallest tasks done.

In Pakistan, while General Pervez Musharraf's taking over the governance of the country was no doubt undemocratic, it sidelined the corrupt so-called democratic politicians. He has also been able to rein in the extremists religious elements (who would have otherwise controlled the national politics), which could auger well for peace sustainance between India and Pakistan. Further, he has been bringing in the madrasas into the mainstream of the public education system. What is particularly welcome (and essential for the subcontinent) is his imposing a minimal qualification of Bachelor's degree for any political candidate. Should then Pakistan have been suspended from British Commonwealth of nations for not having democracy, even though premature opening-up the national politics to party-based democratic elections would have had peril of a hard-line religionist regime coming into power?

The international community and human rights groups are wary of dictators, and rightly so. This is because in most instances they tend to be megalomaniacs and impose a personal-cult following, entailing their people having to study their books on their humbug social views (as in the case of dictators of Libya and China). Hence, while it may be frustrating to live under a corrupt party-based democratic system, it is far more precarious to accept an impervious dictatorial regime (as in the case of North Korea). Nevertheless, the solution is to not go from capitalist democracy to dictatorship but to socio-economic democracy and cooperative capitalism.

Centuries back, many European nations colonized African, South American and Asian nations, to capture their resources. Today also, this persists; the only difference is that the *predators* and their tactics have changed somewhat. It should be such that each country can adopt and follow an independent non-aligned political policy with a global outlook, without the threat of punishment by being either trade boycotted or even invaded and occupied (especially if it is rich in natural resources) in the supposed cause of "liberation from a dictatorial regime". During the transition period from PPCD to economic democracy and professional governance (SED & PRG), international political ethics demands that all nations sign UN-enacted resolutions:

- committing each nation to adopt and implement (1) internal policies augering for the all-round welfare of their inhabitants, and (2) foreign policies respecting all people's rights and needs for dignified living;
- for human rights implementations in their lands;
- for prevention of terrorism by government regimes on their people, such as what happened in Iraq (under the Saddam Hussien regime) and in Cambodia (under the Khmer Rouge regime);
- preventing stronger nations from invading and occupying weaker nations, such as the occupation of Afghanistan by the Soviet Union;
- for assuming collective responsibility of all nations for "decent living (food and water, clothing and housing, healthcare and education, employment and social security) for all," in stages with to-be-achieved milestones;
- according governance autonomy and/or "nation" status to those communities demanding and justifying it, such as the long-delayed granting of nationhood to the Palestinian territories;
- for ensuring that their democracy is not dominated by their business corporations and/or by small socially privileged elite groups;
- that surveillance be effected on private corporations, to ensure accounting transparency and to not gainfully use the stock market to artificially raise their stocks and worth;

- for non-proliferation and dismantling of nuclear weaponry and other weapons for mass destruction;
- for non-stationing of troops by one country within another country.

While safeguarding the sovereignty of states from foreign intervention, we should at the same time ensure that the local to regional socio-political system is such as to prevent miscreant regimes (such as the Taliban and Khmer Rouge) from coming into power and tyrannizing their people. In our socio-political set-up, from the FSCs at the grassroots level up to the world-government level, there can be no scope for such criminal regimes to come into power, because at the FSC level itself, the societal sectors decide who their representatives will be in the local government. Further, at the world government level, there will be ongoing surveillance of the FSCs to check that ignoramus and dogmatic clerics do not get into Legislative councils.

9.4 Ethics of nations and the power of ethics

All along in the realms of history, the behavior of nations has reflected the personality of their chief politicians (prime ministers or presidents). In most cases, the aggressive policy of a nation has not been shared by the majority of its citizens. On many occasions, the inter-nation wars, border conflicts, ethnic riots and killings are attributed to the chief politicians of the warring nations. For these professional power-obsessed politicians, everything and all policies and maneuverings have only one objective, to get elected by hook or by crook and thereby have another legislative term in power.

On the other hand, in our SED & PRG framework, the relations among nations as well as the political environment within nations (as cultivated by the legislators) will reflect the opinions of the various (professional, services and residential) sectors of the community, who in turn will be concerned with how they can do the utmost for the good of the people. There would be no need for governance executives to emotionalize the people with prejudicial (racial and caste, geo-socio and pseudo-patriotic) sentiments (as is currently the case in so many countries), because the legislators would no longer need to act in the interests of their political parties. They will be closely interacting with and answerable to their respective electoral associations, and then among themselves to enact public policies conducive to the community's progress. In such a set-up, inciting people with prejudicial sentiments would of course be deemed as opposing the maintenance of peace in society. Also, in the framework of our SED & PRG, it would not be possible for oxymorons and morons to bulldoze their way into central-stage politics, neither for cruel dictators (like Saddam Hussein and General Pinnochet) to take over as rulers of their countries, nor for religionist clerics to misguide people into regarding them as guardians of society.

This then brings us to the issue of the ethics of how a nation should conduct itself in international politics. Of particular concern is how should a superpower government regime think and relate to other countries, so as to not propagate its own interests but act for the noble cause of this earth being the peaceful home of the one indivisible human family, with common needs and aspirations for a cooperative progressive living. Throughout history, nations have become superpowers with extended empires, which eventually have crumbled. So nothing lasts, be it a civilization or an empire, a palace or a house. What outlasts human conquests, assets and constructions are noble ideas and ways of living that uplift people's minds. In fact, history bears testimony that when public leaders or superpowers become overbearingly dominating as well as arrogant and ruthless, their downfall is eminent — pride comes before fall! So how should a nation (i.e. its leaders) behave?

9.4.1 Principles of intra- and inter-nation peace

Some of the attributes of a peace seeking and maintaining nation are:

- it must provide a home and haven for its citizens, a place where they feel comfortable to live in, a place where there is freedom and fairness, secularism and opportunism (not just to become rich, but to be able to do noble deeds for the society), morality and security;
- its society must be a cradle of noble values, embedded in the sovereignty (not of the politicians, but) of the people, in facilitating their march to a neo-humanistic stance;
- it should provide autonomy in governance to all its member states or provinces, and promote the attitude of "all for one and one for all" among its member states and for its inhabitants, in the form of public policies;
- it needs to be consistent in its outlook, i.e. it should advocate and promote equivalent benefits for its own people as well as for the people of other nations;
- it should not exploit and bully its weaker neighbors, nor attempt to dominate them by conquest or economically;
- its international policy should not be dictated by self-interest, but by what is in the best interests of the people of other nations;
- it should build a cooperative network with its neighbors, by cooperating with them in the sharing of knowledge and know-how, in trading of resources

and products, and in all that it takes to be a good and reliable member of the global family of nations;

- it should not have a competitive attitude with its neighbors, but rather have a policy to promote collective progress for all the people of its neighbors.

Together, the above attributes constitute the eight-fold principles of peaceful exsistence. Let us say that nation A behaves neighborly with nations B, C and D (i.e. develops all forms and levels of the cooperative policies with them), and that all the nations A to D in turn develop cooperative relations with their respective neighbors. Then, in this spirit, the entire region will become a regional cooperative of nations. Imagine what an uplifting scenario that would be, in comparison with the prevalent inter-nation attitude and culture of self-interest and suspicion, competition and domination.

9.4.2 The power of ethics

In terms of promoting peace, we could complement Norway's role. Norway is not an economic power or a political power; it does not aspire to be so. It has not been particularly attractive for would-be immigrants, but it could claim to be an international capital of peace. From arranging a peace accord between the Aceh province and the Indonesian government to the 1993 peace accord between the Israelis and Palestinians, from brokering peace agreements between the Tamil Eelam nationalists and the Sri Lankan government (in 2002) to the Croatia-Yugoslavia peace settlement, Norway may well be regarded to be the world's leading peacemaker.

What makes Norway such a successful peacebroker? The answer is that it follows most of the above-mentioned eight-fold principles of peaceful existence:

- it has no colonial past and no grand designs on other countries;
- it has no ulterior motives to capture and/or control the natural resources of another country;
- it does not follow the biddings of the big power cartelling nations, nor does it get penalized for not doing so;
- it does not have strategic military alliances, nor does it attempt to exert dominance over other countries;
- its citizens enjoy a good standard of living, and yet they are not arrogant;
- it does immense humanitarian work in so many countries, but does so without parading it;
- it conducts its peace-bringing missions efficiently and without fanfare, and yet does not lobby for its own people to be nominated for the Nobel Peace Prize; and

- it is so well respected by so many nations, and that is verily the power of its political ethics.

9.5 Hyperpower consciousness and the conscience of a hyperpower

9.5.1 Hyperpower consciousness

Is the Norwegian brand of international politics unrealistic because of not promoting self-interest? Should not a hyper (militarily) powerful nation define its own brand of internationalism:

- ensure that it always stays as the most powerful military country, and is also the most economically powerful nation;
- make strategic coalitions for hegemonic undertakings in all the regions of the world, as well as diffuse potentially powerful nations and nip their aspirations in the bud;
- make all nations understand that, if they wish to develop some military capability, they would be better off doing business with its weaponry industry;
- warn emerging countries that their pursuit of high-tech military capabilities will be disastrous for their national interests, to thereby dissuade potential military competitors;
- remind nations and its political heads (especially the developing countries) that being on its side will be rewarding for them;
- make nations open up their markets to its multinational companies, and get them engaged in free trade treaties, so as to create more exports for its agricultural and industrial sectors;
- make it clear to all the nations that if they are not supportive of its policies, then they are automatically against it;
- make its self-interests to be the basis of its foreign policy;
- implement its national security policy on many fronts, by spreading its own brand of internationalism based on its values, culture and national interests;
- be not bound by any international system of law and justice, but to in fact make and propagate its own system of laws, and to essentially be a law into itself;
- be an imperial power, and create its own world-government with itself as its capital.

Should this brand of internationalism and world government be cacophonous to other nations, especially to the Nos. 2 to 5 nations? Perhaps all of these nations (1 to 5) would prefer to be involved in an oligopolistic brand of internationalism. However, in order to review the histories of such internationalism, let us flip back the pages of recent history to the second half of the 20th century, when duopoly between the United States and the Soviet Union dominated global policies. It took just nanoseconds of human history for communism to implode. Let us go back just a bit more to view the end of the so-called British empire, when Britain was forced to withdraw from its colonies. Its political chess game in the Middle East to set up favorable political regimes (under the guise of pro-democratic sentiments to camouflage its covert strategic and oil interests) culminated ignominiously by the rightful taking over of the Suez Canal by the Egyptian government.

So then, what is the right attitude? Europe has taken a very progressive step in forming a European Union, thereby simulating our proposed concept of regional federation moving towards the eventual formation of globally-representative World Government, supporting people-centric democratic governments in all the regions of the world. Perhaps, it might likewise occur to other continental groups of nations that being civilized implies moving away from living by strategic alliances and secret weaponry, to recognize that the most important formula for peace is not to be a superpower but rather to be a super habitat! How should we solve this seemingly oxymoronic conundrum?

It is most heartening that Europe has taken the lead in the formation of our proposed neo-humanistic order of regional unions or federations comprising of independent nations. What now remains is for similar groups of nations to (at the first instance) deepen their democratic and people sovereignty base along with governance autonomy at the community level. Then slowly, the regional union would come to comprise of bordering states, in which the people sovereignty (at the FSC level) would be the prime social order. At the other end of the global political structure, it would seem that once the formation of regional unions or federations is in place, it would be natural to think in terms of a world government of parity among nations. In the meantime, while awaiting this juxtaposition, let us put down some guidelines for the conduct of a superpower nation, for the development of some essential conscience.

9.5.2 Conscience of a hyperpower

In addition to the above-mentioned eight-fold principles of peaceful co-existence and cooperation among neighbors, a superpower nation has added responsibilities:

- it should not be a hypocrite, in having a big arsenal of weaponry while bullying other nations with trade sanctions for not signing a non-proliferation treaty;
- it should not engage itself in subversive activities to dismantle the military build-up of other nations;
- it should respect the rights of other nations to disagree with it on international issues (such as free markets). It should not expect other nations to bow to its wishes, nor should it threaten them with dire consequences;
- it should be impartial in its policy and attitude to other nations; it should not condone lack of democracy in resource-rich friendly nations that are allies, while punishing other nations for lack of democracy so as to gain control of their natural resources;
- it should be a champion of human rights for its own people as well as for the people of other nations, and treat them respectfully;
- it should not promote its own brand of internationalization, based on what is in its own best interests and on how other nations can acquiesce to its demands;
- it should not attempt to even economically colonize other nations;
- it should not issue imperialistic edicts, and expect nations to bow to them;
- it should not pressure and bully other smaller nations to vote in its favor in the UN Assembly on all international issues;
- it should comply with the international code of ethics and criminality, with regards to the conduct of its political leaders as well as its military and peace-keeping forces, in not demanding immunity for its own people for their actions;
- it should not violate international law, by conducting a pre-emptive war (except as an act of self-defense) or by forcing the members of the UN security council to authorize pre-emptive war in violation of the UN charter and law (prohibiting crimes against peace and requiring breach of peace to be settled by peaceful means);
- it should not flaunt its superpower status on the international stage, but rather behave as an entity ready to help other nations to develop and advance (based on the outlook of universalism);
- it should be a role model, in propagating a universal system of laws based on cardinal virtues.

A superpower should set an example to all nations by committing itself to universal jurisdiction. A superpower strength is: (i) not its military-quotient (MQ) and in its military bases in various strategically located countries so as to establish its sphere of influence and contain other competitive nations, but in its emotional-quotient (EQ) in being genuinely interested in the welfare of other nations, (ii) not in its acquisitions capacity (AC) to covertly obtain weaker nations' natural resources, but in its assist-quotient (AQ) in helping other nations to develop.

9.6 Quality of life

It is important to draw up a charter on international political ethics as well as on the ethics and responsibilities of nations and superpowers. We need to also develop an international political structure to promote the lofty concept of a family of nations and communities, bound together by the common objective of providing the maximal scope for psychic evolution. In that respect, our proposed global political world government framework (of FSCs, economic blocs, self-reliant zones, regional federations and world government) has, in fact, been conceived to provide:

- local autonomy in governance, with independence in policy enactment and legislation;
- cooperation among FSCs in all spheres, for mutual benefit with neighbors;
- parity among all the nations;
- a safe world devoid of threats of weapons of mass destructions, and security from territorial encroachment; and
- constitutional human rights and people's sovereignty.

Nevertheless, even in this neo-humanistic global political framework, it is at the grassroots level of an FSC or a nation that the people's quality of life is to be assessed. So let us draw up an evaluation scheme for quality of life quotient of an nation, which could also apply to an FSC.

The Quality of Life Quotient (QLQ) of a Nation:

Item	A Worth 10 points (maximum validity 10 and minimum validity 0)	B Worth 10 points (maximum validity 10 and minimum validity 0)	A − B (ranging from −10 to +10)
1	The extent to which it caters to fulfilling the primary requirements of living.	The extent to which wealth is concentrated and not evenly distributed.	
2	Its constitution protects and endorses human rights.	Only politicians and the wealthy have the privileges of the society.	

3	It caters to the continual upliftment of its people.	Its politicians have no regard for people's welfare.	
4	It has a high literary rate.	Its people progress on their own, in spite of governmental obstacles.	
5	It provides scope for all-round fulfillment of its people.	It stifles the average person's initiatives.	
6	It has a delightful ecological environment, and contributes to global environmental protection.	Its cities are slums, and its rural areas lack even basic amenities.	
7	It has an independent public and foreign policy.	It is a an opportunist, and does not follow any guiding principles.	
8	It is secular by constitution and in its outlook.	It is a religious state.	
9	It has a low crime rate.	It is controlled by the mafia.	
10	It has high GDP and income level.	It exploits other countries resources for its own development, and/or intimidates other countries.	
11	It has a record of standing up for the progress and welfare of other nations.	It has a dismal record of colonization (of plundering its colonies) and/or racism and/or suppression of minorities.	
12	It has an efficient judicial system, from which even common persons can expect justice.	Its judicial system is either bureaucratic and/or unjust and/or corrupt.	
13	It has a competent and caring governance.	Its politicians (and political parties) are incompetent and corrupt.	
14	It extolls democracy.	Its democracy is in the hand of powerful capitalist corporations and the armament industry.	
15	It provides good living conditions.	It is rife with corruption, making it particularly difficult for the common person to survive.	

16	Its quality of life and constitution are based on noble values.	Its does not emphasize human rights and people's welfare; its quality of life is based on money and affluence.	
17	It abides by UN legislation, and does not try to dominate other nations to vote in its favor on international issues.	It does not abide by the Charter of Human Rights and Crimes Against Humanity; it demands immunity for its politicians and armed forces, from being prosecuted by the International Criminal court.	
18	It is most likely to adopt (1) the neo-economics of cooperatives, and (2) socio-economic democracy of a party-less governance system.	It is either entrenched in communism or big-time capitalism.	

The quality of life quotient (QLQ) is formulated as:

$$\mathrm{QLQ} = \left\{ \frac{\left[\left\{ \sum_{J=1}^{18} \text{Item } j\,(\mathrm{A}-\mathrm{B}) \right\} + 180 \right]}{360} \right\} \times 100$$

$$= \left\{ \frac{[\text{Item } 1\,(\mathrm{A}-\mathrm{B} + \text{Item } 2\,(\mathrm{A}-\mathrm{B}) + \cdots + \text{Item } 15(\mathrm{A}-\mathrm{B})] + 180}{360} \right\} \times 100 .$$

This chart can provide insight into what aspects are lacking in a nation's society. Based on the above formula, the QLQ of a nation can range from 0 to 100. If a nation can even merit a QLQ > 50, then it is deemed to be an acceptable place to live in. On the other hand, nations having QLQ > 75 may be considered to be desirable to live in, and deemed to be respectable members of the global community of nations. However, a nation having QLQ < 50 is deemed to be in dire need of reforming its societal values and governance system.

9.7 In the fast lane to world government

We have expressed concern over:

- the deteriorating political ethics among the so-called democratic nations;
- the UN record of only acting when it is in the interests of its controlling nations;
- UN inability to deal with poverty and disease, lack of education and healthcare in developing countries;
- UN priorities being wrapped in the priorities of the powerful nations and not in the priorities of the big Third World population;
- powerful nations placing themselves outside the jurisdiction of the International Court of Justice (at the Hague) and the International Criminal Court (established in July 2002);
- the increasing trend to facism and human rights abrogation in the bastion(s) of democracy;
- the abysmal ethics of the industrial corporate culture virusing the political governance culture of nations as well as that of the World Bank and the International Monetary Fund (and even the World Trade Organization), because of the intricate links between these cultures as well as these of like-minded people at the helm of both cultures.

Under these circumstances, the future of human civilization on our Planet is bleak, unless we adopt the political framework of the world government (WLG), as detailed in another chapter. Let us, however, highlight some of its features. The world government will have governance departments (such as of law, healthcare trade, etc). Each of these departments will have divisions catering to and financially supported by the regional federations. Nevertheless, the world government will only have a role of monitoring and safeguarding the people's sovereignty, security and quality of life. The primary implementation of the neo-humanistic principles of cooperative living and enlightened governance will be at the FSC level.

Even then, in the absence of the political parties, the size of the FSC governance structure will be small, so as to keep the cost of governance as small as possible. If we were to add up the total number of state level legislators and national level ministers in all the nations today, then the total number of legislators and ministers in our neo-political structure will be much less. In other words, we will be converging to a cost-effective system of governance.

Military power of a superpower can threaten and destroy.

However, the power of ethics of a superpower can provide security and peace.

Nevertheless, it is better to be a superplace than a superpower.

When the new era of people-serving political system (involving cooperative economics and collective capitalism along with civilian democracy and people-oriented governance)

and political reorganization of the world regions into regional economic common-markets and world-government (providing equal status in globalization to all nations),

replaces the current era of people-ruling (as opposed to people-serving) political systems (involving competitive economics and individualistic capitalism along with oligarchic democracy and political party-centered governance)

and politico-economic hegemonism of militarily powerful nations (and permanent members of the UN security council),

only then we will have genuine peace (based on equal opportunity for all the people of all nations to enhance their potentialities and live fulfillingly),

and full-bloom human civilization.

10

From United Nations to World Government

This chapter delineates the momentous transformation of the United Nations General Assembly and Security Council (with unequal empowerment of nations) to World Government (for parity among nations).

10.1 The United Nations Charter

We, the people of the United Nations, have determined:

- to save future generations from the scourge of war, which twice in our lifetime has brought untold sorrow to mankind;
- to reaffirm faith in fundamental human rights, in the dignity and worth of human persons, in the equal rights of men and women and of nations large and small;
- to establish conditions under which justice and respect for the obligations arising from treaties and other sources of international law can be maintained; and
- to promote social progress and better standards of living in a larger freedom.

And for these ends:

- to practice tolerance and live together in peace with one another as good neighbors;
- to unite our strength to maintain international peace and security;
- to ensure, by the acceptance of principles and the institution of methods, that armed force shall not be used, save in the common interest; and
- to employ international machinery for the promotion of the economic and social advancement of all people; have resolved to combine our efforts to accomplish these aims.

Accordingly, our respective governments, through representatives in the city of San Francisco, who have exhibited their full powers found to be in good and due form, have agreed to the present Charter of the United Nations and do hereby establish an international organization to be known as the United Nations (UN).

10.2 UN Millennium declaration and principles values

During 6–8 September 2002, the heads of states and governments, gathered at the UN headquarters in New York, and reaffirmed their faith in the UN. They further chartered the following values and principles for a peaceful, prosperous and just world:

1. to uphold the principles of human dignity, equality and equity at the global level;
2. to uphold the sovereign equality of all states, with respect for their territorial integrity and political independence;
3. to ensure that globalization becomes a positive force for all the people of the world; and
4. to emphasize the following values so essential for international relations:

    - the right of men and women to live their lives and to raise their children in dignity, free from hunger, violence, oppression and justice;
    - no individual and no nation to be denied the opportunity to benefit from development;
    - global challenges to be managed by a fair distribution of costs and burdens, in accordance with the principles of equity and social justice;
    - a culture of peace and dialogue to be actively promoted among all civilizations;
    - the current unsustainable patterns of production and consumption to be changed in the interests of the welfare of the people and future generations;
    - nations share the managing of economic and social development as well as threats to international peace and security; and
    - to live with a sense of universal responsibility, identified with the earth community as well as local communities.

For environmental protection:

On 22 May 2002, the following key principles were reaffirmed for environmental protection, in relation to 2002 — The International Year of Mountains:

- to ensure sustainable development for improving the quality of life within the carrying capacity of the earth's life-support system;
- to guarantee the protection of nature, local and indigenous culture; and

- to strengthen, nurture and encourage preservation of traditional skills, agriculture produce, traditional housing and landscaping, and using natural resources in a sustainable manner.

10.3 For human development and deepening democracy

The 2002 UN Report on Human development is about (1) how political power and institutions shape human process, and (2) what it will take for countries to establish democratic governance systems that advance human development of all the people of the world where so many are left behind. We will employ this forum to delineate how (1) the afore-mentioned principles cannot be sustained in the current global political system, and (2) human development of the people of the world can only be fostered in the framework of our advocated socio-economic and political system. Why are we so concerned about politics? This is because people have to operate within political frameworks, free to determine their destinies and to determine the extent to which they can satisfy their living (physical, economic, intellectual and psychic) needs.

The UN report advocates that developing countries establish democratic governance. Now, why is democratic governance so important? This is because democratic governance implies that all the people have the opportunity to be involved in the policy-making and implementation frameworks to advance their development. However, and particularly in developing countries (with a high illiteracy rate and low political and moral consciousness), democratic governance by political parties merely empowers the elected legislators and ministers to occupy political office, and employ it to serve their own self-interests. It may not even be so unfair to state that most of the elected members of state and national parliaments have no concern over people's welfare and do not even have the acumen to address the needs of their people.

Hence, the present democratic system has to be replaced by our formulated system of having the various functional and economic sectors of the community elect their most capable representatives to best govern and fulfill the needs of their respective sectors. Then, these elected governance executives will be responsible to their sectors for promoting the welfare of the people in those sectors, e.g. education and healthcare sectors. Additionally, mechanisms would be in place for the elected legislators to periodically meet and exchange information with representatives of the community sectors, in order to promote a close synergy between the community sectors and the legislators, so as to ensure that public policies reflect and represent the informed and knowledgeable views of the community. We refer to this democratic system along with, the cooperative system of business organization, as socio-economic democracy (SED). As regards governance, it can be said that good governance for human development requires: (1) the fostering of fair and accountable institutions that protect human rights and basic freedoms, (2) governance systems that are not only accountable to the entire civilian population base, but can also elevate the mindset and enhance the knowledge-profile of the people, and (3) enabling all people to participate in making decisions that shape their lives and empower people to press for beneficial socio-economic policies.

Unfortunately at this point of time, all of this is mere idealism, judging from the reality. In so many developing and developed countries, there is no accountability of, for instance, money collected and corporate donations for election campaigns. People's participation in political policy-making is out of the question in the political party system of democracy (PSOD). Political parties will never allow idealism as well as people's priorities and welfare to interfere with their priorities, i.e. to get elected over and over again, and use their politician status to enrich themselves. However, in our SED & PRG (socio-economic democracy and professional governance) system, the elected (independent-thinking) professionals will be accountable to their associations and agencies for their performance. Further, because of the absence of political parties, there will be no question of alliance among this new type of legislators or neo-politicians (in the name of the party) nor will they be expected to (in the interest of party politics and strategy) sentimentalize and mislead the public.

The current democratic system is supported by capitalists — it is no wonder that it is normal for legislators to be wealthy economically but not necessarily intellectually. The UN report argues that democratic governments better respond to the needs of poor people, are better able to protect people from economic catastrophes and can cater to human rights better than authoritarian rule. Nevertheless, it is also stated that there is no correlation of economic growth and distribution with either authoritarianism or democracy. With regards to democratic governance being responsive to people's needs, one only needs to note how much the people mistrust politicians (particularly in developing countries), who always come around to make big promises only before election campaigns. It can be safely said that, in the majority of the so-called democratic countries, the people have to fend for themselves (to even have access to water, let alone drinking water), because they get zero assistance from the legislators (who are busily engaged in making money as fast as possible).

It is also odd that over the last 100 years, political scientists have only been able to provide a choice between democracy and authoritarianism for the people. Inarguably, one fact of today's democracy is that money in politics subverts democratic institutions when it exerts undue influence on who gets selected and what the legislators vote for. From the United States to India, big corporations provide a big percentage of the funding for the political parties. It is no wonder that in Europe and the US, the membership of political parties is severely declining, out of this disillusionment with corporatist democracy. In our SED & PRG system, the question of money for politicking definitely does not arise.

In fact, the increasing public distrust of capitalist corporations is synonymous with increasing public distrust in political parties. The increasing consciousness among people of the "realities versus misplaced idealism of corporatist culture" will result in the reforming of capitalist corporations into cooperative corporations, and of capitalist democracy into socio-economic democracy, in accordance with the psychology and needs of the various socio-economic sectors of society. In this system, only the professionally competent people (with added CAS* degrees) will be elected by the sectorial constituencies.

10.4 Globalization

The 2002 UN Millennium Declaration of the heads of nations advocates that globalization needs to become a positive force for bringing people together towards a common denominator of living standard. However, the world is becoming even more fragmented between the rich and poor, as well as between the powerful and the powerless.

This is why, anti-globalization protests in industrial countries and on the part of developing countries are driven by the demand for responsiveness to the needs of poor nations and people. However, the prime concern of people with the globalization movement is that it is controlled by the same countries that have either been colonial powers or have economic colonization designs. These countries have been the bastions of business corporational control of democracy (of capitalist democracy) in the own lands, and would like to see a similar brand of democracy in all the developing countries. However, when capitalist corporatism has been indicted for corruption and public deception, and when the public mistrust of the present day democratic process and its politicians is at its peak, who will trust the globalization process put forth by the same group of nations and indirectly by their powerful capitalist corporations (with questionable ethics)?

Globalization can only achieve the remit of poverty eradication and convergence to near-uniform living standards when there is a structured and transparent system

*Community Administrative Science degree, mentioned in Chapter 7.

of movement of resources (and know-how) and products (and produces) between nations, after the socio-economic democratic system is in place. Suppose that an IT company in affluent nation A wants to open a branch in developing nation B, so as to utilize its IT professionals. Currently, it could employ people in nation B, pay them very low salaries, and have the technology sent back to nation A. However, if the socio-economic democratic system is in place, then this kind of exploitation of the labor of nation B will not be possible, because this multinational company would have to be cooperatively structured and managed.

Let us take another example of a pharmaceutical company (in an affluent nation C) wanting to establish a herbal drug manufacturing plant in a developing nation D. In the current setup of immoral business adventurism, it could be possible for this multinational company to form a partnership with a local capitalist, systematically utilize the locally available herbs for drug manufacturing, and even patent the technology. This could then encroach on the rights and customs of the local people, who would have been using a home-made form of this technology for centuries. Now, in our socio-economic democratic system, it would be mandatory for the local people to be involved in their land's natural resource development and conversion into products. Further, engagement and exploitation of low-wage labor would be prohibited, and the salaries payable to the local people would have to attain on par level (with the salary structure in the developed nations) within a certain time frame.

When our proposed re-organization of regions (starting with developing regions) into self-reliant economic blocs and zones is in place, it will enable the developing countries to assist and cooperate with one another, and thereby raise their educational and agro-industrial levels as well as elevate their civil and community services. All of this will enhance the social and knowledge capitals in the developing countries. At this stage, the socio-economic-political situation would be appropriate for effecting equitable and democratic globalization.

10.5 Political alliances and national security

Political alliances between nations generally implies alliances for mutual self-interest. This invariably leads to groupism in international politics. Also, when the alliance is between a developing and developed (as well as militarily powerful) country, it implies subservience of the former to the latter. This has a danger of abrogation of human rights in the developing countries.

Nowadays, all nations are being compelled into forming political and even military alliances. As it is, in many developing countries, there is very little conscience among the politicians to bother about policies for public welfare and progress. Now, when strategic military alliances again return to the center of national policy-making, there is the added danger of compromising human rights for supposed national security, in addition to a compounding of unconcern for the public.

As regards to national security, it is deemed that security forces are in democratic control, in democracy. However, in many developing countries, there is popular disillusionment with the politicians because of their poor ethics. When distressed people start protesting, then security forces are employed by the government to restore order, resulting in violence against civilians. Then, it is the poor people who are the primary sufferers. It is estimated (as per the UN report) that in the 20th century, governments (i.e. government forces) killed almost a billion people, at a rate for exceeding that attributed to dissent terrorism over the past four years.

In these circumstances, in some countries, the military heads take over control of the government, to restore law and order and to supposedly remove the corrupt civilian government and legislators. Once that happens, regaining democratic control is very difficult, as in the case of Myanmar. This reversing of political systems and events, from communism to democracy and then again from democracy to military rule, exposes the inadequacy of the present day capitalist democracy.

10.6 Influence of the UN?

Frankly, the structure of UN, according permanent status to a few military powerful nations, is intrinsically flawed, because of the self-endowed privileges by certain nations. This is why the UN is controlled by these permanent member-nations of the UN security council, and has only intervened when it has been in the interests of these nations. Otherwise, the UN has had to turn a blind eye to many genocides within nations as well as atrocities committed by nations and in particular by the militarily powerful countries. Why did the UN fail to intervene when an estimated 1.4 million Afghan citizens died during the Soviet Union's occupation of Afghanistan, and when Vietnamese lands were being napalmed by the US? On 8 April 2004, a memorial service was held in the Rwandan capital of Kigali, to mark the 10th anniversary of the start of the 1994 genocide. Only a handful of leaders from beyond the African continent were present at this function, signalling continuing Western indifference to their and the UN failure to stop the 100-day massacre of some 800,000 Tutis and Hutu moderates by the ethnic Hutu extremists.

The structure of the UN has been such that it has neither had political authority nor adjudicational mandate. For instance, it took the UN six years to get an agreement from the Cambodian government to even set up a tribunal to try Khmer regime leaders for genocide (of an estimated 1.7 million people) during their 1975–79 reign of terror. The UN Office of Human Rights simply does not have the mechanism to impose justice within its member nations. At best, the UN Human Rights system can collaborate with the regional human-rights commissions such as the European Court of Human Rights (part of the 44-nation council of Europe) and the African Commission on Human Rights and People's Rights (under the Organization of African Unity).

The UN has been sidelined and/or used at the convenience of the permanent member countries of its Security council. Where were those morals-preaching, democracy-touting and human rights championing, self-proclaiming "civilized nations", when the native African people were being terrorized by the "civilized" apartheid regimes of South Africa and former Rhodesia? What was the UN doing when Afghanistan was Soviet-unionized for a decade? Decades after the brutal scourging of the people of Vietnam and their lands by chemical weaponry, the civilized nations have erased these war crimes from their conscience and their history.

State terrorism and crimes against humanity committed by some South American nations dictators pale into insignificance compared to the terror-stricken and state crime-ridden decades that the people of the big communist-imperialist regimes and of the two big apartheid regimes had to suffer. Why could not the UN have intervened and prevented these mega-scale state terrorisms? The answer is because either the crimes against humanity were committed by some of the UN security council's permanent member nations (and their allies), or the UN system does not have jurisdiction over stage sovereignty to prevent gross crimes against humanity.

So this is why the formation of the world government is a necessity:

- so as to draw the curtain down on the hegemonial era of big nations making decisions for small nations on all matters, ranging from environmental and ecological safeguards to nuclear weaponry development and control to globalization;
- in order to initialize globalization by the remit of "food for all, health for all and education for all," because only after this base has been established, can we move to free trade and open markets;
- in order to replace the World Bank and the International Monetary Fund with regional banks and monetary funds, for regional development (without economic policy imposition);

- so as to prevent a powerful country from encroaching on someone's territory or from forcing another country to provide it a military base;
- to legally define human-rights as well as human-rights violations and crimes-against-humanity, so that there is no legal ambiguity in denominating such violations;
- to strictly enforce human rights implementation within all nations as well as in inter-nation matters;
- to develop a universal legal system to take to task all human-rights violators and perpetrators of crimes against humanity, regardless of the level of political office held by these criminals and the status of their countries in the UN Security Council;
- so that the people of all nations can live in peace and dignity.

10.7 International Code of Conduct

It would appear that subscribing and adhering to an international code of jurisprudence would be healthy for all nations. It would equally judge all heads and militia of nations. It would deter politicians from making super-patriotic and/or insensitive racist and/or religious statements to incite people into religious and/or war frenzy and mass killings. Further, no one or nation can have immunity from being judged by the international code of political ethics. However, judging from the opposition of some militarily powerful nations to the International Criminal Court, it appears that there is a huge non-negotiable double standard between the most powerful nations and the rest in the concept of an international code of political ethics as well as an international code of conduct even in times of war, so that:

- no nation indiscriminately bombs another nation and its civilian population;
- a nation bombing another nation be held accountable for loss of civilian lives;
- even prisoners-of-war are treated in a civilized manner (because it is their commanders who may have been responsible for their actions);
- even the peacekeeping forces be held accountable for their conduct.

There are many other spheres of double standards:

- in environment degradation protection, and sustainable development;
- in non-proliferation and disarmament;

- with regards to the attitude of the powerful and industrialized nations, as to what should constitute an acceptable living standard for themselves and for others as well as the acceptable salary structure for their people compared to the salary scales in poor countries;
- with regards to concentration of, attention on, and funding for warfare versus funding for deleting poverty and disease (such as AIDS).

The concept of international code of conduct can only be implemented if the authority of the International Court of Justice is recognized in all the nations of the world. That is not possible in the current UN setup. Well in that case, and in the face of this huge hypocricy, there can be no other alternative except to bring about our world government political system.

10.8 The vision and mission of the world government

The vision of the world government (to be different from that of UN) would be that:

- humanity and/or suppression of any kind would be intolerable;
- inter-nation interactions are to be for the mutual benefit of the people of all nations, with the goal of achieving uniform living standards and quality of life;
- intra-nation governance and societal structure are to involve people of all strata in all the sectors of society, so as to converge to distributive justice.

The world government mission would be to provide neo-humanistic global governance, ensuring:

1. protection of human-rights and prevention of ethnic racial and religious disharmony and conflicts, by means of a global code of jurisprudence;
2. that all communities develop their own people-oriented public policies and constitutions;
3. global equity in living standards, through education and sharing of knowledge;
4. that all the global regions function as cooperatives, by
    - means of cooperative trading in assets and resources,
    - providing assistance to newly emerging FSC(s);
    - providing relief to any community or state in times of natural calamities (ranging from drought to flooding to earthquakes); and
5. that every community and region has fair governance (with competent and dedicated elected governance officers) in all matters of people's living.

10.9 World government structure

We are advocating that the world government adopt the functional agencies of UN, such as UNESCO, UNICEF and UNDP. Some new agencies would need to be established, to deal with Human rights, Humanitarian law and Jurisprudence for crimes against humanity. The UN General Assembly and Security Council would be replaced by the World Government Parliament (WGP) and the Global Security Council (GSC). Both WGP and GSC would have the authority to preside over all the nations and regions of the world.

The world government parliament will comprise of ministers with the full range of portfolios required for this apex governance. The ministers for each portfolio will be elected by that portfolio's ministers of regional federations. In other words, for instance, the world government law minister will be elected by the law ministers of regional federations. In this way, all the world government ministers will be linked to their FSCs. A major point of difference between UN General Assembly and the World government is that the latter will have full-fledged ministries (or departments) associated with all aspects of intra and inter community, bloc, zone and federation matters.

For instance, the world government ministry of law (WGT-MOL) will deal with the constitutional frameworks of these matters. It will also ensure that there be no violations of people's code of rights in any community. The WGT-MOL will also keep an overview of the conduct of the legislators, through its ministries of regional federations, economic zones and blocs and FSCs. Nevertheless, the WGT-MOL will respect the governance autonomy of the FSCs.

Now, the question of financing the world government arises. Nations may not want to finance an additional government. However, the choice is between having an inept UN not meting out justice uniformly and the world government functioning as a just and fair government and not as a group of national representatives (with no jurisdiction over the sovereignty of belligerent nations). One type of financing is that the world government ministers' salaries be paid by their respective federations and that the various regional divisions within each ministry (i.e divisions dealing with matters of different federations) be supported by their respective federations.

This policy can work only after some measure of global uniformity in living standards and salary scales has been developed. Until then, in the initial period, the more developed regions would need to provide the support of WGT for all its governance activities and role. This disparity between the North and South nations can be evened out faster, once the (to be adopted) Code of International Business and Trade is effected. As per this code,

- the developing nations and/or their FSCs would charge prices for natural resource exports, that also reflect the utility value and importance of the products of the resource;
- the labor costs in developing countries would become on par with that in the developed countries.

10.10 Globalization and the peace program

There is a close synergy between high performing universities and societies. Universities can play an important role (i) in developing the ideals of a society and its institutions, in all realms of human thought and endeavor, and (ii) in elevating the human mindset to conceive noble ideas in all the functional sectors of a society. Hence, the world government ministry of education (WGT-MOE) has a tremendous scope to work locally, regionally and globally to implement the WGT vision and mission. Particularly, the WGT-MOE can play a paramount role in accelerating the advancement of developing countries, such as in:

- knowledgeable human-resource development and capacity building, so as to empower the people to bring to bear a high level of know-how for cooperative solutions of local problems;
- implementations of scientific and technological advancement to elevate the indigenous industrial acumen, health-care delivery level, community infrastructure and living standards of the people of developing countries;
- facilitating environmentally conducive and sustainable development;
- implementing socio-economic democracy and professional governance, to cater to people's welfare;
- heightened cooperation among the nations (and people) of a region, to promote economic self-reliance (and economic common-market) among the developing nations of the region.

In order to implement these objectives, the WGT-MOE can help the universities in developing countries to establish community-impacting academic programs in "regional self-reliant economic development" (RSRED), involving:

- capacity building of developing countries;
- culturing technological base and indigenous industrialization in developing countries;
- enhanced agricultural and food processing technology and capability;
- community services infrastructure-building in education and healthcare, food and water supply, electrical power and transportation;

- food and drinking water for all, housing for all, healthcare for all and education for all.

Finally, on the important and highly debated issue of Globalization, the WGT-MOE can work with universities in both developed and developing countries to institute Inter-university (inter-faculty) graduate programs in "Globalization," so as to formulate the concepts of:

- people's empowerment in sustaining resource development on their lands;
- mechanism for providing equivalent salaries for equivalent jobs in different parts of the world, and minimum-salary purchasing-capacity for the basic requisities for dignified living;
- developing countries forming economic common-markets and political cooperatives, so as to assist one another and share know-how, in order to improve the living standards of their people;
- resolution of regional conflicts as well as of autonomy aspirations of marginalized communities, by forming functionally-sustainable communities with autonomous governance;
- regional free-trade blocs to assist regional economic development as a basis of globalization;
- constituting globalization on the foundation of a more even economic and industrial base among the regions of the world.

Throughout history, power without justice has caused power abuse and led to tyranny. In our present UN setup, no one pays heed to justice without power. However, justice combined with authorization, in our World government setup, will make the just (and weak) secure and the strong ethical.

The idealistic concept of United Nations implies that all nations unitedly work for the welfare of the people of all nations, so that all the people have equal opportunity to develop their potentialities and contribute to this noble objective. However, the sad reality is that the political-party heads of a few nations are ruling and controlling the destinies of the people of the world, through unpopular policies that are inimical to their welfare as well as unpopular among their own people. The big majority of the nations of the world have become spectators of this global political game of big-time players.

At the same time, the political-party heads of most nations have also been guilty of using the democratic platform for their personal political power and monetary gains. Their civilian populations are only pawns of these supposedly democratically elected political-party leaders, who live on the fruits of the labor of their people without even developing mechanisms for their people to reap the benefits of their own labor.

At this time, the people and even the intelligensia seem helpless to envisage and effect a civilian-based democratic system along with the complimentary supportive economic-political globalization set-up. It is hence up to the educators and university academics to develop and cultivate the blue-print of a neo-humanistic democratic system and globalization set-up, in which the earlier inunciated ideals of the world government can be fulfilled.

When, as a result, the benevolent intelligensia are elected by the civilian sectors of communities to become guardians of civilian democratic governance under the aegis of a world government system, then only can we expect to have a neo-humanistic civilization — from US and UK to India and China, from Russia and Georgia to Spain and Italy, from Panama and Columbia to Chile and Argentina, from Tanzania and Uganda to Liberia and Nigeria, from Libya and Morocco to Saudi Arabia and Iran, from Japan and Korea to Indonesia and Australia.

Section III

Real Democracy and Neo-humanistic Global Order

11 Socio-economic Democracy: Governance, Economic and Financial Policy

11.1 Failure of democracy

Political democracy is a misguided concept for most developing countries, and not only for developing nations but also for industrialized nations. In political democracy, one expects that the most competent candidates will be elected. However, this requires that the electorate is well-informed, educated, politically conscious, and capable of making independent decisions. In most developing countries, there is a high incidence of poverty and illiteracy, and the electorate is swayed by glib talks of insincere, and/or incompetent and/or corrupt politicians, and is pressurized to voting for them.

In most developing countries, the stage has come when many inhabitants have contempt for the politicians, because elections come and go while their basic problems of water supply (for drinking and irrigation) and sanitation, electrical power and transport facilities, healthcare and education never get solved. Hence, political democracy has become a farce in most developing countries, and the same applies to most high-development countries.

Even in developed countries, democracy is primarily only political democracy and not socio-economic democracy. It is not possible for competent, sincere and visionary people to get elected, unless they run on party tickets with substantial financial backing. That powerful business corporations finance the political elections is itself contrary to true democratic governance principles, because they then expect governmental decisions and policies favorable to their operations; furthermore, they expect to get shielded by the government from fraudulent businesses and financial practices.

These are only some of the aspects of (the so-called present-day) democracy that need to be altered. The first one is the political party system, which makes it impossible for independent thinkers to get elected and entails considerable energy dissipation in inter-party squabbles. The second is the linkage of the capitalist system to this type of political party system of democracy, which involves big-time capitalist corporations making big donations to political parties in order to protect their interests through favorably elected-party policies and legislations. This rent-seeking behavioral syndrome, by which these corporation-donors get unfair financial benefits due to favorable government policies of taxation and regulation (such as concerning smoking), is endemic to this capitalistic democratic system.

So what is intrinsically wrong with capitalist-democracy, why cannot it be termed as genuine democracy? In capitalism, there is a social division based on financial capital. In mass elections, the only way to reach the masses is by effective mass propaganda, which requires financial capital; so, how can we call this democrary? Further, the elected politicians form themselves into elitist society, commanding a higher standing in the community. This goes against the very tenet of democracy. Active civilian evolvement in public issues and policies is a basic requirement in democracy. However, in supposed citadels of democracy, only the government society is supposed to think and govern, while the civilian society accepts its lot to follow and be governed.

11.2 Protesting in the face of repression: treason or patriotism?

Democracy cannot be sustained by capitalism, even though democratic politics has all along been linked to capitalism, in the form of colonization (for centuries until the middle of last century) of resource-rich former colonies and thereafter by economic exploitation of developing countries because of cheaper cost of their human resources. In fact, cheap natural resources and human resources have been the curse of developing countries. Why? Firstly, their cheap resources (whether it be oil or timber, diamonds or uranium) are enticing to the super-capitalist countries. Secondly, many of these poor countries need development capital and technology to bring them out of the dark caverns of poverty. At the same time, many of these resource-rich countries (of Africa, Asia and South America) are in the stranglehold of incapable, corrupt and even terrorizing regimes. Some of these regimes sell off their countries' resources cheaply for arms purchases. Others approach the (so-called) world banks for development loans, a big fraction of which gets siphoned off into the personal accounts of their political leaders. The improper lack of tangible development makes the debtor countries become defaulters. Then, they approach the (so-called) international fund agencies to overcome balance of payments. In doing so, they are forced to be signatories to some stringent conditions that are not necessarily in their national interests, such as having to sell even their national industries (such as hydro-electric power) to MNC(s). All of this, combined with devaluation of their currencies, makes them even poorer.

So then, what is the solution to this dilemma? Primarily, it is education as a form of national wealth to create home-grown development, or (even though undesirable) to at least provide the human resources for MNC(s) to come and help develop natural resource industries. Education also provides socio-political consciousness to the citizens, and makes it more difficult for them to be controlled by the politicians' mafia, which is so dominant in many developing countries. However, it is doubtful that education alone can bring about democracy in many countries under militarist regimes (e.g. Myanmar), communist regimes (such as North Korea and China), and religious regimes (such as Iran). What is also needed is governance morality under the influence of the civil society.

Where civil society groups constitute the society's conscience and its functional sectors, there democracy has a bigger potential. Where the civil-society organizations are not allowed to develop (let alone have their voices heard) by imposed restrictive legislations under the pretext of social stability, their people cannot experience the cool breezes of freedom. The people of Hong Kong are now concerned with the sincerity of the "one country but two systems" formula, after their July 2003 pro-democracy demonstrations were denounced by the Chinese government regime and they were warned against political activism. The Chinese government considered Hong Kong to be an "economic city," not a "political city." The "one-country two-systems" formula is itself an absurdity and an insult to the people of China, because it implies that the people of the mainland have lesser freedom and privileges than the people of Hong Kong. Not trusting this hypocrisy, the government of Taiwan has begun preparations for a new constitution for Taiwan, inspite of threats of military action from China. However, the industrialized nations of the world are supporting China's contention that Taiwan is part of China (even though they know very well that Taiwan's democratic system cannot be contained within China's autocratic communism system), because of China's economic market potential and military strength. Such is the hypocrisy of international politics!

Around the same time, the younger and bolder generations of Iran are protesting against the big mindset gap between the religiostic government regime and the people representing the civil society. Their contention has been that the government institutions lack a public base and appropriate view of people's problems. In both Iran and China, the government's attitude has been to downplay the social discontent and attempt to correlate the unrest to economy and unemployment. In another part of world, the Russian government has conveniently equated the Chechen Republic's fight for separatism to terrorism on the part of some rebel groups, inspite of young Chechen women sacrificing themselves as suicide bombers in desperation for freedom.

This brings us to the issue of Patriotism. In a country where there is a distinct separation of the civilian society from an alienated government society, distinctly different views of patriotism are held by the two societies. On 5 July 2003, China lost a role-model patriot in General Zhang Aiping. He played a big role in China's military modernization and in the establishment of China's nuclear arsenal. Yet, during the so-called Cultural Revolution, he was arrested and imprisoned under the charge of being a counter-revolutionary revisionist for opposing Chairman Mao and socialism. Even after spending six years in prison, he got back into the governance society, and administered China's intercontinental ballistic missile program. But then in 1989, he again angered the government establishment by affirming the patriotic sprit of the Tiananmen-square civilian protestors, and opposing the ensuing imposition of marital law. This is what patriotism is all about: fearless upholding of cardinal principles for the welfare of the society even in the face of repression.

11.3 What is socio-economic democracy?

In an ideal democratic political (or policy-making) system, governance is to be carried out democratically, and policy decisions are adopted as a consensus. The party system of politics makes a mockery of this, since the policies are enacted by the party in power in seclusion and secrecy, and a lot of lobbying is carried out to convince the opposition party members to vote in favor of the policies and/or bills. So essentially, a big number of elected members are sidelined from political decision-making, and cannot hence effectively represent their electoral constituencies. It is however argued that opposition parties are necessary to keep a check on the party in power, which in itself is a conundrum and an admission of poor integrity of politicians.

In a real democratic system, there needs to be involvement of the electorate through their representatives in all aspects of governance, in a knowledgeable way. In other words, the professional associations of agriculturists, educators, medical practitioners, lawyers, financiers and bankers, agriculturists and industrialists and the citizens in general can have direct involvement in policy framing through their elected representatives of their associations, agencies and councils. In this way, informed opinion and consent is involved in policy enactment, as opposed to the ruling political party making all decisions (in the present framework) and incompetent party members having the main say in the governance of various portfolios. It is difficult to expect intelligent and independent-thinking people to be shackled to political party policies, of having to act in unison in the interests of the party and of conforming to the so-called party discipline; it all sounds too moronic!

In the present party-based democratic system, the election campaigns are costly, and subsidized by big industrial and business corporations (with the idea of investing to in turn elicit policies favorable to their business interests). In other words, the present party-based democratic system constitutes an alliance between the political parties and the capitalists; this scenario applies to the developed countries (United States, United Kingdom, Japan, Germany, Italy, etc.) as well as to developing countries.

In this system, it is apparent and inevitable that a few very affluent people dictate public policies and reap economic benefits. At the end of the day, democracy should provide a fair distribution of economic benefits as per one's contribution and value to the society. This then brings us to the concept of socio-economic democracy, and how to enact a system in which the general people can be involved in economic development and have a share in socio-economic benefits as well as influence governance through their elected representatives.

So, for grassroots socio-economic democracy (SED), we need to organize all the community's functions (i.e. community services and business enterprises) in a cooperative way, in the form of cooperatives, professional associations, agencies and townships citizen councils. In the framework of this cooperatively working and living societal system, (i) all the people working in corporations will be forming micro-cooperatives, by virtue of which they will all have the incentive of being involved in the performance of their corporations, and share its profits and losses; (ii) all the people working in specific sectors of the community (such as journalism, legal progression, education, etc.) would form associations; (iii) all of the people who do not come into this category, such as those who manage the house and family would form residential councils.

Now each of these associations, agencies and councils (representing all community functions and activities) will vote two candidates, for the general public to then elect its one representative to local governance. Further, there would be a mechanism for all the elected governance executives to regularly and periodically meet with their sectorial agencies (separately as well as together), to discuss and debate public issues and develop policies based thereon. Thus, all the community people will have a say in public policy decision-making, through these grassroots organizations. In this way, both economic and political democracy will be implemented hand-in-hand. It is, hence, fair to say that socio-economic democracy propagates political democracy.

11.4 Socio-economic principles

Progressive development of society requires optimal utilization of human potentialities. For this purpose, the socio-economic policy of our socio-economic democracy and professional governance system will be governed by the following set of principles.

All of human potentialities need to be utilized

Our industrial sector has no doubt helped to generate physical wealth. However, because the know-how is not made widely available, the developing countries stay poorer. The knowledge capital needs to be widely shared, so as to enable every person to have access to livelihood. The reason for the non-development of human knowledge and technological capacity (and hence of financial capital) on a big scale is because of absence of morality and neo-humanism, and because economists are not used to thinking in terms of knowledge and spiritual resource or capital, as recognized by the Progression Utilization Theory or PROUT*. However, while knowledge resource makes inventions and builds physical capital, spiritual resource can build the moral fabric required for a progressive society.

Minimum living standard

Every FSC is to guarantee employment for local people. Local people are those who are concerned with local welfare, work locally and place their savings in local banks (as opposed to banks in foreign countries), and constitute local ability resource. In a cooperatively structured community, wherein all enterprises and services are run as cooperatives on a not-for-profit basis, it can be possible to have 100% employment. The minimum wage (set by the FSC government) has to support a minimal standard of living, in terms of the essentials of life (food, clothing, health care, housing, basic amenities and education). Further, the FSC Government could provide tax rebates to corporations for employing jobless persons, while the FSC banks could provide loans to new cooperatives of jobless persons to start businesses.

Unemployment

Losing a job and to be unemployed constitutes a tremendous emotional, physical, psychic distress to a person and to her/his family. How should we tackle this dilemma in a benevolent way? It is sinful of governments (such as the state-government regimes of India) to be oblivious of this trauma. It is also unethical for politicians to expect jobless persons to become entrepreneurs while they have secure income, because most people are not mentally attuned to the concept of having and running their own business. Hence, in our people-centered society, the community government would have to take a proactive role, to identify areas or

---

**PROUT in a Nutshell* (Vols. 1 to 21), by Prabhat Ranjan Sarkar (Ananda Marga Publications, Calcutta-39, 1987).

sectors that need servicing and development, to even form government cooperatives of jobless people, get them operational and slowly make them into independent cooperatives.

Services and industrial sector

All local community projects will be carried out by locally structured business cooperatives; newly structured business cooperatives can take loans from FSC coop banks. Government agencies will manage community services, such as healthcare, education and public transport. Certain services, involving a number of FSCs (such as for instance, electrical power and water supply), will be carried out at the economic bloc level. Natural resources (such as mining and crude oil production) stand at the beginning of the product development chain; they would be managed by SEB governments. Big scale natural resource development and conversion of these resources into products will be structured as public utilities, at the economic zone (government) level, at the sites of the resources.

The cooperative industrial sector: All big and medium-sized (large capital and human resource-requiring) businesses (such as manufacturing plants, pharmaceutical, medical equipment companies and even hospitals) could be cooperatively managed. The private sector will include small scale enterprises, such as shops and small scale services.

Agricultural sector

Herein, the raw material inputs (such as fertilizer, irrigation water and fuel) would be managed by public utilities. Agricultural processing industry would be organized as producer cooperatives, the agricultural produce will be distributed by consumer cooperatives, possibly without intermediary distributors in order to keep the prices down and benefit the producers as well as the people.

Land owners and resource developers can have cost-effective food production by cooperating in (1) technology-sharing so as to get maximal land yield, (2) environment preservation, and even (3) in organizing better living as well as healthcare and educational amenities.

Government sector

At the FSC and SEB levels, government participation in the economy would be to develop raw materials (and help to convert them into processed materials), manage public services (such as education and healthcare, water supply and transport security, social and welfare), facilitate and fund community infrastructure (roads, canals and administrative buildings), and frame policies for the conduct of all the community sectors. Government income would be from these key industries, community services industry, taxation and (borrowing by) selling of government bonds. However, the government would not be allowed to run up a deficit by drawing on central banks (of economic bloc and zones) credit. This is also the policy of the European Union with regard to its member nations.

In an FSC, the government would also need to undertake to get the unemployed people working, by setting up work-cooperatives for them. In a newly developing community, the living standard of people would be progressively increased, by (i) attending to the provision of basic living needs, (ii) finding markets for the community's exports, and (iii) by the import of affordable commodities for their consumption. Chapter 5 describes how to set up a functionally-sustainable community, in which cooperatively-structured industrial companies (set up by loans from the COOP banks) would bring revenue into the community to support community services and sustain small businesses.

At the federation level, the role of the government would be in preparing a people-centered (human rights and welfare oriented) constitution, as well as in ensuring constitutional implementation for facilitating the smooth functioning of self-reliant economic zones (SEZs), in providing security to SEZs and in ensuring cooperation among SEZs. The world government will be primarily concerned with promoting and safeguarding the global order, in which the federations will cooperate to ensure the welfare of people of all federations.

11.5 Balanced self-reliant economy

Multi-faceted economies

Social economy deals with the provision of the essentials for living, i.e. for housing, food and clothing, their production, distribution, marketing, storage, pricing, etc.
Knowledge economy deals with the utilization of intellectual and psychic potentialities of people by facilitating innovation, bringing to bear EQ in the management of the workplace, and through the establishment of research and development centers to develop new technologies and transfer the know-how to industry.
Commercial economy entails distribution and utilization of all resources (towards a productive economy) by means of trade, banking and fiscal policy.

Service economy is concerned with planning and administrating of community services, such as healthcare and education, electrical power and water supply.

Balanced economy

Within an SRC, all the sectors of a community's economy (namely, agricultural, industrial and service sectors) are to be developed in balance. The excessive concentration of the workforce in any one sector of the economy can cause economic instability and unemployment. For instance, in a new township built around a natural resource, there needs to be proper living conditions and amenities for the people working in resource development operations; otherwise, people will get disenchanted and leave that township. At the same time (and as illustrated in Chapter 5), the community services have to be sustainable from the revenue generated from the natural resource. Further, in order to minimize production cost, local industry should utilize local resources and raw materials; processing industry is best located where raw materials are readily available.

Economic sustainability

Sustainable economy means (1) developing the local economy, using local resources, local savings, local labor, local initiative, and (2) ensuring that the export earnings are able to pay for the imports and community services as well as sustain the small business sector (associated with consumer needs for day to day living).

There are two ways for developing country (or FSC) to become economically competitive and provide a good living standard for its citizens. One approach (as in the case of East Asian countries) is to create a foreign investment base and an industrial sector of MNC(s). The other approach is to foster home-grown entrepreneurship, as in India. This can be a slower but a more stable process in the long run. Let it, however, be known that India's indigenous companies have made it on their own, without help from governmental regimes.

Indeed, when India's enterprising business-people, professionals (doctors, engineers and lawyers), social scientists and academics get involved in education (so as to raise the literacy level as well as the quality of university education) and take over the governance from the hands of their incompetent and corrupt oxymoronic) politicians (whose prime source of propaganda are the illiterate masses), only then will the country truly prosper. The same is true of other developing countries having a highly educated (resident and non-resident) segment of population. When Indian entrepreneurial industrial culture gets extended to the education sector and communities services sector, then only will India emerge out of its third-world confinement. In fact, India can set an example for a similar civilian involvement in governance to other developing countries of Asia (such as the Phillipines and Indonesia), Africa (such as Kenya and Egypt), South America (such as Peru and Venezuela).

11.6 Resource management

Herein, we will enunciate the principles of resource management.

Multi-faceted resources utilization: As per the SED socio-economic principle, there should be adroit utilization of material, human, capital and technological resources (in relation to the nature of work), for effecting a vibrant economy at the FSC level. Hence, within an economic bloc there needs to be free-flow of these resources, in order to effect a uniformly high living standard in all the FSCs of an economic bloc. Likewise, there should be effective utilization of people's acumen (say, as business and finance managers, scientists and engineers, teachers and social workers, technicians and laborers, doctors and nurses, lawyers and historians), by providing mobility within a regional federation. This will also help to develop a uniform standard living standard within a federation.

Economy can also be knowledge-based and not just based on investment capital. In fact, it is now recognized that the creation of (and investment in) a knowledge-based society will foster a strong as well as more versatile and expanding economy. In other words, a broad knowledge-base resource is a better catalyst for sustained and multi-dimensional economic growth (in this era of continually emerging fields), in comparison with the old-style capital investment-based uni-dimensional economy.

Cooperatively owned and managed industrial enterprises will elicit motivated staff participation. For economic development within an FSC in a developing region, instead of inviting multinationals to set up plants in the community or country, it is better to invite and pay experts in different fields to provide technological know-how to indigenous companies. It may even be necessary to take loans from foreign banks, but that could be the extent of foreign aid. Also, day-to-day living needs can only be catered to by indigenous enterprises, because we cannot expect foreign enterprises to cater to basic needs. Further, in a developing country, the emphasis should be on the use of social capital and appropriate (intermediate) technology for the production of essential goods and services.

Equitable distribution of wealth: The accumulation of wealth above and beyond the needs for comfortable living and self-expression leads to gross economic disparities within and among the regions of the world. Over-concentration of wealth can eventually lead to economic instability. Inequitable distribution of wealth occurs due to an exploitative attitude and/or corruption: in the form of private businesses in which employees are poorly paid (disproportionate to their labor and to the revenue generated) and/or have no profit-sharing, cheap acquisition of land through one's political connections, kickbacks from contractors, politicians influencing banks to give unjustified loans to their cronies.

Emphasis on morality can mitigate this unethical manner of wealth accumulation, and pave the way for more equitable distribution of wealth as well as for better resource utilization by the society. In our advocated socio-economic democracy and professional governance system, all big and medium-sized enterprises will be organized as cooperatives, wherein the difference in salary range is minimized (i.e. the standard deviation is small). Further, cooperatively run enterprises will also provide shares to its member staff. However, these shares would not be available to outsiders, in order to avoid (i) stock market manipulation by shares and currency trading, and (ii) virtual wealth creation, all of which could lead to artificial economy.

11.7 Economic framework

The management of economy revolves around structural policy, industrial policy, monetary policy, trade policy and fiscal policy.

Organizational structural policy

- Each socio-economic zone (SEZ) would be developing its own economic plan, and strive to become self-sufficient in having its export revenue support community services and sustain small scale businesses;
- each self-reliant socio-economic bloc (SEB) governance will have an economic planning unit, to provide advice to the FSCs on the optimal sectorial population distribution within each FSC, so that the different population sectors of a community have equivalent standard of living, as demonstrated by the case study in Chapter 5;
- the community economy will be organized into natural resource sector, industrial cooperative sector and private small-enterprise sector;
- the banking industry will involve the central bank as a public utility, commercial banks as money-keepers and savers, and COOP banks serving as credit unions within the cooperatives.

The monetary and banking system

- Within an SEZ, the banking industry would be structured into tiers: the SEZ bank to function (and to serve) as the central bank for the economic blocs, and the SEB bank to represent the central bank for the FSC.
- In FSCs, there would be commercial banks and COOP banks (having credit unions within the cooperatives).
- Banks would be required to properly manage their loan accounts and savings accounts, so as to maintain a balance between the interest earned on the money lent out and the payable interest on customer's accounts. In other words, banks would not be allowed to extend loans exceeding their customers money deposit; this is so that under no circumstances should a bank not be able to pay out customers wanting to withdraw their bank deposits.
- Each Regional Federation will have a Federation Bank to help maintain stability of federational currency and economic stability (preventing inflation and depression).
- The regional federational currency would need to have a stable standard value linked to the natural resources and products of the region, so as to maintain an adequate purchasing capacity.

Money circulation and trade

To initiate and facilitate roll-over of money in new (and previously impoverished communities, the FSC governments can initiate loans to their cooperative enterprises, for example to agricultural and manufacturing cooperatives. These governmental loans would enable the production and export sector to support community services and sustain small businesses, as well as to recover the money (and pay for loans) by selling and exporting their products. Alternatively, and in the development phase of a community, the SRC government could also buy the agricultural produces and/or products from the producers (and export them), thereby initiating money circulation in the FSC.

Once this process of money circulation gets started, the inhabitants would have the monies to pay for community services (from the government), such as water supply and sanitation, electricity, healthcare delivery and education. Hence, in a newly formed FSC, the process of developing community services (from start-up funds provided by the SEB government, through the FSC COOP banks) and for initiating revenue-generating enterprises would need to go hand in hand. Any time-lag between these two sectors can cause public discontent, and end up in professionals leaving the FSCs.

Within an SEZ, raw materials would be converted locally into products and commodities, as close as possible to the site of raw materials availability, so as add value to the materials and also to decrease the cost of production. For instance, it is more profitable to locally convert petroleum into petrochemicals and export products instead of crude petroleum. Trading in raw materials (in excess of amounts needed regionally) would be at prices that would take into account the need and strategic value of the materials.

Initially, within each self-reliant regional federation (RFD) there would be a common currency, and the world (government) bank would set up the currency exchange rates among the federations. Eventually, when all the FSCs would have near-uniform living standards, then there would be a common global currency.

Prices and wages

The specified minimum wage would need to sustain a minimum standard of living (in terms of basic necessities and amenities). All the cooperatives belonging to each sector of the community (such as the manufacturing sector) would form a professional association, which would have two tasks: (1) to assess the markets for the commodities produced by their cooperatives, and recommend the optimal market-sustainable price for that commodity, (2) to represent that community sector in the community governance. This association will set the prices of their goods, to pay for production costs and dividends on bank loans as well as for acquiring new technology, for expansion of the business and for supporting their associations.

11.8 Capitalist to Cooperative economic model

A knowledge-based economy needs a neo-humanistic outlook,
for the making of an ideal society.

Corporate capitalist imperialism

The super-capitalist system of getting companies assets augmented by the common public, through purchase of their stocks and through rise in their stocks values, has so many pitfalls. It favors big asset holders, who have enough reserves to absorb losses. However, it has been a disaster for the average people, who have been deceived (by the financial consulting companies) into augmenting their assets by investments in stocks and shares. The beneficiaries of this unfair system are the capitalists. Hence, in the collective interest, it is better to end this system of public holdings, to avoid the uninformed or partly-informed public from losing their life savings to fluctuating stock values. In our advocated socio-economic democratic system, the cooperatives will constitute grassroots economic units, and these cooperatives will only issue shares to the employed cooperative members.

Many MNCs (including the powerful fast-food and pop-drink chains) have successfully eliminated indigenous competitors, by their marketing strategies (such as sponsorship of sports events). Yet, in business management courses of MBA programs, their management styles are epitomized as models of success. Today, even in the capitalist camp, there is a jostling for the status of super-capitalists, by financially powerful corporations buying up less powerful corporations invariably resulting in big lay-offs and contributing to unemployment. Verily, this is the beginning of the dismantling of corporate capitalism, and for the emergence of collective (cooperative) capitalism. Our new political economic system will not provide support for the emergence of such predator corporations. In the cooperative management of corporations, there would be no need for such buy-overs of a corporation by another.

If one were to get to the bottom of many past and present international conflicts, the covert reasons will emerge as the desire for gaining control of added resources and markets for their to be exported products, under the guise of national security. In our neo-political global order, engaging people into war under false pretexts (of weeding out terrorism or changing a terrorizing regime) and resulting in killing of innocent civilian populations by the governance-executives of a nation (or an SEB) would constitute a crime against humanity, as per the constitution of the world government.

Cooperative globalization

Whenever and wherever the so-called "economic and financial leaders" meet to discuss globalization, they attract huge and vehement protests from public, who come from different parts of the world (at immense personal sacrifice). In spite of that, these leaders (displaying commendable immunity to peoples' voices and protests) continue their relentless drive to economic colonization in the form of free trade and WTO, while ever so often issuing some condescending and misleading statements concerning the need to assist poorer nations through a free market system.

Opening up markets of nations to receive imports is in fact a very limiting concept of globalization, and perhaps could even be initially detrimental to indigenous economic sustenance local enterprise. However, the true spirit of globalization implies development of knowledge as well as technological and human resources of poorer nations by the richer nations, so as to first create an equitable base for joint inter-nation business ventures and trade. This could be done by having the business corporations of industrialized nations to develop and include corporations of developing countries in their business (R&D, manufacturing and marketing) chains. This could enable fair trading in resources and human services (by setting up uniform international norms of remuneration for goods and services), to eventually pave the way for global economic parity and social harmony.

It is a fallacy for the capitalists and the rich nations to believe in security based on concentration of wealth. Rather, security lies in enabling all the members of the corporation and/or federation (of nations) to be as well remunerated (in proportion to their acumen) and all the nations within a federation having uniform living standards. Indeed, an ideal society is one in which there is a uniform knowledgeable human resource base, and in which most people are cooperatively engaged in promoting the welfare of others (through fair business and professional practices), so that all can express themselves to their full potential.

It is about time that the Third World countries stop asking for aid, and start a solidarity movement for demanding reparation from their former colonial nations for usurping their resources and assets. With regards to their stance on globalization, the only way for fair and ethical (or rather neo-humanistic) globalization to come about is by the Third World nations forming a coalition of Third World nations, for development through self-reliance by:

- free-trading of their assets and know-how among themselves;
- forming a Third World cooperative movement, including the establishment of a Third World development bank and monetary fund.

Let us live prudently by a fair utilization of material and human resources,

Let there be fair trade to enable a just distribution of financial returns,

Let us evolve a noble economic order in which people do not need to immigrate for lack of utilization of their potentialities,

So that all the people can live in dignity and contribute to the making of an inspirational global society.

Peasant hut beside sugarcane fields on Negro's Island, (Philippines)

Hungry children in rags with sugarcane for chewing, on, Negro's Island, (Philippines)

Farm workers toil to feed the people, while they themselves are consigned to live and die in poverty. The governments of developing countries should do everything possible to assist them, and enable them to earn a decent living, and not let them work at the mercy of natural elements and the middlemen who suck up all their profits. For this reason, it is so necessary to install a cooperative system, in which the producers, distributors share the profits. It is difficult to comprehend the hard-heartness and utter lack of compassion of the G-8 countries' advocates of globalization pressurizing the developing countries to stop subsidies to agriculturists.

The G-8 countries are preoccupied with mechanisms to protect themselves from group terrorisms and to exercise control over the developing countries to ensure their usage of their natural resources, so as to maintain their economic standing. They are naturally not concerned with the poverty, starvation and disease issues of developing countries. Hence, the developing countries ought to realize once and for all that unless they form alliances to help themselves and one another by forming regional self-reliant economic blocs, they will never progress. Socio-economic democracy and collective capitalism provide the foundation of a people's welfare-centric society.

12

Truly Democratic Electoral Governance System and Global Political Structure

12.1 Shortcomings of the present democratic governance system

The main drawbacks of the prevalent political and economic governance system are:

- the political party system, making it possible for politically and financially powerful, immoral and incapable people to get elected by party-backing and financial support;
- capitalist domination, lack of economic democracy, and non-participation of the people in economic development;
- impossibility for well-qualified independent-thinking people (who do not subscribe to the manifesto of any party or who do not want their thinking and public policies to be dictated by party politics) to be a part of community or state governance;
- non-participation of people in economic management and governance of the community;
- wastage of public funds on insincere election campaigns;
- wastage of time and money by elected party members in continuing political rhetoric and mud-slinging at other parties; and
- wastage of public funds to pay the salaries of non-functional elected members of parties that are not in power.
- elected party members constituting an elitist government society, a higher standing than the civil society that elects them.

Generally speaking and more so in developing countries, unqualified, incompetent and corrupt candidates run for elections behind their party banner. Candidates get elected, based on the money support provided to them by affluent people and capitalists and corporations. They in turn are obliged to enact policies favoring their sponsors' financial and business practices. In developing countries with much less morals, their sponsors are rewarded by government business contracts. In many cases, the state government ministers have scandalous and criminal records. They have no concept of their political tasks and roles, and become politicians solely to become rich.

Thus, democracy can only be genuine if the majority of the people are literate and politically educated, ethical and moral. If these criteria are not met, democracy is only a sham, and a convenient means for the bold and selfish to become richer and/or more powerful. In the present system of democracy, only people with party and financial backing get elected. Once elected, they spend their tenure-in-office to amass more money and/or influence, as well as denouncing their potential competitors from other parties. There is no scope for independent, educated and experienced, well-qualified and moral persons to get elected without substantial financial backing (in the US, for instance). In other developing countries, one needs to have to make big financial contributions to a political parties, to be accepted as member and be eligible to be nominated as a party candidate for elections; the expectation is that the membership fee would be easily recovered by that politician from corrupt practices.

In the democratic governance system involving political parties, the party politicians are continually obsessed with criticizing and running down the actions and policies of the other competing parties. In that process, they hardly do any constructive public service work themselves. They are also not held accountable for their work and performance or (appropriately) lack of it, which gets dissipated in the overall party policy and performance. This can be verified by the day-to-day performance of the party politicians (of many developing countries that are blacklisted as among top corrupt countries in the world), typified by their core incompetence, apathy for any public service work and total lack of in-accountability: the only nonsense one reads in the media is petty mud-slinging and shenanigans in the form of organized strikes and protests to paralyse the community.

The present democratic system is only a system for people with money backing to get elected. Hence, it cannot be termed as democracy in its true sense. Further, because the system perpetuates capitalism, it does not provide opportunities for intelligent persons with inadequate means to play participatory roles in economic development and governance. So democracy in its present form may at best be termed as political democracy, but certainly not socio-economic democracy.

In the political-party democratic (PPD) system, there is governance by the party in majority. The ruling party can hence indulge in a lot of suppressive measures, such as in financial and home affairs policies. It can even control the judiciary and education, and precipitate the nation into internal (inter-ethnic) as well as external conflicts. It is solely motivated by self-interest and sustenance.

There is yet another disturbing aspect of the PPD system. The elected members of state and central governments make a society unto themselves, distinct from the civil society that elected them. They have a pompous lifestyle and the civilians find it difficult to even meet with them, let alone share their public-policy views with them. Hence in all supposedly democratic countries, there are two distinct societies: the government society and the civil society. The government society members have immense influence and essentially rule the civil society. They are courted by the media, whose prime professional endeavor is to discuss their policies and actions for the civilians' intellectual consumption.

12.2 Socio-economic democracy through cooperatives

In "true democracy", it is necessary to:

- firstly, institute sectorial organization of the community, in the form of industrial (agricultural and industrial cooperatives, distributors and purchasers) cooperatives, associations of professionals (such as lawyers, doctors, educators) and public-services agencies as well as residential councils;
- secondly, abolish the party system of governance and introduce socio-economic democracy by organizing all the functional sectors of the community in the form of cooperatives;
- thirdly, abolish the practice of financial support for election campaigns from donations by wealthy individuals or corporatives;
- fourthly, abolish the basis of stocks manipulation and currency trading;
- enact the sectorial-electoral system whereby competent individuals associated with various sectors of the community can be elected as governance officers (to represent those sectors), and that no single person dominates or dictates the governance body.

So what type of governance system is most suitable to nurture a functionally-sustainable community? In a community, we are advocating the formation of cooperatives in all facets of community functioning, as delineated in Chapter 3. The basis of socio-economic democracy is cooperative structuring of industrial corporations (as for instance involving the formation of producers, distributors and consumers cooperatives), business corporations, community services, large and medium size manufacturing plants, and even residential clusters. When this cooperation involves equal rights for the participating members, equal legal standing, mutual respect for one another and catering to mutual welfare, it is called coordinated cooperation. Socio-Economic democracy can be brought about by such a coordinated co-operational organization of all aspects of societal function (agriculture and industry, municipal and healthcare services, education and judiciary), and incorporating these societal-sectorial cooperatives as associations (for example, teachers' association representing teachers' cooperatives, lawyers' association of lawyers' cooperatives, etc.).

We can have cooperatives and/or associations of professionals engaged in all sectors of community function: business cooperatives (such as medical clinics and law firm conglomerates), farming cooperatives, municipal services, cooperatively owned and managed health centers (from polyclinics to tertiary care centers), teachers cooperatives-owned schools, and cooperatively-owned and managed large and medium size business enterprises (to yield better salaries for employees and better pricing for consumers) and even residential cooperatives. The cooperatives of every community functional sector would then be represented by an association of that sector, as for example Teachers', Doctors' and Lawyers' associations.

So, starting from grassroots, one develops a functionally-sustainable community-economy by organizing all community functions and services in the form of cooperatives: by cooperant modes of living and working, as for example by forming work cooperatives, healthcare and educational cooperatives, food and provisions cooperatives, housing cooperatives and banking cooperatives. These cooperatives will be organized by pooling financial resources, and by obtaining loans from the SRC cooperative bank. The work cooperatives will also undertake to develop housing and community services (hospitals, water and sanitation, electrical power, schools and transport facilities) for their workers and local communities, as well as help to start cottage industries and consumers' cooperative stores, so as to help provide employment for all. The association of cooperatives of each societal functional sector will then elect its most qualified representative to governance, to represent that sectors needs and welfare policies.

The socio-economic democratic system stresses local sustainable industrial and economic development, by using local resources (material and technological, intellectual and spiritual) and local initiatives. In developing countries, the priority would be to produce the basic necessities of living, indigenous produces and products from local resources, for export and revenue generation. For this purpose, large-scale and medium-scale industries and enterprises would be organized and managed as cooperatives. The government sector would be involved in providing social services, in assisting the various sectorial cooperatives (such as by obtaining bank credits for them) as well as in policy-making. These principles have applicability to any economy, both developed and under-developed.

12.3 Neo-system of governance

The present party system of democratic governance is the root of many of the societal ills. In the name of the party, huge funds are solicited and collected. The party system also promotes regimented thinking. As a result, it is impossible for a competent independent-thinking (non-party affiliated) person to get elected to public office. The party system of political governance (PSPG) promotes chronism, nepotism and corruption. In so many so-called democratically governed countries, the political parties are involved in all sorts of financial scandals, in ruthless treatment of people who they are supposed to serve, violations of human rights and crimes against humanity. The PSPG abets cover-ups of scandals by politicians.

In the current multi-party democratic system, huge sums of public money are spent in election campaigns, while a big percentage of government-sanctioned monies for community facilities endup in the coffers of the politicians. So, in the present system of democratic governance, one has to be rich and/or accumulate funding in order to contest elections or get rich after elections in order to recover one's assets spent on the elections. The elected representatives are supposed to be serving the people and the community. However, particularly in developing countries, these representatives act and function (and parade around) as if they belong to an elite class, and the people are nervous to approach them because of the power and influence they wield. There is no doubt that the present so-called democratic governance system constitutes gross neglect and abuse of the people in the guise of democracy.

Essentially, what we are saying is that in the present-day political framework (in democracy and more as in communism, dictatorship and monarchy), there is a big divide between the civil society and the government society made up of elected political-party members, which precludes the involvement of the civil society in public policy development and governance. We are hence proposing the concept of civilian democracy in the form of socio-economic democracy. A community or a nation in which the civil society handles the governance will naturally be more sympathetic to the problems and issues of common people. It will also be able to provide more knowledgeable human resources to the governance system.

We are hence recommending a socio-economic, democratic and party less political governance system. How do we implement that? In order to replace the present miserable system of governance, we propose that each association or agency of a sector of community function (such as of healthcare, jurisprudence, banking and finance, manufacturing industry, agriculture, municipal cooperatives and/or agencies) elect two members, and put them up as well-qualified candidates (of known acumen) for the local government portfolio (represented by that particular association or agency). The general public will then vote and elect one of these candidates (of known integrity) to administer the corresponding portfolio on the local governance board. Hence, a local government will consist of people-elected representatives of, for instance, the primary healthcare system, municipal system, primary education system, industrial enterprises, local banks, sports council and townships' councils.

Then, all these sectorial associations-approved and people-elected SRC government legislators (with adroit credentials for their portfolios) would be able to totally concentrate on their roles and functions, without being entangled in inter-party sledging and squabbles. They will be appointed for a four-year term, be totally responsible and accountable for their department's performance. Their re-nomination on the governance board will be based on their integrity and performance. This system of governance cabinet constitution will ensure appointment of governance board members having adroit qualifications for their posts, while also being totally accountable for the performance of their departments. It will also do away with the system of one person (the local party chief) controlling governance. This new governance system will do away with the multiple party system of pseudo democracy, money-wasting mechanisms, corrupt governance, and introduce real democracy. Above all, this civilian democracy will provide people-centric knowledge-governance instead of political party-centric governance!

There are two added points that we want to make. One is that of a mechanism for the governance executives to meet regularly with the community sectorial associations, singly and collectively. The other issue is that based on community sectorial representations in governance, how do we elect a legislator or minister to be in charge of the external-affairs portfolio. For this purpose, the elected governance council (or legislature or parliament) will elect one of its members for this portfolio, and then have the second elected representative of his/her sector take charge of his/her sectorial portfolio.

12.4 Neo-global governance-electoral system

In order to enable individual SRCs of a Third World region to favorably compete and trade on equal terms with developed countries, the local FSCs need to be brought together under the fold of socio-economic blocs (SEBs), self-reliant economic zones (SEZs) and regional federations (such as the South Asian Federation, East African Federation, etc.), under a world government.

In the previous section, we formulated the electoral system of the FSC legislators. The elected cooperatives' presidents and FSC legislators will, in turn, elect the governance officers of the SEB government, who will then elect the ministers of the SEZ government. This will also be carried out on portfolio basis, so as to ensure and propagate knowledgeable voting and election of competent officers for their specific portfolios. All the SEZs' ministers (associated with each ministry) will then elect the regional federation (RFD) minister for that ministry. Finally, the RFD ministers will elect one person for each portfolio to the world government. We will now further illustrate this electorate system to governance.

Let us consider a regional federational political setup of:

- ℓ FSCs, m SEBs and n SEZs within a regional federation; let $\ell \cong 25$, $m \cong 20$, $n \cong 10$;
- a typical FSC will be denoted by FSC-i ($i = 1,\ldots,\ell$), a typical SEB will be denoted by SEB-j ($j = 1$ to m), and a typical SEZ will be SEZ-k ($k = 1$ to n);
- p ($\cong 100$) = average number of associations (of cooperatives, representing various types of professions), agencies (for community services) and councils (for townships' environmental safety and cultural affairs) within each FSC;
- q ($\cong 10^4$) = average number of members in each association/agency/council;
- r ($\cong 10^6$) = $p \times q$ = average number of inhabitants of each FSC;
- S regional federations under the aegis of the world government.

The associations, agencies, and councils within a FSC can be, for instance:

- educators and teachers association (E&T), medical and doctors association (M&D), legal and lawyers association (L&L), etc.;
- energy and power supply (E&P) agency, water supply and sanitation (WS&S) agency, land transport (LT) agency, postal (POS) services, transport (TRP) services, etc.;
- corporations of agricultural and farmers cooperatives (A&F), manufacturers cooperatives (MF), and banking cooperatives (BK);
- citizens (CT) councils (made up of voting eligible member residents who are not members of professional associations and agencies) to elect government candidates for neighborhood environmental safety and cultural affairs; and
- sports (SP) councils.

12.5 FSC, SED and SEZ governments' establishment

In the previous section, we formulated the electoral system of the FSC legislators. What is now depicted, below, is that the "q" ($\cong 10^4$) members of each of the

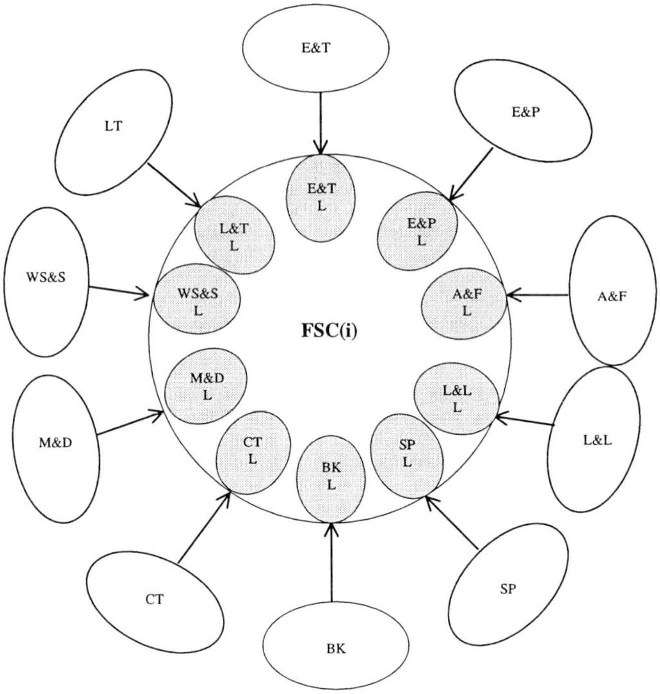

Fig. 12.1 Election of p number of legislators (for p number of portfolios) in an FSC(i); herein L denotes legislator.

p (≅ 100) associations/agencies/councils elect their candidates to the legislature of the FSC (i) government (wherein i = 1,...,ℓ). For instance, the E&T association elects/nominates its E&T legislator, the association of banking cooperatives elects/nominates its banking legislature. Thus, all "p" number of legislators get elected to the local legislature of the functionally-sustainable community "i" (FSC-i), as illustrated in Fig. 12.1.

This form of election will take place for each of the ℓ FSCs (i.e. for i = 1,...,ℓ) belonging to a particular SEB-j. Hence, at the end of this first level of elections, we will have elected for each of the ℓ FSCs (belonging to a particular SEB-j):

- one E&T legislator to handle educational policies and matters;
- one E&P legislator to be in charge of energy and power, and so on (as illustrated in Fig 12.2).

Next, at the SEB level, the ℓ number of E&T legislators (of the ℓ FSCs) will elect their E&T representative to serve as the E&T minister on the government of

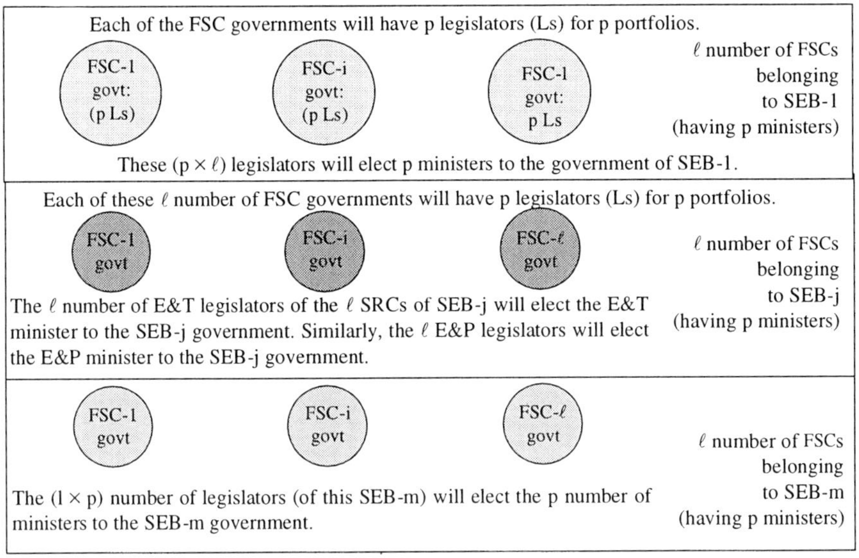

Fig. 12.2 Electoral constituencies of the m number of SEBs.

the SEB-j, to which the ℓ number of FSCs belong. Similarly, the ℓ number of E&P legislators will elect the E&P minister to their SEB-j government. In this way, all the p ministers (of p portfolios) will be elected to the SEB-j government, as illustrated in Fig. 12.2.

Then, at the SEZ level, the SEB ministers will, in turn, elect the SEZ ministers for the p portfolios. Finally, the p number of ministers of each of the n number of the SEZs of a regional federation (RFD) will elect the p number of federational ministers (for the p portfolios). This procedure is illustrated in Fig. 12.3.

12.6 Constituting federational and world governments

At this point, we have an $m \times \ell$ matrix of ℓ number of FSC governments and m number of SEB governments, with each SEB comprising of ℓ number of FSCs. Correspondingly, we will have a total number of $(p \times \ell)$ legislators for each of the m SEBs. The ℓ number of legislators (of the ℓ FSCs) for each of the p portfolios of a particular SEB will elect one minister for each portfolio to their SEB government. Thus, we will have p ministers (of p portfolios) for each of the m number of SEB governments. This gives us a total of $p \times m$ SEB ministers in each of the n number of SEZs, to elect the p number of ministers for each SEZ government, as illustrated in Fig.12.4.

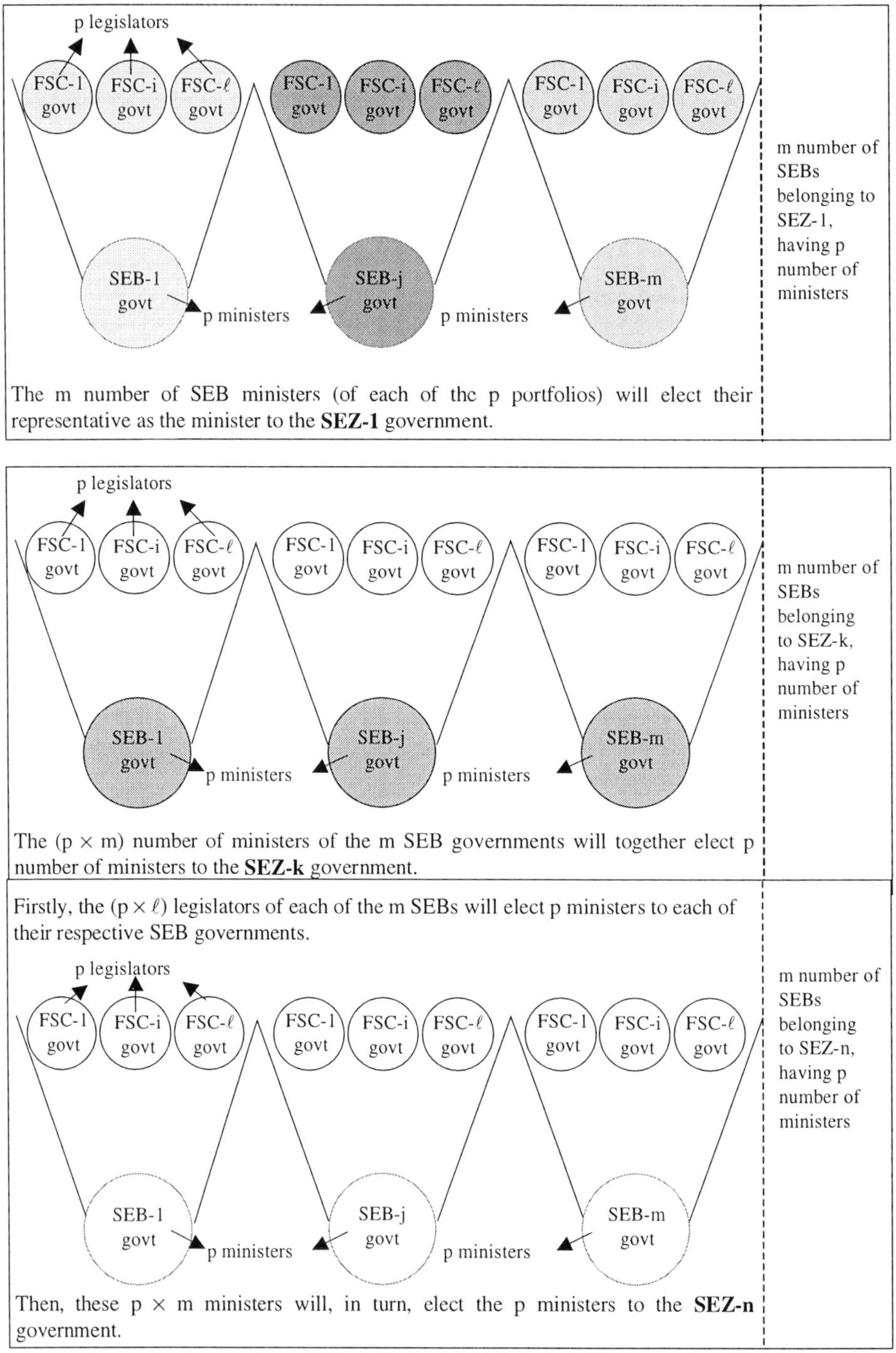

Fig. 12.3 Governance structure at the FSC-SEB-SEZ levels.

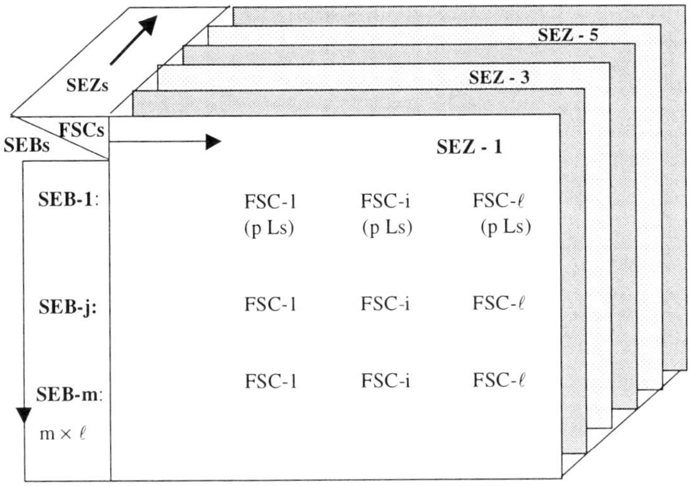

Fig. 12.4 Political structure of a Regional federation of n SEZs. Each of the n SEZs (such as SEZ-1) comprises of m SEBs, and each SEB comprises of ℓ FSCs. Thus, as illustrated in the figure, each SEZ will comprise of $(m \times \ell)$ FSC(s). Each FSC will have p legislators, and each SEB will have p ministers (for the p portfolios). In each SEZ, there will be p SEZ ministers, elected by or from $(p \times m)$ SEB ministers.

Filling in the gap:

It is noted that among the ℓ FSCs of an SEB, one out of ℓ ($\cong 25$) legislators of a particular portfolio will be elected to the SEB government. That particular legislator will have been one of the two elected candidates of that corresponding association/agency/council (in a particular FSC), who was elected to the legislature by the people. So, then, the other elected candidate of that particular association or agency or council would take his/her place on the FSC legislature.

Similarly, a total of p ($\cong 100$) legislators out of $p \times \ell$ ($\cong 2500$) legislators would be elected as p ministers to each of the m SEB governments. So these p legislators would have to be replaced by the elected candidates of their corresponding associations/agencies/councils in their respective FSCs. In other words, in each SEB, additional legislators would have to be replaced in their respective FSCs' legislatures by the second elected candidates of their respective associations/agencies/councils.

At the next level, yet another p ($\cong 100$) out of $p \times m$ ($\cong 2000$) SEB ministers of a particular SEZ would be elected to their SEZ government. So, these p ($\cong 100$) number of ministers would need to be replaced by the corresponding FSCs' legislators, who in turn would be replaced on the

FSC governments by the second candidate of their respective associations/agencies/councils.

Now, for l ≅ 25 and m ≅ 20, if p ≅ 100 SEB ministers are elected to their SEZ government, giving us p = 100 vacancies among the (p × m) ministers of m (= 20) SEBs. Hence on an average, p/m (≅ 5) ministers (of p/m portfolios) need to be replaced in each SEB government from their respective FSC governments. These p/m (≅ 5) ministers would then need to be replaced by elections to be carried out by the (5 × ℓ) FSC legislators of these five portfolios. This, in turn, means that five more legislators would have to be elected in their five FSCs, or be replaced by the second candidate of these fuce associations/agencies/councils.

Finally, we come to the formation of the RFD government. The n number of SEZ ministers, belonging to each portfolio p (for instance, E&T portfolio) of the SEZ governments, will elect the RFD government minister of that portfolio. The RFD ministers will then elect the world government minister of each of the p (≅ 100) portfolios, as illustrated in Fig. 12.5. In this way, all of the ministers would be elected to the world government.

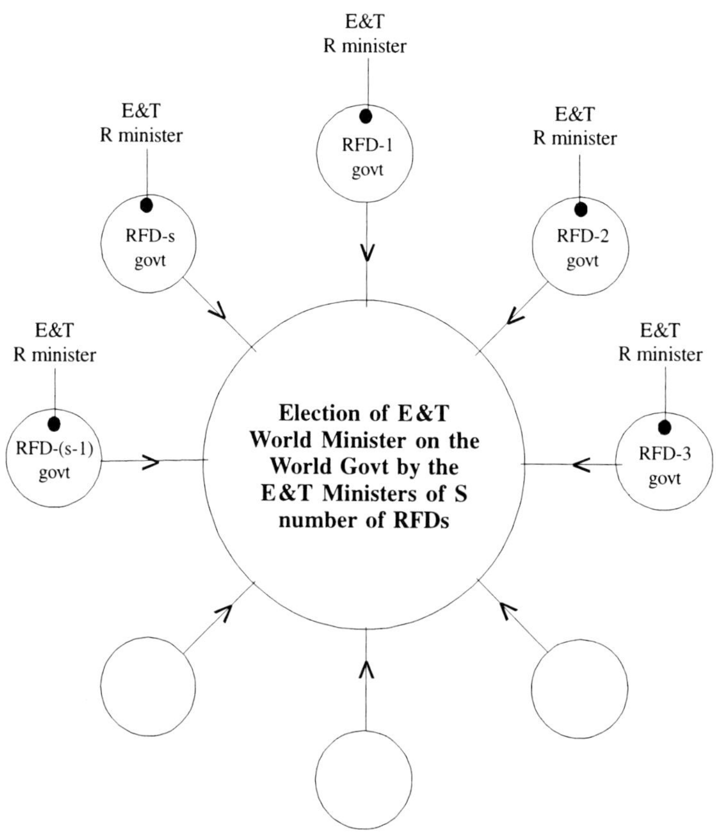

Fig. 12.5 Election to world government's parliament.

12.7 Ignorance factor in conventional democratic system

Let each of the total of ($\ell \times m \times n$) number of FSCs be designated as FSC-ijk, belonging to the kth SEZ, j^{th} SEB and i^{th} FSC. For $\ell = 25$, $m = 20$, $n = 10$, there would be a total of 5000 FSCs in each federation. Each SRC would have p ($\cong$ say, 100) number of sectorial associations (of cooperatives), and each of the p associations would have q ($\cong$ say, 10^4) number of people members. This yields a total of 5×10^9 ($= 5000 \times p \times q$) population for that region (as for example, the East Asian region or federation).

In the conventional political party-based democratic system, all the people would vote for all the candidates. In other words, all the r ($\cong p \times q$) people ($\cong 10^6$) of an FSC would vote for all its p ($\cong$ 100) political candidates. In our neo-democratic system, we would have only q ($\cong 10^4$) people members of each association/agency/council knowledgeably voting two capable candidates for a specific (i.e. each) legislative portfolio. No doubt, all the FSC people would then elect one of these two approved and knowledgeable candidates to be in charge of that particular portfolios in the legislature. So, in the conventional system, there would be $q(p - 1)$ or 990,000 ($= 10^6 - 10^4 = r - q$) additional people voting in each FSC, for each FSC governance candidate, who will be ignorant of the credentials and competency of the candidate.

If we take into consideration that there would be ℓmn ($\cong$ 5000) FSCs within a regional federation (RFD), then there would be approximately 495×10^6 ($= 990 \times 10^3 \times 5000$ or 495,000,000) people voting in ignorance in that region, making it a mockery of democracy! On the other hand, in our electoral system, each legislature candidate would be first elected by only the members of a particular association/agency/council, to whom the credentials and competency of the candidate would be well known. Thus, each of the associations, agencies and councils will present two well-qualified candidates to the general public, who will then elect one of these two candidates to govern the corresponding legislative portfolio.

People of one nation should feel empathy for people of all the other nations, in the true spirit of universalism.

Let the universal refrain be that all people earn equivalently for their labor and/or knowledge, so that:

all the families and communities have equivalent lifestyle;

all people get uniformly respected, irrespective of their geographic inhabitation and other imposed labels;

we all live as one cooperative global family, with everyone attending to everyone's needs.

These slum dwellers cannot be expected to have any hope to improve their lot as long as we have this miserable democratic system, of political parties serving the affluent and corporate sectors of the society. The political parties are like corporations with their own policy and profit making agendas. By contesting elections, they bid for contracts from communities to manage the community resources to supposedly benefit the people. However, in reality they are in this governance business for themselves. Hence, let us all work collectively to improve the lot of these beautiful children, by bringing about a people-centric Civilian economic and governance system, in which all the community's functional sectors are involved in community politicization.

13

Human Rights and Constitutional Guarantees

13.1 Lessons from history

Throughout history, it has happened that in a community and society of people and nations, a strong or clever person or nation has captured economic and/or political power. However, it also follows that in such a society, others continually topple these persons or nations in power. Hence, it has been shown that in hegemonism, there can be no peace, besides it being a primitive way of living. As a general rule, it is dangerous to be "alone at the top", and definitely more secure to live in harmony with one's neighbors on the ground floor.

For sustained peace and enlightened living, it is important to evolve a system, which cannot breed ruthless communist regimes and dictators, nor power-obsessed heads of democratic regimes, as well as not permit political or economic or military hegemonism. In our new framework of socio-economic democracy (and associated electoral system by community service agencies, professional associations and citizen's councils) and the world government, there will be no scope of hegemonism by any individual or nation at any level.

Throughout history, when nations have over-extended their territories and empires, and attempted to dominate people of other cultures and nations, their inability to understand the psychology of those distant and culturally different people has sown the seeds of discontent and led to the break-up of their empires. Hence, small autonomously governed communities of different cultures can co-exist more peacefully than centrally and forcibly governed discontented (and even uni-cultural) communities of big nations.

At different periods of time, different nations have been powerful and have exerted dominance over other nations. However, history has also consistently shown evidence of the fall of the once powerful nations. Hence, imbibing the lessons of history, a powerful nation needs to be a role model of compassion and graciousness, rather than parade its military strength and power by causing massive destruction of weak and poverty-stricken nations or by bullying them to fall in line with its policies and agendas.

13.2 For democratic and political pluralism

Today's EU would like to forget the colonial past of many of its members, who were also engaged in slave trafficking and extermination of ethnic communities. EU's preference for multipolarity is opposed by the US government on the grounds that such a concept of promoting rivalry and competing interests would not auger well for the ideals of freedom. Within EU itself, some nations (France and Britain) are centralists who wish to retain their national sovereignty, while others (like Germany and Italy) are federalists. Nevertheless, there is consensus to the concept of co-leadership.

China's communist governments much advertized governance policy of one nation and two systems (although never been applied to Tibet, for instance) has been meant to placate Taiwan and Hong Kong (prior to its 1997 handover). However, when the Chinese government tried to get its Hong Kong government to surreptitiously push through an anti-subversion Bill (through its handpicked millionaire leader), more than half a million protested on the streets on 1 July 2003 against this legislation, that would curb human rights (such as freedom of religion and speech) and civil liberties. The Chinese state press launched a scathing attack on this display of anti-government sentiments, on the grounds that it sowed the seeds of societal discord. It even hailed the Hong Kong security governance chief as a patriot for her determination, toughness and courage in pushing through this anti-subversion bill. A leading Chinese newspaper even glorified the legislator as a fearless patriot. So this represents the Chinese government's view of patriotism.

On the other hand, on 5 July 2003 when China's former defence minister General Zhang Aiping passed away quietly at the age of 93, the civilian society pronounced him as a model of integrity, even though he was branded as a counter-revolutionary revisionist (the standard communist anti-democracy jargon). For opposing Chairman Mao's socialism and cultural revolution, he survived six years of imprisonment to emerge with unshaken views on political governance ethics and civilian freedom, as a defence minister. Then again in the aftermath of 1989 Tiananmen Square student-rally, he dared to disagree with patriarch Deng Xiaoping's imposition of martial law and even defended the patriotic sentiments of the students' protest. So although he was again hermitized, he gained more respect from people, for his moral courage and patriotism.

Herein, we have a prime example of the big gulf in values and perception of what is noble and patriotic, between the "government society" and the "civilian society." Those courageous and moralist thinkers, who are champions of people's rights and freedom of expression, are the civilian society's models of patriotism. These noble persons are staunchly "democratic" in insisting on the acceptance of a high order of variance in the normally-distributed spectrum of human psyche in society. They are defenders of human rights in not only their country but also for the people of other nations, and are not afraid to publicly oppose their countries' policies that are contrary to these values. On the other hand, the government society considers these civilian society's patriots as anti-patriotic for opposing the governments political policies, and in fact regards the hard-line enactors of such public policies as real patriots.

This is why, it is so important for us to bring about a civilian democratic governance system. Throughout history and even today in the supposed era of democracy, there has always been this divergence between the cardinal values of civilian society (CVS) and the government society (GVS). Up to now, in all GVS-controlled democratic regimes, the "thinking and telling" is supposedly to be done by the GVS, and the "listening and following" by the CVS. In an evolved society, the two ought to merge. When that happens, only then can we have genuine democracy.

13.3 Need for human rights and conscientious governance

In real democracy, the wishes of the people are to be respected. A certain community may have lost confidence in its state government, because its interests have not been served under that government. Then, it is pointless to keep that community in subjugation by force. Rather, for the sake of peace, that community should be given autonomy to form its own government, and to constitute a functionally-sustainable community (FSC).

Communal riots and killings will occur in a nation, wherein narrow sentimentality is rooted and whose political leaders are known to harbor and express racist and castist sentiments. In the prevalent party-based political system, wherein senior party members get the important portfolios (such as home affairs and foreign affairs), it is a tragedy for a nation if a senior party member with a racially biased and/or caste-minded attitude were to be given the home ministry portfolio.

In Ayodhya (India), on 9 December 1992, the Babri Masjid was demolished by Hindu religionists on the grounds that the mosque was built over the ruins of a temple for Lord Rama during the time of the mugul emperor Baber. That incident has since then been the cause of communial violence in India. The ruling BJP party has been accused, by the opposition parties and staunch secular groups, of putting on a mask of moderation while tacitly and covertly encouraging Hindu sentimental fanaticism, which is contrary to India's constitutional secularism. In a country, where there is mass poverty and illiteracy as well as no semblance of mass health-care delivery, where every year so many people suffer either due to drought or flooding of rivers, where so many people live and die on the roads, is it not tragic that political parties are embroiled in such issues?

In India, the people progress in spite of government regimes. One has only to read the leading daily newspapers to find out that conspicuous by its absence is any mention of any people's welfare issue or policy on the part of any politician. The central government and state government politicians are totally immersed in petty inner-party squabbles and election campaigns at all levels. Outside India, Indians prosper academically and professionally. It is said that the percentage of Indian doctors in US, of Indian IT professionals and entrepreneurs in Microsoft and Silicon Valley, and of Indian aerospace engineers working for NASA far exceeds the percentage of US citizens of Indian origin. However, there is no such scope for them to develop professionally in India, why? It is because it is very difficult for international-level professionalism and intellectualism to prosper in India, without corruption and political-party connections.

It is to the immense credit of a few persevering visionaries that their automobile and telecommunications companies as well as IT and pharmaceutical companies have developed into internationally competitive corporations. However, only when such visionaries turn their attention to education and political governance (encouraged by our concept of socio-economic democracy and party-less sectorially representative governance), then we will witness a true resurgence and renaissance in all realms of society in India. That time is not far off.

Inter-ethnic violence and killings in a community is a disgrace to that community as well as to the nation and particularly to its political leaders. It constitutes crime against humanity! The responsibility of such widely prevalent inter-ethnic disturbances rests on the political leaders, who (in order to preserve their popularity with the provocative community) do not have the moral courage to condemn such mass violence and ethnic killings as being primitive and barbaric, immoral and inhuman. Communal killings constitute crimes against humanity, and their perpetrators should be liable to be indicted for anti-humanity crimes.

It is hence so important for the governance members to imbibe values of neo-humanism, oneness and indivisibility of the humanity, as well as the common origin and desideratum of all human beings. Further, people rights and human rights, incorporated in the constitution, should make it legally possible for such ill-motivated and disgraceful political heads and leaders to be brought to justice by the common people.

Aside from that, it is also part and parcel of human rights provisions by a community or nation to except and receive knowledgeable governance. Just as medical practioners are liable to be sued for lapses in medical practice, so also politicians should be liable to be sued by the people for governance mal-practice. Not only is apathetic governance intolerable, but even ignorant governance by dumb politicians constitutes deception and violation of human rights. While awaiting our proposed reformation of the governance system, it is high time that such miscreant politicians are held legally responsible for abrogation of people's rights to competent governance. Only then will they stop running for elections.

13.4 Human rights in a progressive society

A progressive society is deemed to be one that provides, to its members, a socio-economic-political environment to enable fulfillment of the people in all aspects of living and thinking. In order to bring this about, the society needs an enlightened constitution, incorporating statutes to provide for all-round welfare of its residents and to facilitate their all-round progress. Earlier, we have addressed the type of governance most suitable for a FSC, in order to make it into a progressive society? Herein, we will discuss some constitutional requirements and guarantees to ensure that all the people can fulfillingly bring to bear their multi-faceted potentials for mutual benefit, and to thereby fashion a progressive society.

For a progressive society, we would need to promote multi-faceted development and opportunism for its people, through its constitution and public policies, some of which are listed below:

- secularism is promoted and narrow sentimentality (on basis of religion, caste and financial status) is discouraged;
- all human rights are recognized and protected;
- the right to religious practice and conversion is respected;
- animal and plant life are protected;
- equal and fair opportunities are available to all members of the society, to have education and employment, commensurate with one's capabilities;
- all sections of the population have near-uniform living standards;
- no form of discrimination can be acceptable and tolerated, and everyone is to have the right for full development of his/her potential in all segments of the society;
- even the minimum salary is to have adequate purchasing power for basic living needs as well as amenities for minimizing physical drudgery;
- everyone has access to proper medical care, and there is proper social security for everyone: even for those who are stranded or abandoned, incapacitated or handicapped, destitute or alone, old or infirm; and
- psycho-spiritual development of the people is encouraged and facilitated, so as to develop a neo-humanistic social outlook and environment.

It can be easily seen that the constitution and form of governance can have a significant bearing on the progressiveness of a society, and especially in the case of Third World nations. It is obvious that democracy in Third World nations has not succeeded, why? In the name of democracy, so many parties (of incompetent and often corrupt persons) are formed and contest elections by making fake election propagandas, which they have neither intent nor competence to implement. In the majority of Third World countries, many people are uneducated, are not political conscious, and are poor. They are unable to make proper assessment of the parties and their representatives, are generally deceived by them, and can also be duped by small incentives.

Governance involves knowledge of all the complex functions and processes of a society, as well as an astute pulse of how public policies will influence them and affect the peoples. Hence, people involved in community governance or national or regional governance should be highly educated, extremely moral, super-compassionate, and neo-humanistic. Unfortunately, very few politicians have these basic credentials for a public office. In some developing countries (such as in India), the people in charge of governance may not even be educated and sometimes even have criminal records. How can they be role models for their community people?

In most developing countries, the politicians are making themselves rich at the expense of the people, and making it impossible to provide the above-delineated basis of a progressive society. Thus, aside from starting at a disadvantage of (economic, resource generation, industrial and educational) backwardness (due to centuries of colonization and thereafter being bled by their own politicians), the people of developing countries have to contend with disordered and corrupt governance, infrastructure and administrative machinery. There is hence a serious and urgent need to modify the present system of so-called and name-sake democratic governance. We have hence proposed a sectorial-electoral system of democratic governance (devoid of political parties, as described in Chapter 12), which will enable and ensure that competent people are in charge of community functional portfolios.

An eligible governance executive needs to have reasonably high levels of the following quotients:

1. INQ (intelligence quotient or IQ), in order to at least comprehend governance;
2. EMQ (emotional quotient), to have a proper temperament for governance;
3. HOQ (honesty quotient), to not indulge in corruption;
4. SIQ (sincerity quotient), to be sincere to people's welfare;
5. SCQ (secularism quotient), so as to be above narrow religious sentimentality;

6. DMQ (democratic quotient), so as to relate to people's voices; it includes ability to have a lifestyle equivalent to that of an average person whose salary is the mean salary of the community;
7. COQ (compassion quotient), so as to be sympathetic to people's sufferings;
8. CSQ (civilian society quotient), so as to care for the concerns and needs of the civilian society;
9. LGQ (local-to-global quotient), so as to work for local prosperity, in the framework of global unity;
10. NHQ (neo-humanism quotient), so as to be a role model human being, journeying on the mysticism boulevard to self-realization.

For each quotient, we can allocate 10 marks, so that an evaluator has to give marks out of 10 for each quotient. Then the multi-quotient index (MQI) = (sum of the marks of all the quotient)/100. The concept of MQI is quite similar to that of the ISPO index formulated in chapter 7. If a politician gets MQI = 80/100, then he/she gets an A grade as an excellent politician or a governance candidate; a grade B, for 70–80/100, implies a good political candidate; a grade C for 60–70/100 is indicative of a satisfactory politician; a grade D for 50–60/100 indicates an unacceptable candidate; and a grade F for <50/100 is indicative of being totally unfit for governance. It is left to the readers to assess their politicians on the basis of this MQI.

13.5 Economic democratic guarantees for the people

Within a self-reliant economic unit (SEB) and also FSCs, the economic policy will provide the following guarantees.

Fair utilization of human potentialities: Fair utilization of human resources can imply fair renumeration as well as having the right person for a specific role. The key economic guideline for a FSC is to ensure development and societal utilization of all the (physical, intellectual, aesthetic, psychic and spiritual) potentialities of the people. Fulfillment of the people, in being able to either relate to their society (in values and outlook) or to contribute to it, is very important for contented living and a peaceful community. The economic system and policy should not just be able to generate wealth but also distribute it equitably, as well as guarantee freedom from starvation and depravation of minimal living amenities.

Fair distribution of wealth: Unfair distribution of wealth can result from unfair utilization of human resources and suppression of human potential. Especially in developing countries, concentration of wealth has also been responsible for under development. This is why we are advocating cooperatively structured firms and companies. Further, the economic planning needs to aim for 100% employment, and near-uniform living standards for all population sectors of the community.

Social security: Aside from everyone being able to have employment, the minimum salary should be able to support a minimum standard of living, with adequate purchasing capacity to acquire atleast the essentials of life (i.e. food, clothing, healthcare, housing and education). Additionally, healthcare coverage and old-age social security should be available for all people.

Fair election and governance: The most capable people must be administering the various governance portfolios, and the election procedures must make that possible. In order to provide the above-mentioned guarantees, the community living and work sectors need to be organized in the form of work and living cooperatives, along with associations representing professionals as well as clusters of cooperatives and residence councils. Then, the elected representatives of these associations would constitute the civilian government of the community, as a genuine democratic governance.

Fair democracy: The normalization of wealth distribution would be achieved by the combination of business and industrial cooperatives, adroit utilization (and renumeration) of people's capabilities (in relation to work), minimal wage specification (for global business transactions), and stocks being only available to corporation employees. When the people find their lifestyle fulfilling (by maximal expression of their potentialities), then only can we have a fair democracy.

13.6 Constitutional requirements for a progressive society

Most constitutional remits deal with procedures of election and selection of people's representatives in governance. However the role of a constitution is to facilitate all-round development of all people, by (i) means of an excellent primary-to-university education system, in order to help develop and disseminate the ideals of the society in all arenas of human endeavors; (ii) an eclectic and pluralistic society, to provide people maximal oppurtunity to develop themselves and to contribute to their societal progress; (iii) removing all situations of discriminations and persecutions (due to language, culture, race and religion), (iv) guaranteeing that the minimal wage has the purchasing power of the prime living necessities (food and housing, healthcare and education and basic amenities), (v) ensuring secularism, respecting people's rights to pursue and propagate spiritual paths, and (vi) appropriate utilization of human capability, with commensurate renumeration.

The constitution should further provide guarantees in:

- compulsory and free education up to high school, state and central governments commitments to support higher education without interference in curricular development (such as re-shaping history to make it more favorable for the governing of political party's narrow sentimentality);
- managed healthcare for all (either through direct registration with hospitals or through medical insurance companies), and subsidized primary healthcare in poor sections of the community; and
- social security, involving old-age renumeration, and compulsory pension scheme satisfying minimal maintenance needs and healthcare coverage.

The constitution should also incorporate: (1) common marriage and inheritance codes for all religious communities within FSCs and SEBs, with freedom to marry and divorce, (2) ecological protection, involving safeguarding of rights-of-existence and lives of animals and plants, and preservation of forests and wild animals, (3) tribal cultural protection and all-round development, ensuring cultural rejuvenation, education and healthcare for all, and modernization of their traditional means of (land-based) livelihood.

People's participation in governance and economic management of the community also needs to be ensured by (1) structuring both political and economic democracy, (2) local economic planning and people's involvement in economic development through cooperative businesses and enterprises, and (3) ensuring people's involvement and cooperation in all aspects of societal functions: community services (schools and colleges, healthcare centers and municipal services), corporations and industries. Further, to ensure industrial financial stability, shares would only be made available to employees of industrial corporations; outsiders would be prevented from buying and manipulating company shares. Further, stock and currency trading would be disallowed, thereby preventing capital development without any tangible resource development.

Genuine democracy involves (1) possibility of righteous, capable and independent persons to be elected/nominated for appropriate political posts, without party and/or financial backing, (2) elimination of election campaign extravaganzas, (3) legislative assemblies and parliaments to be made up of only well-qualified (elected) persons in charge of portfolios, (4) elimination of petty time-wasting and money-squandering inter-party squabbles, and (5) independence of the judiciary, so that all can be equal in the eyes of the law without governmental pressure or interference.

Combined political and economic democracy governance forum needs to be incorporated in the constitution. All community functions/operations would have to be organized as associations (of for example industrialists' association, agriculturalists' association and teachers association), agencies (such as municipal agency, postal agency, trade and commerce agency) and councils (such as resident townships councils). These associations, agencies and people's councils would be electing their representatives, for the general public to then vote them (as ministers) into the local governments. For example, the teachers association representative would be the legislator for education, the agriculturists' association's representative would be the legislator for agriculture, the townships' council's representative could be the legislator in charge of the security or environment portfolio and so on.

In such a non-party governance system, the public service offices and governance would be in the hands of capable, honest and moral persons. Further, it would be possible for intelligent but independent thinkers to hold public or political offices, because election and appointment to governance would be made through associations (of industrialists, educators, healthcare professionals, cooperation), agencies (such as for public utilities and banking) and councils of neighborhood people (who are not represented by professional associations).

13.7 Specific constitutional requirements at FSC, SEZ and RFD levels

An FSC will be the basic living unit of this neo-global order and society, and hence of grassroots economic democracy and governance. At the FSC level, the constitution needs to particularly guarantee:

- fair and fullest utilization of all human resources in community functional sectors;
- right to employment, and minimal salary to have the purchasing capacity to be able to satisfy basic living needs;
- cooperative involvement of the people in all operations of a corporation: in profit-sharing, occupational health and safety, workers' compensation and pension schemes;
- uniform penal code and social justice for all people, and that too based on cardinal principles (and not on religious dogmas or tennets);
- protection of animals, ecology and environment;
- taxation-subsidized (and hence affordable) higher education, healthcare delivery, public transport and social security; and
- money derived from development of local resources is to be primarily utilized for local development and community betterment.

Then, at the SEZ level, we need to constitutionally ensure:

- free trade among the FSCs and SEBs of SEZ;
- facilitate import and export among SRCs, as well as mobility of human resources, know-how and technology and essential living needs, so as to ensure near-uniform living standards among all the SRCs of the SREZ;
- physical protection, social and economic security, uniform (and non-discriminatory) opportunities for education and employment for all the FSCs' inhabitants;
- accountability of the legislators to the community and its people, for (1) competent governance and benefiting public policies (incorporating available know-how), and (2) honest and transparent administration;
- the right for any socio-culturally segregated community to cede from its FSC, and to form a separate FSC.

At the self-reliant regional federation (RFD) level, we further need to provide constitutional rights:

- for all constituent SEZs of the RFD to have security and protection from one another, to prevent military operations by any one SREZ against another;
- for any endangered SEZ to call on the common RFD low-enforcing military force, for safeguarding its territorial integrity and inhabitants;
- to ensure enforcement of "human rights", and prevent harassment and persecution of any social and/or cultural group;
- to prevent any constituent SEZ from falling behind educationally and industrially and/or socially and economically, because of lapses in governance and/or poor public policies; and
- to intervene in the affairs of such a mismanaged SEZ, by educating its ministers and (if necessary) to restructure its government, by having re-elections for certain ministries/portfolios.

13.8 Knowledgeable governance with sincerity and morality

Without morality, there cannot be progress to an enlightened society and lifestyle, respect for and implementation of human rights, and proper recognition (through remuneration) of people's labour and services. Without such social and economic justice, there cannot be peace!

Effective governance is to be transparent and at the same time invisible. Governing implies winning over the hearts of people. No nation can (and has a right to) forcibly govern a community that it has not cared for, and hence lost its respect and trust. So the basis of peace is to be secure in mutual regard and love.

Human rights imply the right to be treated respectfully and honorably, kindly and compassionately, in the fullest sense of these terms. Human rights is to form the basis of interactions among people and nations, and especially the basis of the conduct of governance executives to the people. Our delineated neo-humanistic socio-economic political democratic order and world government system of globalization offers maximal scope for the implementation of a neo-dimension of human rights.

In the face of a long history of colossal human suffering (imposed by heads of nations and political systems), the solution (at the grassroots as well as higher levels), is to formulate and adopt a political system, wherein the governance persons (elected to administer portfolios):

- do not rule, but serve the people;
- are answerable to, and work for the constituencies and agencies (and associations) that elect them;
- are sincerely carrying out their roles, without fanfare or craving media attention;
- can implement socio-economic democracy, and ensure independence of educational, judicial and public media systems;
- have no scope for corruption or for exercising power over their people, who will have in fact placed their trust in them to competently administer their portfolios;
- cannot have any scope for encouraging discrimination (of any form), and carrying out repression of their own people; and
- uphold human rights in the fullest measure.

At the global level, we need a world government political system, to ensure fair governance, socio-economic democracy, and human rights at all levels.

We need a mindset change in order to effect a people-centric governance, instead of a capitalistic-controlled political-party based governance-administration system.

When people will realize that true democracy can indeed be constituted (as socio-economic democracy) without political parties, by the structuring of a community into functional sectors which would elect their most capable representatives to the community government, then they will come forward to participate in governance.

In such a society, in which the civil society will execute governance policies, there will be ample scope for everyone to express themselves fully. Such a society will truly represent human civilization!

The remains of dozens of bodies that were exhumed from a mass grave (at Sahil Attaf) in the northern Iraqi region of al-Hadar, 105 kilometers south of the northern capital of Mosul, with the help of experts from the US Armed Forces Institute of Pathology are seen on the ground (15 July 2003). The exhumed bodies belong to Kurds (men, women and children), executed by Saddam's regime in 1988, the final year of an eight-year war between Iran and Iraq.

Bodies are exhumed from a mass grave at the Kibeho refugee camp (27 April 1995) to count the dead following the massacre of Hutu refugees allegedly committed by the Tutsi-dominated Rwandan Army (23 April). The Rwandan government put the toll at 338, but the UN has said some 2000 people were killed.

Only our proposed World (people's) government can prevent such tragedies. There are many countries, under oppressive rule of ruthless dictators as well as monopolist royal families (who own their nation's wealth) and fundamentalist clerics, that need to be liberated. In the present setup, it is a dilemma as to how the UN and the nations of the world can oust a tyrannical dictator of a terrorized country. Unfortunately, because the UN charter deals with nations and not with people, it recognizes the sovereignty of nations.

Import sanctions on that country only affect the people and not the rulers. Also, invasion of that country by militarily powerful countries (interested in its natural resources) is not morally justifiable, because civilians get killed in the process by which the liberators turn into tyrannical intruders. Then, the local people opposing their intrusion get to be labeled as criminals, while the invading forces and their country's leaders enjoy immunity from prosecution for crimes against humanity. Hence the UN needs to develop a strategy of dealing with rogue dictators, to remove then from power. In our new political setup, it would be impossible for ruthless dictators to emerge and take over a country.

14

Civilian-Centered Neo-humanistic Global Order

A global order comprises of social outlook and culture, socio-economic system and political structure, banking and trade, constitution and jurisprudence. Neo-humanism entails liberation from narrow sentimentality and adopting universalism, mind upliftment to nobler realms and ensconsement in consciousness.* When the majority of people are infused with this spirit, we can have a neo-humanistic global order. In this chapter, we will deal with all these components in relation to the neo-humanistic global order.

14.1 Neo-humanistic social outlook

The sentimental journey: As social groups started to emerge (in river-valley civilizations of, for instance, Indus, Euphrates and Tigris, Nile, Hwang Ho and Amazon), language and culture became the binding and identity factors. Simultaneously, consciousness of natural and so-called supra-natural phenomena developed transcendental tendencies among some individuals. People started to follow their ideas and doctrines, and thus religions began to evolve.

As social groups started to migrate, they tended to preserve their culture, language and religions. Now as interactions between social groups increased, there arose feelings of superiority of one's language, religion and culture. The tendency to assert superiority of community culture and religion led to wars.

As human habitats started interacting, they acquired narrow sentiments and propensities (resulting from attachments to their communities and cultures), which obstructed their evolutionary journey to their desideratum. Then came about the self-realization that the struggle to move forward by liberating oneself from the influence of propensities and narrow sentiments is the prime endeavor of an enlightened human being.

This liberation of intellect requires a clear understanding and analysis of these fissiparous sentiments as well as the means of liberating oneself from them.

**Liberation of Intellect: Neo-humanism*, by Prabhat Ranjan Sarkar (Ananda Marga Publications, Calcutta-39, 1999.

The factor inciting the most fanaticism and conflicts is religiosity and ethnicity. Socio-religious and socio-cultural intolerance have resulted in genocides, and wiping out of ethnic populations (such as in Australia and US). In India, narrow and prejudicial socio-sentimentality has caused the outcasting of certain communities from the mainstream of society and has led to the problematic and divisive caste system. Ethnic prejudices and intolerance has also caused holocausts in Europe and Asia, while the fusion of religious fundamentalism with the modern pseudo culture has generated psychic tensions as an instigator of terrorism.

Among sentimental problems, geo-sentiments have caused colonization and enrichment of colonial nations at the expense of the colonies. Socio-religious sentimentality has caused unwarranted clashes and sufferings (such as in India and Pakistan, Israel and Palestine), while socio-cultural sentiments have caused fictitious pride and resulting hostilities among cultural groups. National sentiments have led to many wars, time after time. Most of the time, these sentiments are incited by politicians' rhetoric. Politicians drum up euphoric narrow sentimentality to strengthen their own position and popularity. For that matter, no nation can and should claim to be the greatest, no community needs to claim the superiority of its culture, no group of people needs to be recognized as the chosen people.

The neo-humanistic social outlook entails:

- means of raising oneself above narrow sentimentality,
- cultivating a proper societal environment (devoid of cultural suppression, religious impositions, economic exploitation, political subjugation and ecological destruction), for both individual and collective progress, and hence for a progressive society.

As regards to overcoming narrow sentiments, socio-sentiments can be overcome on the basis of the recognition of the common origin and desideratum of all people. Geo-sentiments can be overcome by a universal social outlook that the destinities of all are interlinked. Finally, cosmology and spiritual science inculcates the recognition of "all in one and one in all".

14.2 Neo-humanistic socio-economic system

The adage for a progressive socio-economic environment is "one for all and all for one" and "welfare of all for welfare of each one". In the past century, we have had defective socio-economic political systems of (1) capitalism (epitomized by MNCs), characterized by corrupt corporatism, economic defranchisement of employees and economic colonization, and (2) communism (or state capitalism and terrorism), noted for a big economic gap and lifestyle difference between politicians and common people. In both the systems, the masses cannot participate in economic production and earnings, as corporate partners. On the other hand, in our advocated socio-economic democracy and professional governance (SED & PRG) system, the community people will be working and living cooperatively, pooling their acumen and know-how to optimize their work and living setups. Further, our political substitute for these defective capitalist and communist systems is to (1) have governance executives of FSCs elected by the respective professional associations (such as sports association, manufacturers association, teachers association, bankers association, etc.), and (2) involve the local people in the development of local resources for enhancing the local standard of living.

With the demise of the intolerably repressive communist system of governance, the corporate capitalism has come to the fore, with various wealth concentration means and schemes. It can be noticed that there is an increasing trend of big corporations buying up smaller corporations, with concomitant layoffs of staff under the ruse of rationalization of workforce. Another covert tactic is globalization, whereby the MNCs of developed countries exploit the cheap labor of the Third World countries and export the commodities (from the nations where they are manufactured) to their developed countries. At the same time, the developing countries are being forced to open up imports of consumer goods from developed countries, resulting in enhanced unemployment in the developing countries.

The decrease in the number of companies (due to merges and growing wealth concentration) will make things even more difficult for poor sections of societies to find employment. A time could come when we would have a very disturbingly skewed wealth distribution. The econometrics of this scenario will also reduce people's purchasing capacity. Eventually, this small super-wealthy capitalist group could run out of revenue, resulting in the collapse of the capitalism bubble.

On the other hand, our socio-economic democracy and political governance (SED & PRG) system will provide a wider employment base as well as a bigger market base and purchasing capacity. Within each functionally-sustainable community (FSC), there would be producers', distributors' and consumers' cooperatives. The community services could also be organized as cooperatives of, for instance, teachers, healthcare workers and municipal workers. Socio-economic democracy (SED) puts the local economy in the hands of local people. Concomitantly, economic democracy automatically leads to a new form of electoral system and governance.

In our advocated professional governance system of political and economic democracy (at the FSC level), all the grassroots organizations, associations, agencies and councils of the community will elect two representatives, from whom the public will elect one for the corresponding portfolio in the local government or legislature. In other words, the lawyers' association will elect two of their representatives, out of which the general public will vote for one of them to assume the portfolio of the law ministry. Thus, the local governments of all SRCs would be run by these community organizations' representatives as legislators or governance executives.

However, all the non-elected representatives of community sectors will also be members of the legislature and/or parliament. They will not constitute the equivalent of the opposition party but will rather contribute to the total acumen and knowledge-resource of the legislature and/or parliament, in the development and implementation of public policies as well as in forming a link with the civilian society.

14.3 Neo-humanistic political governance and judicial systems

Earlier, we have stressed that sentimentality leads to a fragmented society, people's suppression and even persecution. Hence, for societal cohesiveness and progress, the antidote to narrow sentimentality is neo-humanism. In the area of governance, neo-humanism implies civilian-centered governance, made possible by the involvement of representatives of the civilian society in governance. Indeed, for a people-centered society, the government or governance society should in fact be a sub-set of the civilian society. For the sustainability of a health democratic system, we want active participation of citizens in public matters that concern them; indeed, this should constitute a constitutionally entrenched right. Such an active citizenship will bring to bear a broad spectrum of ideas into governance practice. As delineated in the previous section, our SED electoral system can help implement this concept of active citizenship.

14.3.1 Governance

For promoting and protecting human rights, a proper constitution is required. However, that itself is not enough. It can be shown that where inter-racial, inter-caste, inter-religious, inter-ethnic conflicts and riots occur, the politicians are behind them either actively or by virtue of the platform of their political party to misuse and misdirect public sentiments and benefit from them.

Additionally, super-power nations are defining and implementing their national interests in ways incongruent with the interests of smaller nations. What has been compounding it all is the super-power economic-politics, whereby most countries feed superpower consumption. The G-8 countries can spend more than their income, and borrow the difference from other countries. The pressure on the governing political party to maintain this consumption demand (with trade imbalance) can force policy decisions acrimonious to peacekeeping. Hence, the root cause of global disturbance is the present day political party-based democratic system based on and controlled by the political-parties.

On the other hand, it can be shown that our advocated neo-political system, of community sectors' representations in governance, can lead to a much more responsible, fair, moral, transparent and efficient governance. This, in turn, can pave the way for:

- secularism and cosmopolitanism, as well as collectivism in capital generation and sharing at the local level;
- a spirit of cooperation for mutual welfare and for a better quality of life at the regional level;
- uniform constitutional laws for all people, primarily based on cardinal values, human rights and social security; and
- world government, with parity among nations and an end to hegemonism, the bane of peace throughout history.

14.3.2 Global Judicial System (GJS)

Throughout the history of human civilizations, the national and local judicial systems and courts have been powerless in dealing with unethical, corrupt and criminal politicians and heads of nations, with regard to crimes perpetrated on their own people as well as tyranny inflicted on other nations and people. The judicial system and the courts have also been inept in the face of racial riots and ethnic killings incited and/or tolerated by the politicians, corruption and bleeding of national wealth by the politicians, misgovernance and misuse of governance by the ministers and political party heads, and getting nations involved in war.

In this absence of a GJS, it has also happened that a super-power country has acted unilaterally to invade a weak country. Inspite of a noble objective to topple a despotic regime, such pre-emptive military interventions cause considerable suffering and deaths among the civilian populations; who is to be held responsible for this carnage? Additionally, prisoners are taken and kept without trial in inhumane conditions, such as the case of several hundred prisoners held in Guantanamo Bay without trial, by being labeled as enemy combatants. While the human rights groups could have been powerless to intervene, how could the United Nations have allowed the creation of such an extra-legal zone? Clearly, the UN has lost credibility as a protectorate of human rights.

Hence, in keeping with our world government global political structure, we will have a global judicial system comprised of local and regional courts for FSCs, self-reliant economic blocs (SEBs), self-reliant economic zones (SEZs) and regional federations (RFDs). The judicial system will also be reformed into making it possible for common people to file cases against political or governance officials for unjust governance or malgovernance:

- for violating people's rights;
- repressions of micro-communities due to their caste and/or culture; and
- engaging people in internal and external conflicts under the false garb of patriotism and national security.

14.4 Neo-humanistic societal culture

After creating the ideal environment for unbarred cultural and aesthetic (and even intellectual) expression, along with economic democracy and self-governance (devoid of the political party system), the stage is set for a neo-humanistic societal culture. In this regard, let us talk about neo-humanism, which involves inculcating humanism for all living entities, as we progress from micro-cosmic imperfection to macro-cosmic perfection. Neo-humanism advocates animal rights' existential value, responsibility for ecological preservation, and cultivation of nobler supra-aesthetic sentiments to impart a universal outlook among all societies.

There are three stages of inculcating the neo-humanist culture. The first is *neo-humanism in-practice* (to help rise above one's psychic defects) and involvement in service to humanity. The second is *collective neo-humanism* of the collective thought process and psyche, so that all the people are inspired to greater neo-humanistic heights. The final stage is *neo-humanism as-a-mission* (through the recognition of all existential phenomena to be within the realm of Consciousness), so that everyone plays a part in the unfolding of neo-humanism. In this exalted stance (the culmination of neo-humanism), the entire humanity can attain its neo-humanist potential and be involved in noble endeavors.

14.4.1 Universalism to replace nationalism

Internationalism is a deceptive concept of rising above nationalism. The concept of nations and national interests is the cause for continuing "cold war". In the United Nations' concept, nations having same religion and similar economic system band together, and these alliances override humanistic considerations. The result is the UN turning a blind eye to issues affecting certain nation's interests. This has resulted in neo-colonization by some powerful countries, victimization of certain communities and smaller nations, and de-culturization of (spiritual) societies (such as of Tibet).

For instance, the UN has been tardy and/or neglectful of peace-keeping and prevention of fighting and mass killing in so many countries, in Cambodia, Congo, Liberia. On the other hand, the decentralization of Tibet is a forgotten issue, the decade-long occupation of Afghanistan by the Soviet Union could not have been ended except by the Afghan people themselves, and the present-day Russian atrocities in Chechnya have been overlooked. The UN has also been neglectful in the resolution of the refugee issue of an entire generation of Palestinian, and in providing state-hood to Palestinian territory. Hence, we need to replace the concept of internationalism with universalism.

In many crises between and among nations, the UN has not been able to act, due to pressures from powerful nations. The superpower nations have been able to impose their dictates freely, because of the inept status of the UN in the present day global political structure. We are hence advocating the setting up of a world government and parliament. In this setup, no superpower nation will be able to act unilaterally. The autonomy and security of all peoples' nations will be protected through our outlined global constitutional political structure, along with the help of regional and global peace-maintaining forces.

14.4.2 Support for local development

Over the years, many developing countries have approached the World Bank and the International Monetary Fund for aid in the form of loans. In return, they are forced to structure certain financial and economic reforms. In general, reforms oriented to transparency and helping the common people are beneficial. However, when countries have to sell off their national resources (such as electric power and water supply) cheaply and open up their markets (reminiscent of the colonial era), it leads to massive unemployment and economic collapse.

It is hence best for countries in a region to facilitate local development in the region. Now and then, there have been calls for an East Asian Economic Bloc (EAEB) along with an Asian Monetary Fund (AMF). However, the EAEB plan has met objections from the United States, fearing that this would trigger the setting up of other such regional monetary funds and diminish the influence of the World Bank and IMF. The formation of such regional economic blocs and monetary funds would protect the regions from currency fluctuations by currency speculators, provide economic stability to the regions, and empower them to chart out their own development destinies.

In our new system, the present name-sake World Bank will be restructured into the Global Bank (as an agency of the world government), which will (in turn) monitor the Regional Federations' Banks. At the FSC level, the banks will foster local business and economic development. The economic bloc banks will sponsor bloc-level industrial projects, while the zone-level banks will support zonal projects, such as hydro electric projects involving several blocs and communities. The key criterion for funding allocation will be grassroots development, for raising the people's living standards and for enhancing local competitiveness through infrastructure development.

14.5 Neo-global order

Our solution for a new global order is through neo-humanism (universalism), neo-MagnaCarta and Socio-economic democracy. Neo-humanism advocates universal outlook, that all human beings (social groups and people of all communities and nations) merit the same social status and right to share the potentialities of the universe and privileges of society. Further, for social justice and fair distribution of economic means, we need to reorganize the regions of the world into functionally-sustainable communities (FSCs) at the grass-roots level. This would prevent neglect of minorities, and enable people with cultural similarities to come together and manage their own economical development (economic democracy), community service and governance.

Above all, the implementation of socio-economic democracy at the grassroots level, with the

- concomitant redundancy of the political party-based democratic system, and
- the cooperatives system of working and living, of generating and sharing wealth, of an enlightened lifestyle and noble quality of life,

will help to bring about a civilized and enlightened global society.

14.5.1 Reorganization of world nations

To promote: local economic self-reliance and civilian-democratic governance, collective capitalism and prosperity, human rights and social security, protection of minority ethnic groups and cultures, neo-humanism and democratic globalization, local to regional peace.

We have proposed a new global order, consisting of the following.

1. A partyless community-sector based selectorial-electoral political democracy at the grassroots FSC level
   - combined with socio-economic democracy or civilian democracy;
   - with a collective-capitalism and cooperative-economic system, auguring for collective prosperity;
   - with a constitution guaranteeing utilization of human resources to their full potential, and minimal purchasing capacity satisfying basic living needs.
2. SEBs comprising of like-minded FSCs (as per their choice) and with a common constitution for all the FSCs, based on human rights and social security. It would be entirely up to the FSCs to decide to which FSC to unite with, in forming an SEB. Likewise, compatible SEBs would come together to form a SEZ.
3. Regional federations (RFDs), comprising of geo-graphically compatible SEZs
   - serving as regional economic blocs, to provide regional self-reliance;
   - having a governance system and constitution to safeguard the integrity of the FSCs; and
   - to promote unbarred flow of information, know-how, trade and human resource among the SEZs and up to the FSC level within the federation.
4. A world government of all the federations to promote universalism,
   - by monitoring (federational) constitutionally guaranteed human rights, social security, peace and justice with in all the federations up to the FSC level;
   - to help maintain uniform and continually upgrading living standards and quality of life in all the regions of the world; and
   - while ensuring administrative autonomy to all the member federations of the world government, and governance autonomy for all FSCs.

14.5.2 Civilian-democratic global order

What does democracy mean? Does it imply that anyone can run for public-administrative office? Does not one need some qualifications and quotients (such as intelligence and emotional, knowledge and professional quotients)? Should the ability to muster big electoral campaign funds be an influential factor? Should someone with no evident or potential capability for governance, such as a movie actor (like former president Ronald Reagan), be able to run for and hold an important public office, such as a governorship of a state (like California?) When another movie actor announced his candidacy for governorship of California (for elections on 7 Oct 2003), and was asked by the media as how he was going to solve California state's acute economic crisis, all he could say was that a plan was being prepared. Inspite of his undeclared views on taxes and spending, urban sprawls and water rights, President Bush indicated that he could make a good governor. On the other hand, it is possible that a professor of political and/or economic science (at one of the University of California campuses) may have for greater knowledge and insights, but not the financial power.

It is obvious that, in the prevalent political-democratic system, financial power counts the most! In other words, we have (what can be termed as) an "affluential democratic system (ADS)." On the other hand, we are advocating a system of civilian democracy, in which the most qualified governance candidate will be elected and invited to take up office. In our neo-political world government-based global governance system, all the members of governments from FSC to world government level would have been elected at the grassroots (FSC) level, by professional associations representing all the working sectors of communities and people's constituencies and living sectors of the communities. This constitutes a truly people-participatory civilian-democratic global order. All these governance executives or officers will not only be among the most competent people to administer their portfolios, but will also be working for:

- collective welfare (instead of being involved in absurd sentiments of party loyalty fanaticism and promotion) in all the sectors of society;
- real globalization to promote uniform living standards both regionally and globally, in place of subversive globalization involving tacit and covert intent by industrialized nations to exploit the cheap labor of developing countries to maintain and promote their high standard of living (at the expense of the people of developing countries).

Is it not a distinct tragedy that in the self-professed role-model democratic system, movie actors and wrestlers can become governors of states? On the other hand, it is equally tragic that in the most populous democratic country (India), film actors and actresses as well as non-graduates can also be chief-ministers of states. That speaks poorly about the veracity of the present form of democracy. Governance is supposed to be the most professionally difficult job in the world, so much so that although practically every university and college in the world offers an MBA degree program, only a couple of universities offer a degree in governance.

Queen's university (Belfast) offers a doctorate in governance jointly with the Institute of Public Administration (Dublin), to enable public policy-makers and public-sector managers to develop their needs of this most demanding profession.

Yet, throughout the world in most democratic countries, the least qualified and even dumb persons are running for and holding governance offices with the support of their political parties, thereby making a mockery of the democratic system and the governance profession. It is because of this flawed democratic electoral and governance-process system and racketeer-politicians abuse of the democratic system, that we are proposing the sectoral-electoral system (SES) professional-governance.

14.6 Politicians decide and civilians suffer — But who adjudicates?

Throughout history, the borders of countries and empires have been drawn and redrawn, as the power of countries and empires rises and declines. While these decisions are of course made by the heads of countries, their people's lives get devastated. They end up living within countries antipathic to their culture and psychology, as repressed citizens or as refugees in foreign lands.

Today, so many displaced Palestinians are living outside their homelands and denied the right to return. The Kurds constitute the largest ethnic minority without their own state. In the absence of our advocated world government, no one wants to support their right to have their own state or autonomously-governed functionally-sustainable community carved out of the borders of Turkey, Iran, Iraq and Syria. Likewise, Kashmiris, Tibetans and Chechnyans are entitled to at least have their own governance and culture, if not their own states.

Why should countries be artificially divided, to suit the interests of political leaders and regimes? Why should there be a North and South Korea? Why should the regimes of countries deny some of their people from leaving if they are not happy there because of its government regime? It is high time that the civilian societies all over the world are released from the bondages of their politicians. However, this can only come about through a worldwide civilian movement for civilian democracy and civilian governance, civilian economic system and collective capitalism, and rights of communities to self-governance.

The pages of history have been tarnished by ruthless political leaders who have made decisions for their personal ambitions and self-glorification, and made innocent civilian populations pay for these decisions with their lives. August 6th marks the anniversaries of the most devastating use of weapons of mass destruction, by the atomic bombings of Hiroshima and Nagasaki, on innocent civilian populations. What is the morality of this instantaneous incineration and lingering death of hundred-thousands of civilians? Some humanitarian groups might argue that US could have demonstrated the destructive power of the atom bomb on an uninhabited island. However, others claim that even after the second bomb was dropped on Nagasaki, the Japanese military leadership was defiant and still refused to listen to the peace factions of the population.

The end result of the decisions made by the government leaders of the warring countries was that millions of civilians were bombed and killed in order to win the war. Is that justified? Should the civilian society be always serving at the pleasure of their governments' leaders, extolling them into patriotic fevor? Cannot there be an alliance of the civil societies of nations to make decisions for themselves, for their welfare? Our proposed civilian democratic system can verily constitute this global civilian alliance, not just to protect civilians but to ennoble human civilization.

It would be in the interests of the moral base and humanitarian law of human civilization, to study the legality of atomic bombings of Hiroshima and Nagasaki and the carpet fire-bombings and burning to death of hundred-thousands of the citizens of Tokyo and the German cities of Dresden, Hamburg and others. In a speech on 31 January 2003, the anti-apartheid icon Dr. Nelson Mandela reprimanded the Americans that "because they decided to bomb innocent people in Japan who are still suffering from the aftermath of the bombing, who are they now to pretend that they are the policemen of the world."

On the vexing issue of US non-involvement in international judiciary for crimes against humanity, for fear of unfair prosecutions of American military personnel and politicians, Robert McNamara (the secretary of defence under US presidents John F. Kennedy and Lyndon B. Johnson) has opined that there is a need for a clear code of conduct for what is legal and illegal even in war. Should not the application of military power be proportional to the objective? Is over-use of military power and burning to death of thousands of civilians in one bombing session justifiable? Was Hiroshima legal; was the US use of napalm in Vietnam legal? These answers are crucial for human civilization. It is for this reason, Robert McNamara feels that US needs to participate in the International Court for Crimes Against Humanity (set up in the Hague), to lay down the governing principles and codes for crimes against humanity in wartime and conflict.

14.7 Time to restore human dignity

Many nations, that were once upon a time the cradles of great advanced civilizations, are today reduced to being Third World nations. It is in the interest of the Third World nations to study the history of how and why they were reduced to this status, because the same reasons continue to prevent their progress today. Interestingly, if we study how and why in history, when two cultures interacted, one became more dominant, we can develop social theories on the ideological compositions (or factors) of those societies (in the form of philosophy and psychology, political governance and socio-economic systems, social outlook and neo-humanistic level), and study how the amount of rigor (and authenticity) of these factors caused one culture to become absorbed into another culture.

It is further possible to address the etilogy of the rise and fall of civilizations, empires and so-called ideologies (such as communism) on this basis. Indeed, the sustaining impact of a civilization is determined by its high mindset and the nobility of its ideology. This is why although all of these civilizations are in physical ruins and antiquity, only those among them have present day influence that inspired a high level of mental transcendence. In this regard, religiosity is an impedement to human progress on the neohumanistic trail. Indeed, constitutionally religious nations constitute an insult to humanity and human civilization.

It is certainly appropriate for nations to have pride in their ancient culture and civilization. However, no nation can afford to bask in its past glory. What is important is what these nations are today, what their culture is today, their level of corruption and their narrow sentimentality, their compassionate values and their human rights record. In certain non-secular nations, religious and ethnic minorities feel insecure, especially in the face of a rising tide of misplaced fanaticism and intolerance, in the false garb of fundamentalism and piety. These minorities' people are treated as (and feel like) second- and even third-class citizens. These nations are also seen to have poor records of honesty in public life and governance, backwardness in education and living standards.

On the other hand, nations that have advocated inter-religious, cultural and ethnic tolerance and respect, have benefited from being the receptors of some very smart and noble immigrants from their former nations. These people emigrated in their quest to live in a more just society and where one's family and community importance is not relevant (so long as they could get fair value for their work and acumen), which their own nations could not provide them because of their corrupted societies. In so doing, they have enriched the societies of their newly adopted countries. Hence, these people may now be in a much better position to be in the forefront of the long-awaited march to neo-humanism.

If only the developing nations' public leaders and politicians had been less involved in their power attainment and/or wealth accumulation, and instead more dedicated to their people's welfare, these nations would have been delivered from poverty. If the developed nations' politicians and affluent members of the society had been more concerned about the welfare of their brethren in other parts of the world, then today the Third World nations would have been a much better place for their long-time abused inhabitants. However, these politicians misused the system and their positions, and now people have not only lost faith in them but also in the so-called democratic political system of elections, supported by the governance and capitalist economic system. This is why it is now time to restore human dignity (after the gross victimization of humanity), by means of our advocated collective capitalism, socio-economic democratic system and world government. This neo-humanistic civilian global order will help to eliminate the poverty, provide global social security and lead to sustained peace.

It can start small, by some inspired people

wanting to be idealistic and to do noble things.

Soon, more and more people imbibe this spirit.

Then a wave of idealism starts sweeping the human habitats,

lifting all minds to higher levels of nobility.

Eventually, the entire sky becomes effulgent with the light of neo-humanism.

Section IV

Towards Universal Renaissance

15

Neo-humanistic University System

15.1 Justification and need

We have been talking about the socio-economic democratic system, professional political governance system (of elected professionals in the various functional domains of the society), and a world government system, constituting a neo-humanistic global order. In order to develop such a conscientious society, we need to have the societal mainstream people thinking neo-humanistically and brought up in an enlightened environment. For this purpose, they need to have a neo-humanistic education. This then is the raison d'etre of the Neo-Humanistic University (NHU) system: to educate a new generation of forward thinkers and future societal leaders, who (in thinking differently from the present day self-glorification seeking character of most political leaders) will be committed to people's interests and welfare.* It is these intellectual moralists who can create a benevolent and knowledgeable (and even a spiritualized) society.

How else can we term, except as primitive, our present day global society:

- that has such enormous and immoral socio-economic inequalities;
- in which 99% of the people work (unemotionally) as employees of (and to produce wealth for) less than 1% of the people;
- wherein less than 5% of the nations dictate the economic and political destiny of the remaining 95% of the nations;
- where politicians (supposedly elected to administer various societal functional domains and portfolios) get glorified by the people and the media;
- in which there are so many displaced persons and refugees;
- in whose apex United Nations Security Council, a few nations can veto any proposal contrary to their interests, leaving weaker nations at the mercy of these stronger nations;

**Discourses on Neohumanist Education*, by Prabhat Ranjan Sarkar (ISBN 81-7252-128-6, Anada Marga Publications, Bangkok 10240, Thailand, 1988).

- wherein people still believe in and are made to abide by draconian laws;
- which justifiably permits only qualified medical doctors to medically treat people, but prescribes no qualification for political administrators in charge of all the policies and frameworks governing the people's way of living and destiny; and
- wherein there is no unified concept (let alone implementation) of human rights based on cardinal principles.

Added to all of these anomalies and lacunae is the absolute need for education to address the illiteracy rate in most developing countries, which is not only responsible for their continuing under-development but also for the narrow divisive sentimentality that has caused communal and ethnic riots and mass killings in so many developing countries. There is hence a dire need to liberate people from the psychic bondages of religiosity and narrow sentiments associated with caste, race and even nationality. Indeed, we need a renaissance in our social outlook and collective psychology.

It is to, thereby, bring about a universal renaissance in our society, in our way of thinking, in our values and in our moral principles, that we are advocating the establishment of the NHU system. In the framework of this NHU system, it is proposed to establish autonomous neo-humanistic universities in different continents and regions of the world, to educate the new generation of neo-humanist world citizens. Such a value-laden education system will make people more civilized, elevate their psychology and behaviorism, provide them political consciousness and enable them to be conscientious.

15.2 Charter

To provide:

- a vision of a universal society;
- a curriculum to project a neo-humanistic world order;
- an education that will develop refined intellect, free from narrow sentimentality;
- an education to enable students to address the needs of the society; and through it all, to develop the ideals of a model global society, wherein all the members are proceeding (and also helping others to proceed) to enlightenment.

To bring about:

- a universal outlook, people's democracy and psychic rejuvenation of all people;
- enlightened and democratic globalization, whereby the needs and aspirations of all the people of all the nations are addressed;
- an enlightened global society, in which all people get equal opportunity to maximally utilize their potential, to make glorifiable contributions to the community and society, and attain higher level of consciousness.

15.3 Academic programs

15.3.1 Unified Bachelor's degree program

In today's world and in order to address the needs of the pluralistic society of tomorrow, we will have to deal with many new and multidisciplinary arenas of endeavor. For this purpose we are proposing a composite multi-disciplinary Bachelor's degree program, to provide the basic educational requirements for graduates to understand and contribute to the various activities of human society. For this purpose, the curriculum will consist of a certain number of core and elective courses from the following course streams or groups (totalling 150 semester credits or academic units):

- Humanities (including neo-humanism)
- Socio-economic Sciences (and neo-humanistic global order)
- Physical and Biological Sciences
- Engineering Science and Technology
- Computer Science and Information Technology
- Ecology, Environmental Science and Technology
- Small-scale farming and Agriculture Science
- Small-scale Business and Enterprise Development
- Law and Jurisprudence (based on cardinal principles)
- Health Science and Healthcare Delivery
- Cosmology and Spiritual Science
- Community Development Internship

If after this Bachelor's degree, students wish to specialize in particular fields (such as engineering and law), then they could study for two more years towards a Master's degree.

15.3.2 Graduate programs

Herein, some of the thematic areas can be:

- Self-reliant Community Development
- Energy-conserving and Environmentally-conducive Engineering
- Biological and Medical Physics and Engineering
- Healthcare Engineering and Management
- Agriculture and Ecology Protection
- Neo-humanistic Education
- Socio-economic Democracy and World Government System
- Philology
- Holistic Medicine (emphasizing holistic approach to healthcare, including Ayurveda, Allopathy, Homeopathy, Acupuncture and other systems)
- Law: Criminal code and Jurisprudence (based on cardinal principles), World Government and Constitution (for a progressive global society)
- Cosmology, Spirituality and Evolution (Integrated Theory of Consciousness, Matter and Mind)

15.4 Research institutes

15.4.1 NHU Institute of Consciousness, Psychology and Behavioral Science

This Institute will deal with:

- the science of consciousness, the genesis of the big-bang, the basis for the continuing expansion of the universe;
- the transformation of inorganic matter into organic matter and life entities, and the origin of mind phenomenon;
- the mechanism of enhanced density of ectoplasmic matter, i.e. the evolution of the mind;
- the relationship of the psychic constituents (cakras and nadis) of living beings with their propensities and behavioral traits, as well as the basis of psycho-somatic disorders;
- the science of intuitional practice (meditation) as a means for psycho-spiritual evolution, and as psycho-therapy for behavioral disorders;
- neuro-feedback methods and virtual reality systems for treating neuro psychological disorders (such as depression, schizophrenia and dementia).

15.4.2 NHU Institute of Peace

The charter of this Institute would be:

1. For the formulation and implementation of socio-economic democracy, whereby the community functions would be organized into cooperatives, involving all levels of workers as partners in creating and sharing wealth.
2. To develop a neo-concept of electoral system, whereby competent representatives of the community would constitute the local governance system.
3. To setup a neo-political system involving autonomous self-reliant communities, within economic blocks and regional federations, under the aegis of a world government.
4. To set up a neo-charter of people's rights, which would:
   - prevent heads-of-nations from persecuting minority and ethnic groups, and
   - hold heads-of-nations accountable for duress meted out to the citizens, due to personal interests as well as due to negligence in incorporating available know-how in public policy decisions.
5. To contribute to international peace by:
   - helping to diffuse conflict situations within and among nations,
   - objectively solving international conflict situations, and
   - enabling global parity in incomes to people performing similar jobs in all parts of the world, in the true and equitable spirit of globalization, thereby preventing industrialized nations from economically exploiting developing countries.

15.4.3 NHU Institute for Third World Development

1. This Institute will be concerned with:
   - alleviation of poverty and famine,
   - ethnic minority welfare and advancement,
   - setting up self-reliant communities, within regional federations, and
   - peaceful co-existence of autonomous communities and nations within this socio-economic political framework.
2. The role of this institute would be to develop postgraduate teaching and research programs, oriented to poverty elimination by establishing self-reliant communities, involving local people participation in their community activities. Such a framework would involve the university academics in people's capacity-building and in cooperatively-run community services, ranging from cooperative

housing development to water supply and sanitation and from healthcare services to primary education.
3. The institute would constitute a triangular synergy between the university academics and researchers, non-governmental organizations and the government departments' officials. In other words, the university academics would be involved in the formulation and implementation of government initiatives, through the self-reliant community development programs. Such a scheme would enable the university academics to impact the communities and also elicit government funding for such R&D activities, thereby enabling training of young researchers to work (in the future) as community services professionals in communities.

15.4.4 NHU Law Institute for a Universal Constitution

Mandate: To formulate and help to legalize the constitutional requirements for a progressive global society. Some of the functional themes of this Institute are defined herewith.

1. *Constitution, to:*
   - provide guidelines and policies for people's welfare, and
   - facilitate all-round (trifarious) development of all people.
2. *People's welfare promotion, by*:
   - removing all situations of discriminations and persecutions (due to language, culture, race and religion);
   - guaranteeing basic living necessities (food and housing, healthcare and education), and
   - recognition and remuneration for all types of services rendered to society.
3. *Secularism implementation, by:*
   - respecting the rights of people to propagate religious and spiritual paths, as well as to initiate people into spiritual (religious) paths, and
   - structuring legal codes based on secularism.
4. *People's participation in community development, by:*
   - structuring both political and economic democracy, and
   - ensuring people's involvement and cooperation in all aspects of societal functions: community services (schools and colleges, healthcare centres and municipal services), corporations and industries.

5. *Economic and financial policy, entailing:*
   - people's involvement in economy generation, through cooperative business and enterprises;
   - proper utilization of (and renumeration for) people's capabilities;
   - non-manipulation of stock market, stocks and currency trading;
   - balanced economy, involving the various (industrial and commercial, community services and knowledge resource) sectors of society.
6. *Guaranteed minimal requirements of living, by:*
   - recognizing that everyone (artists, spiritualists, etc.) has the right to contribute to society, for which the society should provide fair remuneration;
   - specifying the minimal wage, to be periodically revised;
   - ensuing the minimal wage to have adequate purchasing capacity, to be able to afford the basic requirements for living.
7. *Education policy:*
   - compulsory and free education through high school,
   - no political interference in curricular development, and
   - local, provincial and central governments obliged to support higher education (without political interference).
8. *Healthcare policy:*
   - three-tier system of healthcare: primary, secondary and tertiary;
   - managed healthcare for all, either direct registration with hospitals or through medical insurance companies;
   - free primary healthcare in villages;
   - medical insurance companies obliged to register all people, irrespective of their health status.
9. *Social security policy:*
   - old-age remuneration, and
   - minimal maintenance needs and healthcare.
10. *Marriage and inheritance laws:*
    - common marital and legacy codes for all religious communities, and
    - freedom to marry and divorce.
11. *Ecological balance and animal protection, to:*
    - safeguard rights of existence and lives of animals and plants,
    - preserve forests and wild animals, and
    - ban the killing of domestic animals for food.

12. *Public service offices and governance:*
    - to be held by capable, honest and moral persons;
    - to make it possible for independent thinkers to hold public offices;
    - non-involvement of political party systems in governance, and
    - primary selection to governance through community associations (of industrialists, educations, healthcare professionals, railway and shipping professionals, etc.).
13. *Reparation procedures for:*
    - the previously enslaved and tyrannized communities, against corporations and agencies having a history of association with these crimes against humanity;
    - the refugee communities, against nations responsible for driving out these communities from their homelands;
    - the victims of mass ethnic killings, against dictators of nations responsible for these crimes against humanity;
    - communities subjected to health hazards due to fall-outs from weapons of mass destruction, against nations responsible for crimes involving killing of innocent civilians as well as property and land destruction; and
    - former colonies, against their colonial nations for crimes entailing looting of national wealth and resources as well as killing of freedom demanders and fighters.
14. *Independence of the judiciary:*
    - so that all can be equal in the eyes of the law, and
    - there is no governmental pressure or interference.

15.5 University education for a progressive society

15.5.1 Renaissance in human civilization

The history of human civilization is replete with instances when it has faced a critical dilemma of having, to forge a new path out of widespread chaos. Today is no exception, as human civilization stands at crossroads. On the one hand, lies the suffering planet divided by narrow sentiments and religious dogmatism, defective self-centered socio-economic and political philosophies, which are creating problems in every sphere of life. On the other hand, lies a lofty and sublime ideal of cosmic fraternity, based on neo-humanism, justice and truth. The path for establishing one universal human society (free from all dogmas, superstitions and disparities) is also strewn with innumerable obstacles. The challenge before us is to follow a pragmatic path, that neither ignores the human sentiments nor forgets the cosmic ideal.

Now at the frontiers of cosmology is the growing recognition that what underlies matter and the physical universe is pure consciousness. This constitutes the basis for the origin and destiny of all human beings and all living entities. From the emergence of primitive organisms to human beings, there is an increased unfolding of consciousness. All human beings have to undertake the evolutionary journey from the first expression of humanism to the cosmic desideratum. The societal structure, in all expressions of human thought and fields of human endeavor, should facilitate this progression. The role of university education, is to provide the ideas and ideals, information and knowledge to undertake this journey of mysticism (from imperfection to perfection), to help foster a neo-dimension of civilization.

15.5.2 Education and knowledge for liberation of intellect and self-realization

An important objective of this neo-humanistic system of education is to liberate the student's mind from all bondages of narrowness and meanness. Every aspect of the environment is to inspire higher consciousness. Some features of the neo-humanistic educational system, are as follows:

- All aspects of the student are to be developed: the body and intellect, creativity and intuition.
- Education is to be value-based. Students are to be encouraged to: (1) develop selfless attitudes and the psychology of service, and (2) be responsible for the world around them, not only for humans but also for animals and plants.
- The status and role of teachers in the NHU system is to be given the highest importance. Teachers are to be role models for the students, embody the values of wisdom, selflessness, service and compassion.
- Education is to prepare students for global citizenship, with the ideal that a true society is one in which all individuals move together so that no one lags behind, the students are to be inspired to work for social justice and upliftment of the downtrodden.
- All the subjects (e.g. physical and biological, geographical and environmental sciences) to be taught holistically, emphasizing the inter-relation between all aspects of nature.
- The interlinking of the destinies of all living beings is to be emphasized, so that ecological principles of collective life can be explored, and a true ecological awareness is cultivated among the students, to enable them to nurture their environment.

- The role of science and technology is to alleviate living standards, while safeguarding the environment and promoting cultural expression, so as to develop a synthetic outlook of life.

The NHU will also incorporate the enlightened ancient concept of GuruKula, where students studied under the close guidance of sages, while (1) imbibing knowledge of different faculties ranging from philosophy to history, agriculture to medicine, numerology to cosmology, and (2) acquiring moral strength, character and high ideals.

15.6 University as a community development agent in developing countries

The bane of developing countries continues to be rural under-development and urban degradation. For Third World liberation and poverty eradication, the proactive involvement of universities in state government projects is required to:

- foster rural development and urban rejuvenation, in order to fulfill the 2020 vision mandate of food, housing, healthcare and employment for all;
- evolve into a socio-cultural, agro-industrial and egalitarian model.

As can be noted, the expectations and demands on university education are enormous. However, in most developing countries, the educational budget is inadequate to meet these demands. Nevertheless, in state government budgets, provisions are made for various items, such as transportation, agriculture, industry, communications, defence, etc. Hence, it is proposed that the state governments involve universities in the planning and implementation of all the programs and missions. Hence, universities and state governments can take the lead in setting up such models of university-state government partnership.

State governments to involve universities in state development programs: For successful implementation of these programs as well as for regional and state development in general, it is very essential for state governments to empower universities involvement in governmental projects and regional development schemes. We need to implement this concept of state governments and universities working together to solve community and regional problems, such as in natural resource management, agro-industrial development, rural development and urban improvement, ecological preservation and environmental protection.

Universities need not be merely looked upon as tertiary level degree-granting institutions. University faculty and students constitute immense and innovative resources that need to be harnessed by state governments for economic development and improving the living standard and quality of life of the inhabitants. This concept of state government-universities cooperation and collaboration will bring funding to universities and involve postgraduate students in exciting community-oriented research and development work, with significant benefits accruing to the states.

University-governments collaboration: The benefits of such university-state government collaboration would be that:

- state development projects will be solved at significantly less cost to the state government;
- the role of universities would be enhanced to regional development institutions; and
- the universities would be directly involved in agro-industrial, healthcare delivery, community services and economic development — thereby, the students would be inspired to do graduate studies.

15.7 Third World development academic (graduate) program

The NHU system would advocate a unique multi-university Third World development program, to develop the template for development of regional self-reliant federations.

15.7.1 Objectives

Today, as the gap in living standards between the north and south countries widens, what is the solution for developing countries to catch up with the north (or developed) countries and to achieve the 2010 objectives of: food for all, clothing for all, housing for all and healthcare for all, as the basic living requirements?

15.7.2 For self-reliance

Individually, it is difficult for any developing country to raise its socio-economic level and attain the above-mentioned objectives through natural resource, agricultural and industrial development. The technological gap between any developing country and any developed country is so big that it is difficult to attain trade balance, and hence have available resources dollars to (i) develop technologically for cultivating natural resources as well as for agricultural and industrial development, and (ii) provide mass state-subsidized education in all spheres of human thought and endeavor, for development of psychological and cognitive, socio-economic, scientific and technological-health and life-style, political and governance acumen.

The only rational solution is for the developing countries to attain self-reliance, by pooling their efforts and resources, to:

- help one another in natural resource, agricultural and industrial development;
- institute cooperation in trading in natural resources, agricultural produce and industrial products, required for socio-economic development; and
- through it all to attain the above-mentioned 2020 objectives.

15.7.3 Academic collaboration

For implementation of the self-reliance concept, we are proposing academic collaborations among the universities of developing countries (such as of South America, Africa, South Asia and East Asia), to provide the basis and foundation for cooperative social and resource, industrial and economic development. This academic collaboration would have to be in all fields, and will include:

1. Science, engineering and technology, especially in areas relevant for:
    - basic development, such as electrical power, drinking water, healthcare delivery and rural resource development,
    - hi-tech development, such as in food processing and preservation, materials and manufacturing technology, biotechnology and genetic engineering, and will include setting up of a multi-national centers for technological and industrial development, to help incubate new companies and indigenous industrial development.
2. Commerce, trade and business development, towards industrial and economic integration, involving alleviating trade tariffs among the developing countries of different regions (Africa, Asia and South America).
3. Humanities and social sciences, to help bring together the conglomerate countries of regions into federations, so as to bring about economic competitiveness and parity with the affluent nations (and their hegemonism); to inculcate a sense of unity in diversity in socio-cultural heritage, and ensure solidarity within a diversity of cultures, religions and ethnic backgrounds.
4. Medicine and healthcare, so as to help institute medical educational curricula and delivery systems, suited to the needs of the region and especially to address the rural healthcare needs.

5. Law and jurisprudence, so as to develop (1) the constitutional infrastructure for collaboration in trade and commerce, multinational companies' operation, sharing of resources, and all other required towards the evolution of a unified federation, and (2) civil and criminal law codes based on cardinal principles.

15.7.4 Curriculum

The program will consist of courses in:

- The Concept and Need of a Regional economic zones and federations,
- Intra-Federational Cooperation in Science and Technology (and industry),
- Intra-Federational Trade (trading currency and tarriffs policy),
- Federational Fiscal and Monetary Policy,
- Federational Defense Policy (including federational peacekeeping force),
- Federational Law and Jurisprudence,
- Federational Parliament (jurisdiction and mechanism of representation), and
- Federational Constitution.

These courses as well as research and theses topics would be aimed at stepwise developing and implementing the comprehensive policy and framework of self-reliant regional federations (such as the East Asian, South Asian, African, Middle Eastern, South American and West Asian Federations), with the intention of having it fully operational by 2010! Verily, this can constitute the road map for (i) self-reliance and prosperity of the present day developing countries, so that by 2010 they can no longer be labeled as Third World countries, and (ii) democratic globalization.

15.8 Impact of NHU on society

1. *Enlightened lifestyle:*
   The NHU system would bring people to an enlightened way of living.

2. *Neo-humanism:*
   The NHU Institute for Neo-humanistic Economic Political System and Global Order would be a bastion and propagator of neo-humanism. It would be called upon to: provide consultation and advice on issues of socio-economic politics, act as arbitrator for international issues and conflicts, and prevent ethnic wars and holocausts.

3. *New realms of psychiatry:*
   The NHU Institute of Consciousness, Psychology and Behavioral Science will conduct research on cosmology (origin and expansion of the Universe, mechanism of life origin and evaluation), link between Yogic science (of cakras) and behaviorism, and neo-psychiatry formulations.

4. *Education:*
   The NHU Department of Education would be engaged in developing an electic system of education for inculcating a sense of oneness with nature, in developing a unified approach to the study of physical and biological science, study of humanities and social sciences to develop a spirit of cooperative living.

5. *Championing the cause of human rights and justice:*
   The NHU Law Institute will develop and implement the most comprehensive chapter of human rights to enable people to live in dignity.

6. *Self-reliant community development and poverty eradication:*
   The NHU Institute for Third World Development would be actively involved in developing:

   - political decentralization and socio-economic democracy, involving people's participation in wealth creation and sharing;
   - a party-less electoral and governance system, involving only the most competent and qualified representatives of the community's professional and cooperatives' associations in local governance; and
   - the means for progressive enhancement of living standards.

7. *Catalyzing a world order:*
   The NHU Institute for a World Government System will help to develop a new world order, characterized by:

   - self-reliant communities;
   - political decentralization and economic democracy, through the formation of self-reliant (locally governed) communities;
   - regional federations: such as European, African and South American; and
   - world government parliament.

Let us develop a lofty system of university education,

To cover all realms of human thought and endeavor,

To provide knowledge of nature, human beings and living entities as well as of supra-natural phenomena,

To observe forms of cooperation in nature and apply these forms to human habitats,

So as to develop a template for sustainable peace in society.

Nalanda, where the ruins of the great ancient Nalanda University have been excavated is situated at a distance of 90 kilometers south-east of Patna by road. Nalanda University, founded in the fifth century by the Gupta emperors, had thousands of students and teachers. Nalanda was a great center of education. So many students from foreign centers of learning and foreign countries were attracted to this University. The Chinese scholar Hieun Tsang received here the Indian name of Mokshdeva.

In ancient universities, the professors were "rishis," who (in imparting both worldly and spiritual knowledge) concerned themselves with the "total education" of their students. These universities were centers of life-long learning. Let us develop a Neo-humanistic University system, combining the highest traditions of ancient and present-day universities.

16 Replacing Hypocrisy by Straightforwardness

We have been discussing the etiology of socio-psychic marginalization of people and economic-political marginalization nations, and its solution in terms of a new regional and global order. Now, with this raising of consciousness, let us share some of the startling hypocracies of our times, and indicate how our new system and order will eliminate these dichotomies and bring about a new era of human dignity.

16.1 Maintaining humanism in spite of persecution — a hallmark of being civilized

Teachers are expected to be and respected as role models of character. Most of us remember and respect so many of our teachers who have moulded our values and attitudes to life and living. However, political leaders and heads of states have not merited similar respect, and yet they are in the position of controllers of our destinies, lifestyles and peace. It is hence time for us to evolve a system, wherein and whereby only the most competent and moralistic people are elected to be in charge of governance.

Both the systems of communism and fascism have in fact imposed terrorism on their own people, in the deceptive guise of labor power and nationalism. On the other hand, colonialism and imperialism (by the self-acclaimed civilized nations of today) resulted in centuries of physical, psychological and economic repressions of the innocent people of the Asian, African and South American continental nations. Likewise, today's political and economic hegemonism incites antagonism among the "subservient" nations.

Recently, South Africans and secular people of the world mourned the passing (at the age of 90) of the anti-apartheid hero Walter Sisulu on 7 May 2003. It is no secret that apartheid was supported by the capitalist regimes, while the developing countries could only be passive sympathizers. Hence, it was left to African freedom fighters to stand up to the tyranny of white racism. His illustrious humanist colleague Nelson Mandela said "together, we walked side by side through the valley of death, nursing each other's bruises, holding each other up when steps faltered. Together, we savored the taste of freedom." To this, we can add: together, they decided to forgive their white torturers, and invited them to join hands to rebuild the South African society and nation. This is the hallmark of a real humanist, of a civilized person, of a role-model politician!

All of these repressive systems have bred desperate means of protest against long-term injustice inflicted by their perpetrators. In the heydays of repressive communism, colonization and apartheid, any form of even mild protest by the local and native people was tantamount to terrorism and branded as treason. Yet some bold liberty-loving people were desperately driven to protests actions branded as terrorism, and even open confrontation with their repressive rulers and systems at the risk of losing their lives. While at that time, the colonial and apartheid regimes' political heads justified executing these protestors and freedom fighters as terrorists and treason culprits, history later on labeled them as martyrs who died for a noble cause.

It is to the immense credit of those people and communities, who were subjected to centuries of apartheid and colonization, to show so much temperance to their oppressors and live peacefully with them. It is they who are demonstrating how to be and act civilized, while the former apartheid and colonial community claim to being civilized and champions of human rights. Unfortunately, this practice, of demanding that the suppressed people of occupied lands be civil and peacefully negotiate their freedom, continues even today.

16.2 Setting straight the historical record of maritime discoveries and atrocities

Today, Western countries celebrate and honor world navigators, who sailed from Europe to discover new lands rich in resources, to bring these resources to their nations. Historical records show that the local communities and their chiefs warmly hosted these famous navigators, and even bestowed lavish gifts on them. Yet, they in turn had no desire to be gracious traders, but only had the intent to pillage these communities and colonize their lands. In spite of that, those native populations (many of whose civilizations were systematically wiped out by the "civilized invaders") are remembered as barbarians, while these invaders are respected for bringing civilization to the discovered lands.

History (rewritten since the bygone colonial era) bears testimony to what happened to the native populations of these newly discovered lands, in the form of genocide of epic proportions, of ethnic massacres and wipeouts, land occupation and annexation, and inhuman treatment of the native populations of unimaginable scales. Yet today, these historical records are not even mentioned in history books, while these navigators are revered in the self-proclaimed "civilized countries"! However, even if the barbaric record of these western navigators were to be kept hidden, there is no excuse for falsifying the historical record of maritime discoveries. Historically, Chinese and Indian navigators considerably predated earliest European maritime (oceanic) voyages of discoveries.

From 1405 to 1433, the great Chinese Admiral Zheng He is said to have made seven marathon voyages to countries of Asia, Middle East, Africa and even America. The scientific and engineering dimensions of these voyages of discovery can be assessed from the size of his flotillas of more than 200 ships weighing around 1000 tons and a crew of about 27,000, in contrast to Columbus' first expedition of three ships of the order of 100 tons and a crew of 87. The retired British naval commander Gavin Menzies has scientifically concluded, in his book "1421", that Admiral Zheng He's commanders not only "discovered the not-so-new world" in their epic expeditions of 1421–1423, but also discovered Greenland and sighted Australia long before any European discoverer did.

According to Menzies, records of maps and charts dating back to 1424, depict Australia, Cape of Good Hope, the Andes, and the Pacific and Atlantic coasts of North and South America. These maps required methods of determining latitude and longitude or the coordinates of places with reference to some global coordinate system. It is these maps that were later on employed by the European navigators. Sadly, the European navigations resulted in colonization of the lands "discovered" by them. In many cases, the native populations were almost wiped out.

The colonization era, however, continues in different forms, in the garb of globalization, World Trade Organization (WTO), World Bank, multinational corporations, military bases and economic sanctions. It is, hence, high time for the Third World nations to establish a Global Anti-Colonization Coalition (GACC) against all covert and overt forms and schemes of colonizations and forced dependency.

There are many nations that have either monarchy or communism form of governance. Nevertheless, none of these self-styled "democracy advocate and custodian nations" dares to criticize them, why? This is because it is in their economic interests to stay in the good books of these nations with monarchy and communist forms of governance. However, if a weaker Asian or African nation does not strictly follow conventional democratic-electoral norms, that nation becomes outcast and economic sanctions are levied against it.

It is indeed ironical that the most eloquent demanders and self-styled custodians of democracy and freedom are the political heads of those very nations, who:

- either forcibly colonized and ruthlessly ruled these nations, on whom they now threaten to apply economic sanctions and whose assets they want to freeze;

- imposed state terrorism not only on their own people but on so many other nations, in the garb of communism;
- have a dubious record of slavery and virtual extermination of their native populations.

Hence, before they start preaching, let these present-day self-acclaimed custodians of freedom and democracies display at least some measure of humility, and at least apologize if not provide reparation to those victimized and abused communities and nations. By this act, they will, to some extent, demonstrate their admission of their past ignominious record and portray honorable future intentions.

16.3 From pseudo democracy to real democracy

In today's so-called democratic system, the political party concept is debilitating to efficient governance and to real democracy. In fact, it is an insult to the intelligence and conscience of governance members, to have to subscribe to political party policies and vote along party lines, or otherwise be rebuked or even expelled from the party for indiscipline. It is also detrimental to governance for all the members of the ruling party to generally vote in one bloc, and for the opposition members to likewise vote in one bloc on public policy issues. Often, party members misbehave and cause pandemonium in the parliament. This is not just a disgrace to their intelligence and standing, but also to the political structure.

Can one imagine such a ridiculous party-based organization in academia or in business corporations? It would stymie intelligent and innovative ideas, and result in a dismal failure. So why have we accepted and tolerated such an absurd system in (of all the setups) governance, wherein we want the most intelligent and moralistic society representatives to bring to bear all of their acumen into making the society as progressive as possible.

When public policies are based on political parties' interests, they are not generally favorable to the societal and people's welfare. They are generally based on self-interests of the concerned parties, and are aimed at maintaining party popularity among their supporters, by catering to their financial interests or narrow sentimentality. In this outdated "political party system of pseudo democratic governance", many charlatans get into governance, by sheltering themselves within parties; this is because most people vote strictly along party lines, without much knowledge of the party candidates backgrounds. Then, when these party members get involved in scandals, they are also shielded by their political parties, and continue to stay in governance. What a farce!

Indeed, a prime reason for the former colonized countries to still remain undeveloped (more than a half century after gaining independence), can be attributed to their incompetent and corrupt political leaders. They have "mastered" the art of manipulating the democratic system for their own benefit, by getting themselves elected in spite of their dismal governance record and financial credibility. While all government staff have to retire by a specified age, these career (and lifelong) politicians never retire, even when they are demented. In the name of democracy, we essentially have politicians' rule, in most so-called democratic countries.

Further, it appears that only one person can make decisions, namely the prime minister or the president, with the help of his/her close associate. The case for invasion of Iraq was prepared at the wish of the heads of US and UK governments. In this process, the UN was sidelined. However, the UN could have done little to cause a regime change, by removal of the oppressive regime leader from his post. When Pakistan and India decided to restart peace talks in February 2004, a statement issued by the Pakistan Foreign Ministry attributed these talks to the political will of President Musharraf and Prime Minister Vajpayee. Does it not, then, make sense for us to have a system having an intrinsic political framework to incorporate people's interests and welfare in policy and decision making!

In our proposed socio-economic democratic system (of community organization into cooperatives and neighborhood councils), elections to governments will be carried out, in the first instance, within and by professional associations (of cooperatives) and agencies (such as for municipal and postal services) as well as councils (for neighborhood environmental development and safety), and thereafter by the general public. Thereby, each governance portfolio officer will function in the best collective interests of that particular sector of the community. There of course has to be a mechanism for all the governance officers to discuss and debate important policy issues put up by their respective officers. However, even in these discussions, there will not be bloc voting, and the attitude would be to converge to the best policy structure for the community and people (since party interests will not be a contending driving force behind debates and voting).

16.4 For a competent and moral governance system

In an ideal democratic governance system, the ministers holding various governance portfolios should be the most knowledgeable people in their respective fields. In the present day democratic political system, that is not possible because the various governance portfolios are given to "loyal" senior (elected) party members. However, in our proposed socio-economic democratic electoral and governance system, only the most capable persons (of neo-humanistic bearing) will be elected to governance.

People (and their welfare) should be regarded to be more important than politicians. Today, politicians hold centre-stage and "govern" the people, who are virtually treated as "subjects" of these politicians. Rather, these politicians should work dutifully (without attracting prominence) at their governance portfolios, for the welfare of the people. This can only become possible in a truly democratic system without political parties, whereby the most qualified people in their respective fields are first approved and shortlisted (through elections) by their respective professional associations, agencies or councils, and then by the general public. By this process, the people elected would be able to bring to bear the state-of-the-art know-how in their governance roles.

In all fields (such as medicine, law and engineering), one has to qualify by undergoing training and passing examinations. It is an irony that governance, arguably the most difficult job to hold and requiring the highest degree of acumen (and morality), has no such educational requirements, thereby enabling incompetent opportunists to get into governance positions, involving shaping the destinies of nations and communities. It would, hence, be appropriate for a postgraduate degree programme in governance to be developed for those aspiring for a public service career.

The curriculum of such a "governance degree" programme in Community Administrative Science (mentioned in Chapter 7) would include subjects dealing with all the facets, workings, sectors and constitution of a functionally-sustainable community (FSC), as well as its role within a regional federation and world government. In this way, every member of governance at all levels (from FSC to Federation level) will be knowledgeable in both the local and global affairs, so that he/she can function both locally and globally to optimally promote the welfare of his/her community.

It is a time-honored tradition for medical graduates to take the Hippocratic oath to practise ethics and non-discrimination in providing medical care to all people. It is all the more important for governance members to take a similar oath of non-discrimination, commitment and dedication to all people.

16.5 Towards equal partnership in brokering global peace and security

It is not only immature but also irresponsible for political leaders of nations to proclaim the superiority of their nation over all other nations. Such statements do not contribute to the noble concepts of the global village and compassion for all humanity. Further, they breed wrong values of arrogance among the citizens, and in fact plant the seeds of inter-nation hostility.

In the present day global political order, only a few industrialized countries have been developing arsenals of weapons of mass destruction, while demanding that others do not do so, on the pretext of their not being responsible nations. In fact, the powerful hegemonial (self-proclaimed to be responsible) nations even levy economic sanctions on these so-labeled "irresponsible" nations. If then this hegemonial political order is replaced by our proposed world government political order, it will lead to a far more just and civilized global order. In such a global political framework, all nations and all people will be equal brokers and partners of harmony and peace.

Throughout history, nations have been waging war on one another. In all of these periods, the leaders who declared war cleverly exempted themselves from fighting in the war. While portraying themselves as guardians of the people and protectors of freedom, they took their nations into wars, and thereby subjected their people to tremendous suffering. Our proposed neo-humanistic world government system will bring an end to this disgraceful era of exploitation of their people by their political (warlord) heads.

In order to bring some miscreant terrorist leaders or groups (harboring in some lands) to justice, it is not justifiable to destroy the lands of the people and to kill innocent people by weapons of mass destruction, for which generations suffer from ill health as well as psychologically. Based on all of these terrible happenings, it is better to have a global political system in place, which provides a preventive and even a deterrent political infrastructure against terrorism of the people by the regime. Our world government system will undertake to prevent and preserve global peace and security based on the lofty concept of neo-humanism.

16.6 From power-centric dictatorial hegemonism to global democracy and parity

In recent years, there has been so much rhetoric about the danger of some "irresponsible countries" having weapons of mass destruction, because their political leaders are not responsible and not amenable to permitting international inspection and/or dismantling their weaponry. The political heads of responsible countries (who are the pioneers and leaders in armament technology) feel that it is in their interests, for the protection of their people, to move into these countries and dismantle and/or destroy their weaponry, and even displace and replace their heads through military intervention. The US and UK used this as an excuse to invade Iraq, without first confirming their existence. In doing so, they miscalculated the reception that they expected to receive from the Iraqis. On the other hand, the US adopted an appeasing attitude to North Korea's admitted capability to develop nuclear weapons, why? Is it because North Korea does not have oil, or is it because its situation is too precarious for US to tackle?

Intervention to remove oppressive regimes and rescue the oppressed people can be deemed to be in the collective interest. However, it is better to have a system in place (such as our system) by which governance heads cannot become dictatorial and are serving at the bequest of the people. In any case, why did these very punitive stick-wielding nations not bother to change the terrorist communist and apartheid regimes and their heads. Nevertheless, military intervention is invariably accompanied by killing of civilians and destruction of their habitat; hence (if their political head does not kowtow), would military intervention be considered to be a humane option to be exercised? Likewise, would it be ethical to destroy the lands that harbor some terrorists making up a minute fraction of the population; considering that the land is the joint property of all the inhabitants (destroying lands is tantamount to destroying their houses and means of livelihood)? Would that be tantamount to crime against humanity? When the police go after supposed criminals, could they justify bombing the entire area where the criminals are hiding? For all of these reasons, is it not better to have a uniformly applicable governance system that cannot permit irresponsible and power-craving persons to become heads of states?

In any case, it would be very appropriate to record all the instances of usage of devastative weapons (resulting in mass-killing of innocent civilians and making their land environmentally unsafe for years to come) during this 20th century. We would then be able to assess how responsible are those self-acclaimed responsible nations. Indeed, this kind of double standards of only a few countries possessing sophisticated armament technology, while dictating others to sign a non-proliferation agreement (under threat of economic sanctions being levied for non-compliance), does not auger well for global harmony.

In our neo-global political structure, no governance executive would be able to become a dictator; no nation (i.e. its leader) would be allowed to embark on weaponry development, especially at the expense of unfulfilled people's needs; no nation will be allowed to intimidate other nation; and no nation (and its politicians) will be above and outside international laws for civilized conduct.

The uni-polar hegemonial global order is humiliating to the nations of the world. In our proposed world government system, there will be no scope for any one nation to dictate others. It will also not be possible for two nations to be involved in long-term acrimonious relationship and/or warfare, or for one ethnic group to forcibly displace another ethnic group from their land, and have to rely on only one super-power nation to come to their rescue. It will be the world government that will provide security and maintain peace and not some super-power countries.

Further, our socio-economic democratic system will not permit any one person to don the mantle of the voice and decision-maker of the nation. In fact, in this socio-economic democratic setup, governance officers (i.e. ministers) will have the same status as common citizens, who are appointed to discharge certain roles for which they are paid. In other words, the curtain will finally come down on this ignominious era of political leaders making decisions that bring suffering to their people, deceiving the people into thinking that they are their guardians, and expecting to be hero-worshipped by the people.

16.7 For obviating terrorism

From the beginning of human civilization, people have been struggling in their search for peace. However, all along, they have been thwarted by inimical ruling regimes, in the form of persecution, oppression and terrorism. Indeed, it is fair to say that, all along, civilians have been terrorized by the ruling regimes. We hence need a holistic definition of terrorism in order to encompass state policies of marginalizing some communities (because of their caste and/or ethnicity), making some religious groups second-class citizens, keeping people poor and ignorant, leaving people jobless and depressed, keeping women uneducated and dysfunctional, and encouraging inter-religious riots and ideological persecution.

Based on this broader definition of terrorism, the percentage of people in any one community who have all along been living in terror can vary from 5% to even 50%. Hence, the ruling regimes have been the original terrorists. Further they have caused suffering to 5%–50% of their populations. Hence, the mayhem that they have caused is much greater in proportion compared to the group terrorisms that we are witnessing today. This is why, we cannot expect these political parties' governments to even contain (let alone eradicate) terrorisms committed by defranchised groups, because these political parties and their political-businessmen (i.e., the party-politicians) are indeed the raison-d'etre of the terrorist groups. Hence, in order to end all forms of terrorism (both State and group terrorisms), let the civilians decide their own living conditions and public policies for all of the societal sectors, in the form of civilian democracy (as outlined by us).

Indeed, democracy is a grossly misused concept. Even today, very few so-called democratic countries can be legitimately termed to be democratic. In the US, without substantial funds, one can never get elected to any public office. Further, democracy demands consistency in how one treats the people of other countries in relation to one's own people. In other words, it is neither ethical nor democratic for the US to terrorize the innocent civilians of weaker countries (such as Iraq) in order to bring their regimes under their democratic control. It just will not work because, from a collective-psychology perspective, nationalism sentimentality will not tolerate foreign occupation even for bringing about democracy. Hence, we cannot classify the US as a democratic country.

On the other hand, in India (the largest democracy), many of the supposedly democratically elected chief ministers and parliament members are incompetent, corrupt and even uneducated. The political parties in power have no constructive program for the people (such as in education, healthcare, industrial development, agricultural assistance, etc.). It is also deplorable that, when so much needs to be done to improve the living conditions of people in India, some political parties have been tacitly acquiescing to religious disharmony so as to further their political support.

There is also another nation-category of constitutionally religious countries, who automatically forgo the right to being regarded as democratic. This is because, in these countries, people subscribing to religions other than the state religion are second-class citizens. It is indeed shameful to human civilization for a country to be a constitutionally religious republic. Finally, there is a fourth category of nations comprising of a great majority of South American, African, Middle-Eastern and Central Asian countries, in which there is not an adequate critical size of secularly minded, educated and politically knowledgeable population to permit credible democracy.

Hence, in the face of this global lacuna in democracy, it is paramount that the civilian populations become proactive in establishing civilian democracy. Herein, we need to make a distinction between our concept of civilian democracy and the pseudo civilian democracy as is practised today. The democracy that we have today is primarily a tussle between political parties to gain governance control by gaining people's votes. In this forum, the political parties (and their member-politicians) are just like business organizations (and their executives) anxious to gain governance contracts. Hence, we could denote this prevalent democratic system as "Democracy Business" and their members as political businessmen.

In contrast, our civilian democracy system will intrinsically involve the most competent civilians from all the community sectors to be involved in governance. For this purpose, we have outlined the electoral framework to establish civilian governance councils. Only civilians can have a pulse of the day-to-day problems of civilians, and not political businessmen (namely the party-politicians). When we will have civilian representative governments, there will be no need for some civilian groups to become terrorists, because civilians groups can better communicate with the civilian sectors' representatives in governance. So our proposed civilian socio-economic democratic governance system will bring about an end to terrorism, not just to overt terrorism but also to covert terrorism. Then only, can we build a civilized society.

Indeed our, life journey provides us with an endless sequence of "second chances," and hence an unlimited scope to do as much good as possible for as many people as possible. However, in order to acquire the wisdom of utilizing these second chances, instead of staying closeted within our mind (with its embedded prejudices), we need to acquire heightened consciousness (in association with cosmic consciousness). We can then progress along ethereal highways, to higher and higher dimensions of living. In this process, we will conceive of noble ideas in all realms of living, which can contribute to higher and higher levels of civilization.

16.8 Towards a global neo-humanistic cooperative

What kind of a present day socio-economic (global) order is that in which (1) a big segment of the world population does not have even the basic necessities of life, in which so many people are embroiled in violence due to ethnic and religious intolerance, and so many communities have had their religious culture suppressed and destroyed, while (2) among the so-called successful and affluent people and nations, the family structure has broken down and the children grow up in a forlorn environment. This scenario does not merit being called a society, because the import of society is "living cooperatively and moving in unison to the desideratum".

Humanity has been bleeding, and sorely needs the soothing and therapeutic balm of a neo-humanistic ideology. So many genocides have been committed in this very century, and that too by precisely those very leaders (of nations) who have signed peace memorandums. The prosperous nations keep meeting to strengthen their material assets and economies, under the aegis of the WTO and the agenda of globalization — a pseudo term for neo-economic colonization. In the meanwhile, the people in the developing countries of Asia, Africa and even South America keep living in poverty and squalor, in despair and sadness.

The phenomenon of globalization, as advocated by the industrialized G-8 nations, is an exploitative device by the affluent nations, and tantamount to neo-colonization by the G-8 nations. These nations' business corporations have been taking advantage of the cheap (under-paid) labor of developing nations to get their products made inexpensively, and are now even demanding free (tariff-less) entry of these very products into the high-density population markets of these poor nations. However, the real implication of globalization is that people in different parts of the world performing work requiring similar skills must be paid comparable salaries. Only such a mandate can help benefit developing countries, and implement more uniform living standards across the world. Once some parity in living standards (across the regions of the world) is achieved, then we are ready to implement free trade.

Finally, the establishment of the world government will ensure socio-political economic stability and security throughout the world. It will put an end to hegemonism and dictation of global policies by the powerful nations to the other nations. It will obviate the need for armaments build-up, and divert more funds for community services. Secret development and stockpiling of nuclear and biological weapons arsenals will be outlawed. Intelligence and espionage agencies will also be outlawed, because they will have no place in this new system of global cooperation and goodwill. Furthermore, no circumstance would justify one self-reliant economic zone (or nation) to attack and destroy another self-reliant economic zone (or nation); indeed, destruction of another land and killing of its people would be regarded as a most serious offence and crime against humanity.

The combination of socio-economic democracy, collective capitalism, and the world government system will bring all the communities of the world into one global cooperative, typifying a neo-humanistic order, of a universal family of (cooperatively organized) communities. The world government constitution will also illegalize persecution of ethnic groups and cultural minorities. This is because global human rights protection laws of the world government constitution will supercede local and national dictates. Also, local constitutions and jurisprudence will have to be based on cardinal principles, instead of on cultural-religious dogmas and narrow socio-sentimentality. Indeed, our global neo-humanistic socio-economic political order will enable the setting up of a universal society.

16.9 Progressing to a neo-humanistic civilization

In order to cooperatively develop a progressive human civilization, involving the noblest human expressions, we need to develop a neo-humanistic psychology that transcends all forms of pettiness, divisiveness and primitiveness. Humanity is not just a phenomenon unique to our earth; rather, it is a phenomenon of the universe. Humanity cannot be divided into narrow geo-socio-religious-economic-political compartments; that is being contra-progressive. Hence, in order for the civil society, to evolve into an enlightened society, we need to reject the platitudes of self-styled political and religious guardians of society.

Indeed, the civil society can develop a glorious future for itself, by rising above the narrow attitudes and prejudices imposed on it by its economic, political and religious controllers. The civil society can thereby evolve into a universal society whose public policies are conductive to universal welfare, when its units minds are elevated above narrow sentimentality; how? In a human being, there are neuro-endocrine regulatory pathways, psycho-somatic regularity pathways and spirituo-psychic regulatory pathways. One needs to activate these pathways in order to have a healthy body and an elevated (depropensitized) mind. Such a liberated mind can then have tremendous scope for attaining macro-cosmic perfection.

In order to always do the right thing that is conductive to others' welfare (and hence to one's own welfare), it is necessary to understand the purport of our earthly sojourn, to appreciate life as a continuum: an eternal journey from micro-cosmic imperfection to macro-cosmic perfection. Journeying on this cosmic trial, a depropensitized liberated mind is free to acquire all the macro-cosmic attributes. Only such an elevated mind can conceive of noble ideas and policies for human welfare. Verily, a society can be deemed to be progressive when it is comprised of such noble minded persons reaching out to all those lagging behind and moving in unison to their ultimate destination.

16.10 Travelling light to our destination

Just as each day can be regarded as the first day of the rest of one's life, one can also be conscious of the possibility of it being the last day of one's life. Then one will be conscious of doing as much good as possible to as many people as possible.

Living materialistically at the expense of others or profiting from others' under-remunerated labor constitutes a low dimension of living. Living as self-styled and self-proclaimed moralists and guardians of the people is not any better! The ideal way is living unassumingly, and serving without publicizing it. The cooperative way of living involves having this attitude.

Honesty is the best policy, and humility is the best attitude! The best policy for a corporation is to function cooperatively, knowledgeably and transparently to provide service to its customers. The best materialistic policy for the people of a community is to live modestly. The best policy for a nation is to look after the interests of its people and to inculcate the spirit of one for all and all for one, as well as to adopt a universal outlook and thereby engage itself in a cooperative relationship with its neighboring nations.

Let our minds be illuminated by that mystical Pole star, gaining knowledge on how to "travel" and applying it to guide one another.

Let us all move enchantedly through the night, to reach our destination at the break of dawn.

24 December 2003 — A Palestinian family sits on the ruins of their destroyed home in Rafah Refugee Camp.

The super-powers and also the UN have lost all credibility for turning a blind eye to this ongoing state terrorism, and for being only concerned about group terrorism. The tale of state terrorism is as old as human civilization, and has been ongoing in every region of the world. Because group terrorism is linked to state terrorism, both have to be solved as a collective problem.

In some regions, there are two generations living as refugees. The super-powers do not care about all of this. They primarily want to be safe from group-terrorism, and want to establish an international pact to fight group-terrorism. The United Nations is controlled by the permanent member countries of the Security Council; hence, it cannot act outside their jurisdiction. This is why we need a benevolent World government, under the aegis of which the most comprehensive "charter of human rights and crimes against humanity" will be developed and implemented.

17

Sustainable Global Peace with Equitable Globalization: Strategizing the Role of the University in Society

17.1 Humanitarian law and progressive equitable political order

In military operations, war crimes are committed on civilians by military personnel under orders from the heads of their nations. Likewise even in day-to-day governance, civilians have been traumatized by the political heads of their states, by their corruption, unfair public policies, non-comprehension of the ideals of what a society should be and by their primitive psychology and mindset. Throughout the annals of human civilization, civilians have been victimized. Even the so-called great architectural wonders of the world were built at the cost of civilian lives. Indeed most nations' ruling regimes and leaders have been guilty of crime against civilians, war crimes and crimes against humanity. Because the civilians have been the victims of crimes on civilians including war crimes, it is hence appropriate that the civil societies of all the nations come together, to undertake to define human rights jurisprudence (HRJ) in reference to human rights. This is the only way to "combat" and eventually prevent this hypocrisy on the part of heads of nations who pose as champions of human rights but perpetrate atrocities against civilians.

While HRJ can be employed as a deterrent against civilian abuse, it would be better to have a system, which will prevent human rights violation. In order to promote this "preventive jurisprudence" (as opposed to punitive jurisprudence), we propose structuring a party-less political system in the form of a civilian-sectorial electoral and governance system (CSEG) system. Such a CSEG system would keep the control of the entire governance structure in the hands of the civil society. Not only can it prevent dictators from emerging from the ranks of political parties or from the military ranks (due to the corruption and failures of the ruling political party), but also it can provide safeguards against democratic dictators (i.e. heads of political parties in power) who control all decision-making affecting civilian lives.

The second role of civil society, as part of preventive jurisprudence, is to delineate the principles of human rights, such that not only oppressive politicians but also incapable politicians can get indicted for failing to deliver proper governance to the people. This is akin to medical litigation filed by patients against their doctors for carelessness or inappropriate treatment measures. In a similar way, a legislator failing to administer governance at professional standards should be liable to prosecution, and more so because a legislator influences the lives of many people by public policies by (what can be termed as) "unprofessional governance." This new process will deter non-professionals (with only personal interests) from entering the political governance arena until our CSEG is implemented.

For defining "crimes-on-civilians," we need to define the governing principles of "humanitarian law," such that politicians are held responsible for causing anti-social disturbances, such as inter-ethnic riots and killings because of their ethnic bigotry and religious intolerance, as for instance Hindu-Muslim riots over the mosque (or temple) in Ayodhya (India). In this category of crimes, we need to also take to task politician dictators for crimes-against-humanity, for their ruthless and mass killing of their nations' civilian populations, as happened under the communist regimes of the Soviet Union and China. So for the sake of preventive jurisprudence, would it not be better to have a political system whereby oppressive political leaders cannot ever come into power. In this regard, our system of societal sectorial representation in governance can mitigate the coming into power of ruthless dictators and power usurping (supposedly democratically elected) politicians.

We next demand (herewith) liability for prosecution of military commanders and heads of nations by members of civil society, for "war crimes" involving indiscriminate killing of innocent civilians in both declared and undeclared wars. Finally, we need to rectify the global political system wherein militarily powerful nations can justify and glorify their invasion of smaller countries (whose leaders have been tyrannical and responsible for the disappearance of thousands of their people), while appeasing the ruthless heads of other not-so-militarily-powerful nations. Currently we have unfair global systems of (1) economic hegemony, whereby economically strong nations can enforce trade policies on economically weaker nations, (2) military hegemony, in which militarily powerful nations can dictate the foreign policies of weaker developing nations, and (3) discriminatory persecution, whereby strong nations decide to police and apply sanctions against certain nations and regimes that do not respect human rights (and especially rights of women as human beings), while appeasing other human rights abrogating nations because of their natural resources or military power.

We cannot continue to have such a superpower dependency for promoting civilian welfare. We certainly need a fairer system in which non-caring and oppressive regimes in all countries are replaced by socially democratic regimes — the United Nations has failed to play this civilian protector role. It has been a bystander in many belligerent abrogations of human rights and mass-killings, and interfered in only a fraction of these situations under the concurrence of the few permanent member nations of the UN Security Council.

We hence need a more equitable system of maintenance of civil liberties in the form of a new progressive equitable political order (PEPO). This order will entail (1) installation of socio-economic democracy (of cooperative working and living) and civilian societal sectors' involvement in governance policies for their respective sectors; (2) the setting up of functionally-sustainable communities (FSCs) in which the above-mentioned civilian democracy and governance would be implemented at the grassroots level, and whereby marginalized communities (as well as communities incompatible with dominant culture of their nations) can have governance autonomy and even sovereignty; (3) the establishment of self-reliant economic blocs and zones constituting common markets of compatible FSCs (and also as dissipaters of regional and global economic instability propagation) serving as local economic catalysts and sources; and the (4) setting up of a world government to provide an equitable political order (devoid of hegemonism). This will constitute the neo-political order, to promote a more humane system conducive to flourishing of heightened human expression and civilization.

17.2 New global order

At the start of 2004, it appeared that the noble issues of "more education and human rights along with better health and better life for all" no longer hold centerstage. The UN's guiding principle of collectivism in addressing these and other humanitarian needs has been mocked by today's lone super power. Self-aware of its powerful economy and the most formidable military strength, the post-2002 US ruling regime embarked on an aggressive international policy of exercising its political influence over all the world regions, under the legitimacy of freeing the people from oppressive regimes. However, this unilateral drive to impose freedom and democracy is only concentrated on select military weak nations (Afghanistan, Iraq and Iran) of the Middle East region, to the exclusion of other autocratically-ruled monarchist Middle East nations and of course of the militarily stronger nations (such as North Korea), let alone much stronger empire-nations of Russia and China (in spite of their dismal human rights record). Therein lies the hypocrisy of its supposed altruism.

The unilateral initiatives on the part of US have aroused anger and invoked terrorism against it. Now, it appears that the only global socio-political agenda of the US is the war against terrorism, to the exclusion of the humanitarian issues of eradicating disease and poverty as well as cleaner environment and sustainable development. The post-2002 American regime has walked away from the Kyoto

Protocol, attempted to create a global market for itself under the guise of globalization, has redistributed its military bases, has forced other previously militarily non-intervening countries (such as Japan) to get involved with Iraq, and has baulked at countries (France and Germany) refusing to support its unilateral militarism. It has even forced countries to contribute to the rebuilding of Iraq, which is tantamount to making them contribute to the cost of contracts to be given to American companies for rebuilding of Iraq's community services that it has unilaterally destroyed in attempting to dislodge its tyrannical dictator.

All of this has invoked two primary forms of repercussions. On the one hand, it has made Islamic countries more anti-American, and made terrorism cells more angered and resolute. As a result, the world's stronger military power has now found itself even more threatened by terrorism and has had to enforce heightened security measures (such as air-flight cancellations, which other countries have not needed to institute), which could even effect its economy. It is indeed an irony that the lone superpower has had to impose restrictions at home, because of its obsession to control the world. This could eventually result in severe restrictions on the American civil security and the confiscation of its human rights tradition, in the guise of the Patriot Act under the pretext of homeland security. The other type of reaction to the current American doctrine of "preventive war and proliferating military bases" comes in the form of an expression on the part of some countries of the need of yet another new world order.

Throughout history, ancient kings and modern political leaders have disregarded civilian treatment ethics and human rights, such as: (1) humanitarian codes of treating civilians with respect and dignity; (2) codes of ethics of doing battle, by abusing and torturing prisoners, by raping and killing civilians, and by indiscriminate nuclear and chemical bombing of civilian populations (such as in World War II and Vietnam); (3) human rights, by mass-murdering civilians (in communist empires), by creating extra-legal zones (such as at Guantánamo Bay in Cuba), by labeling conscientious civilians as risks and threats to security; and (4) any semblance of humanism, by ethnic cleansing and killings (epitomized by the total destruction of the indigenous civilizations of South and Central America by the Spanish regimes and the holocaust on the Jewish populations of Europe (by the Nazi regime of Germany).

It is no wonder that today's world is at the brink of revolutionary disarray and global terrorism, irresponsible use of hi-tech weaponry (by the superpower) to eliminate any form of nationalistic protest against occupation of their land, and massive repression of civilian society in the "heartland of freedom." The need for a comprehensive code of internationally applicable humanitarian law is greater than ever before, particularly in the face of the American disparaging the International Criminal Court and all that it stands for. In the past, many international orders have been declared as a result of great wars, such as the treaties and declarations after World War I and at Yalta and Potsdam after World War II. So now, what kind of a new world order do we want and need, which will be even more comprehensive in defining industry and trade ethics, socioeconomics and governance, freedom and human rights, international relations and cooperative living trends?

In this context, many are in favor of some form of "humanistic capitalism," while some propose disintegration of both unipolar and bipolar global political systems, in favor of a cooperative outlook. Others feel the need of a global security system, or better still a number of regional security systems, like the North Atlantic Treaty Organization (NATO). Others see a need for an ideology of peace, in some ways akin to the platform of "non-violence as an organizing principle of society" by Doris Kucinich who is running for the US Presidency. Could we then incorporate all of these noble societal labels into a grassroots-embedded local-to-global societal ideology, representing all aspects of human thinking and living? We can combine these concepts into one unifying concept of a neo-humanistic socio-economic-political order, to look after the welfare of all the people and promote sustainable peace. Indeed, this is what we have been talking about all along.

We need an ideology that will deliver us from fear: fear of unemployment and poverty, fear of deprivation of food and shelter, fear of uncared-for ill-health and disease, fear of being prosecuted at work by the government for exposing human rights and democracy in all aspects of living and working. We need a noble ideology that will provide us freedom from deprivation, symbolized by (for instance) the situation of the Caribbean Island of Haiti. As we celebrated the 2004 New Year, 200 years back an army of African slaves led by Jean-Jacques Dessalines defeated French colonial forces, to make their beautiful island-country the mother of independence from colonial rule and the first black republic. However, today 200 years later, Haiti is one of the poorest countries in the world, with the majority of its people unemployed, so many suffering from AIDS, and its people living in repression and depression.

On the occasion of this 200th anniversary of independence, the president of Haiti (unpopular as he is) outlined a program to liberate Haiti from poverty and political discord. Sadly, this plan is contingent on a US$21 billion sought from France, for the payment that Haiti was forced to make to France for its independence. There are many other countries like Haiti, that no one talks about and cares about, that do not figure as top priority in the global political agenda or the agenda of the Group of Eight (G-8) most industrialized countries who are totally obsessed by the fright and fight of terrorism.

Using Haiti as an example, how can we implement our proposed global order: (1) of civilian socio-economic empowerment and democracy, signifying civilian governance; (2) grassrooted in functionally-sustainable democracies, self-reliant economic zones and regional unions; (3) under the aegis of a globally–caring Parliament of World Government; and (4) promulgating neo-globalization through collective capitalism, by involvement of developing countries as industrial partners in international capitalism.

17.3 Cooperative globalization based on International capitalism

Globalization, implying global common market, is perceived by developing countries to be a form of neo-economic colonization. The concept of the global common market demands that the countries have an open door policy to imports from other countries. Developing countries are apprehensive that it would make local goods and products non-competitive, and put their indigenous industries out of business. It is their contention that it has taken considerable effort for their indigenous agriculture and industries to develop, since gaining independence from their political colonial rulers. These gains would be nullified if they were to now be subjected to another type of colonization! Their indigenous enterprises have not yet attained the standards of products and goods of long-time industrialized nations. Hence, competition of local products with imported goods may not be fair at this point of time, and it would take some years of international exposure for local industries to attain a degree of competitiveness.

With so much present day rhetoric about globalization, it is to be recognized that the starting point of globalization movement is to even out the huge differential in living standards throughout the world. Free trade and open markets can only be beneficial to all people (and not just to the affluent nations) if all the people have near-uniform living standards, so as to be able to compete on even terms. Hence, it is a moral obligation for the developed nations to first contribute to the upliftment of the poor nations, so that the entire world becomes a global seamless cooperative community. From thereon, people throughout the world would keep ascending to higher and higher levels of human endeavor and cooperation to an egalitarian universal society of the world government, in which freedom and liberty will be ensured and human society will ascend to higher dimensions of civilization.

To this end, in order to accelerate the process of international industrial standards, it is proposed to develop neo-capitalism of "business-partnerships," whereby multinational business corporations set-up business-partner units (BPUs) in the developing countries. This entails employing and training people to work in these BPUs, whose products and performance would necessarily have to be of international standards. To some extent, this process has already begun due to the economic benefit derived by American corporations from out-sourcing and off-shoring labor-intensive IT-oriented jobs to cheaper-wage countries, such as India. Even some pending surgeries in the British Healthcare Systems could be carried out in India. However, the full impact of this inclusion of developing countries in the MNC business chain would be gained only when the high-tech R&D and manufacturing activities become a part of the operational chain.

In other words, in the industrial sector (involving commodities, appliances and all items of daily-living usage), the developed nations' industrial corporations would create local units in developing countries and make them part of their business chains by training their employees in all realms of business. While this process would be cost-effective for these MNCs, it would also help to enhance the overall acumen and standard of the indigenous agro-industrial sector. Thus in five years time, the indigenous enterprises would become internationally competitive, and globalization would then be more equitable and acceptable at that time.

Another important component of globalization is trade: as to what constitutes fair trading from the viewpoint of developing countries. For this purpose, it is proposed that WTO set up trading partnerships, whereby inter-nation trading (INT) sectors are delineated and coordinated by INT committees of WTO. The role of these INT committees would be to identify (for all the trading sectors) the exporting and importing nations (based on their production capacity, consumer need and market absorbility). Then, the INT sectors' committees would undertake to regulate (1) what items can be exported by a group of countries having the requisite need and market to import them, and (2) what items should not be imported into certain countries that already have them, so as to protect their local industry.

The setting up of regional trade zones involving setting up regional tariff-less regional markets, would be initiated after Step 1 of "international capitalism" has been in place for a few years. This regional free-trade (RFT) would gradually expose indigenous businesses to foreign competition standards, and further help human-capacity building and sustainable professionalism in the face of regional competitiveness. A combination of business and trading partnerships along with RFT would, in a relatively short period of time, bring about preparedness within developing countries for globalization in business and trade, towards a global market.

This entire scheme may be termed as "regionalization," as a prelude to "neo-globalization." In the framework of regionalization, regional economic blocs (such as our SEBs) would be set up to foster regional economic self-reliance. In other words, these regional economic blocs would have adequate regional resource capacity and diversity for sustainability. The self-reliant economics of regional economic blocs would provide regional economic stability as well as economic stimulants to the global economy. In this way, the global economic framework would be transformed into a multi-polar economic system.

In order to implement this scheme, so as to enhance and accelerate the competitiveness of the industrial sector of developing countries, we are proposing a UNESCO-sponsored educational program to foster not only industrial and trade business-partnerships between industrialized and developing countries but also business-partnerships in community services development. This education program would also encompass the legal aspects of international business partnerships. Thus, taking into account the scope of this program, it would be termed as "Community-development and Economic Partnership (CDEP) program, involving:

1. Universities in developed and industrialized countries setting up branches in poor countries, or establishing dual-degree programs with universities in developing countries.
2. Development of inter-university "Technopreneurship degree" programs, whereby an industrial consortium would be setup for the development of technologies and for starting indigenous companies to manufacture and market these technologies, and thereby establish international companies (structured as cooperatives) in these developing countries, to thereby raise their industrial standards (and hence the living standards of the people).
3. Offering of degree programs in "community-services development" in the developing countries, and involving their universities in partnering their governments in developing community services.
4. Offering of degree programs in the cooperative economic system, based on collective capitalism (grassrooted in functionally-sustainable communities), at the regional and global levels.

17.4 Community Development and Economic Partnership (CDEP) program

The CDEP program would be an inter-faculty multi-disciplinary program, involving participation of all the faculties of a university. Each CDEP program would involve a university in a developed country (referred to as the "lead-university") adopting a university in a developing country (referred to as "partner-university"). The roles of the various faculties or colleges of the lead-university and partner-university are defined below, in terms of the programs to be administered by them.

1. *The Industrial Technopreneurship Partnership (ITP) Program:* The Science and Engineering Faculties of the lead-university would set up dual-degree programs with the partner-university (in the developing country), at bachelors and masters degree levels. This would constitute the foundation of the PhD

program in Industrial Technopreneurship Partnership (ITP). For this purpose, some industries in the developed country would be motivated to set up an industrial consortium (IDC) to support the PhD research program in technology development and the launching of indigenous companies (with the IDC as well as the doctoral student and their research supervisors as partners). This ITP program would play a key role in industrial resource and revenue development, around which other programs would be centered.

2. *Free Trade Partnership (FTP) Program:* The Business Faculty of the lead-university in the developed country would be in charge of administering this program with its partner-university in the developing country. The academic foundation for entrance to this program would be a Bachelor's degree in Business Administration. Faculty members from the lead-university would set up the program in the partner-university, and could spend a semester or two teaching courses there. Also, faculty members from the partner-university would be invited to spend a semester or two at the lead university, to help them develop the requisite expertise and know-how in subjects of their interest. The doctorate program in FTP would involve a thesis on the setting up of free trade between the two countries in the products of the joint-partnered companies set up by the ITP program. At this stage, we would progress from indigenous industrial development to export-revenue generation.

3. *Community-Services Partnership (CSP) program:* This would be a multi-disciplinary program, involving all the faculties of the university. The lead-universities would be setting up this program at the partner-universities. It would entail developing business partnerships in all community services: water supply and sanitation plants, electrical power plants, healthcare delivery system, civilian and freight transportation systems.

4. *The International Capitalism (ICP) Program:* The establishment of the above programs (of ITP, FTP and CSP) would contribute to International Capitalism (ICP), setting the stage for cooperative regionalization leading to cooperative globalization. This dual-degree ICP program, between the lead-university and partner-university, would be administered by the Social Sciences department of the lead-university. At the PhD level, the students would research and write dissertations on the setting up of the above mentioned partnered business enterprises.

5. *The International Business Law (IBL) Program:* The IBL program would be administered by the partner-university's law faculty. The academic foundation of this IBL program would be a bachelors degree program in Jurisprudence. The IBL JD program would entail courses and dissertation involving international

laws, governing (a) the functioning and dispute-settlement of partnered companies, and (b) free trade between the countries.

17.5 From exploitative political order (EPO) to a progressive equitable political order (PEPO)

The characteristics of our to-date's Exploitative Political Order (EPO) and our proposed Progressive and Equitable Political Order (PEPO) are described in the below Table:

	Exploitative Political Order (EPO)	**Progressive and Equitable Political Order (PEPO)**
Economic Systems	Capitalism, ruling regime ownership, Communism.	Collective capitalism of cooperative ownerships.
Political System	Capitalist-democracy based on political parties, Socialism, Communism, Monarchy, cleric regime.	Socio-economic democracy (without political parties) and civilian governance.
Process of Appointment to Public Office	Elections to Governance subsidised by business co-operations and wealthy donors, Dictatorship, Sham elections.	Sectorial and Public elections of the most capable representatives of the community sectors to Governance assembly.
Public Policy and Governance	Public policy and decision-making totally controlled by political or ruling regime, to the exclusion of civilians.	Civilian professional governance system, by professionals who are experts in their respective portfolios and concerned about people's welfare.
Political Order	Sovereign nations, empire nations and superpower nations; First World countries, Third World countries; United Nations.	Functionally-sustainable communities (FSCs), self-reliant economic blocs (SEBs), self-reliant economic zones (SEZs), regional Federations (RFDs), world government.
Socio-economic Scene	Majority of the world population deprived of the basic requirements of living; minority owning majority of the wealth.	Civilian democracy and governance (CDC) creates potential for more uniform living standards and dignified lifestyles.

Political Scene	Groupism among nations, based on self-interests; domination of some nations by others; superpower hegemonism; United Nations Assembly, a site for under-the-table diplomatic maneuverings to obtain backing over national and international issues.	Potential for political parity among communities and regions; members of governance councils representing the interests and policies of civilian society; members of parliament of SEUs, SEZs and RFDs are all elected by grassroots community-sectors' agencies and associations.
Internal Sociology, International Relations and Peace Status	Considerable tension among people due to internal discontent, acrimonious relations between nations, and inter-nation conflicts; emergence of terrorism as a big threat.	Potential for sustainable peace within and among nations.
Investment and Trade	Countries interested only in procuring investments from other nations' and in forcing their exports on other nations.	Trade between nations to be based on mutual need and benefit.
Globalization	Globalization philosophy based on covert and overt attempts at economic colonization.	International capitalism to promote equitable globalization.

17.6 Towards sustainable global peace

It is proposed that the entire CDEP program be adopted and funded through the UN agencies: UNESCO, UNDP and UNICEF. This would be an excellent forum to promote comprehensive sustainable development of developing countries. The CDEP program would enable doctoral students of both lead and partner universities to work on internationally-partnered industrial and community services development.

In stage 1, the CDEP program would promote joint business ventures (in industry and community services) between the people and corporations of industrialized and developing countries. In stage 2, the CDEP program would contribute to the establishment of regional self-reliant economic blocs, constituting cooperative regionalization. Then in stage 3, after the regional economic blocs have developed respectable standards of industry and community-services for economic sustainability, globalization could be instituted as a natural consequence.

Commensurate with stage 3 would be the opening of the mind-set for the establishment of the world government. The existing UN agencies would continue to function under the patronage of the world government, and thereby acquire legal empowerment. Under the patronage of WGP, the hitherto unfulfilled mandates of all the UN agencies would be accomplishable. New agencies would come to the fore, as for example Civilian Human Rights Agency (CHRA) and Civilian Human Rights Courts (CHRCs), based on the to-be-formulated humanitarian law. Once all of these programs and institutions start functioning, the process of sustainable global peace will have begun!

The involvement of the people of industrialized countries in developing industries and community service in developing countries (as part of their international business chains) will create good-will among the people of developing countries. This in turn, will unite the people of the world, and create an unprecedented wave of global social harmony. Then, people from different parts of the world will directly relate to one another, free from the mental quagmire of prejudices cultivated in them by their governmental regimes. This coming together of the civil societies of the world will herald the beginning of the era of global civilian coopeation and harmony!

The history of human society is replete with the autocracy of ruling regimes and dogmatism of the cleric society imposed on the civilians. Human begins now need to resolve to promote and fashion a nobler and more compassionate society, by having a civilian governance system which is free from the prejudices of political parties, dictates of autocratic regimes, and impositions of ill-suited socio-religious codes by cleric groups. Further, in order to provide the ambience for cultivating noble expressions and ideas, we need to have peaceful living conditions.

In this regard, a neo-humanistic outlook and equitable globalization are the precursors to our having global peace. Real globalization entails all the people of the world living harmoniously as one extended family. In that cooperative spirit, everyone contributes to everyone's living needs, thus easing the burden of their quest for uninterrupted peace!

In order to cultivate the ideas of such a neo-humanistic society, we would need to lift our minds beyond the mundane to the supra-mundane, by dissolving our self-centric psychology into the cosmic domain. Then as we collectively progress on the enlightened neo-humanistic sky-way, we will have sustained global peace!

The *Cyrus cylinder* on which was inscribed the "Edict of Rights and Special Privileges:" The First Charter of Human Liberty!

Cyrus the Great conquered ***Babylon*** *in 539 BC. In 1879, a British archaeologist discovered at* ***Babylon*** *the* ***Cyrus Cylinder****, on which was written "There shall be no slaves in my kingdom. All are free to choose their religion. I will never let anyone to oppress others. I implore Ahura Mazda to make me succeed." This cylinder is with the British museum at London and its replica is with the United Nations at New York. Until the stone cylinder edict of Cyrus was excavated in* ***Babylon*** *in 1879,* ***Magna Carta*** *of Great Britain (written in 1215) was deemed to be the First Charter of liberty.* ***Cyrus*** *was the first king who granted all his subjects the freedom of workship and the right to live freely. His declaration may be seen to be the forerunner of the present-day Bill of Human Rights.*

When ***Cyrus*** *conquered Babylon in 539 BC, he marched through the city gates without any resistance or bloodshed. It is said that as the rebel Babylonian governor led the Persian army into the city, the people spread sheaves of barley on the streets and turned out in throngs to see the great Zoroastrian king,* ***Cyrus****, enter the city. He liberated the Jews from Babylonian captivity and gave them Persian moneys to rebuild their temple in Jerusalem. In gratitude to this act of generosity, the Jews have always referred to* ***Cyrus*** *as the "anointed one," sent by their God, Yaveh.*

The political Capital of the Zoroastrian Empire, founded by Cyrus the Great, was Persepolis. It was built and maintained from 518 to 331 BC at about 75 kilometers from Shiraz, South-west of Iran. The glorious days of the mighty and benevolent Zoroastrian Empire, that had prospered for 1,200 years (from 550 BC), came to an end in 641 AD. There were blown away by the Arab wind. After the ***Arabs*** *over-ran* ***Zoroastrian Iran*** *and started forcibly converting* ***Zoroastrians to Islam****, extremely few Zoroastrians stayed on, and some went to Indus-ind. They found hosts, both welcoming and kind. Among them many prospered and brought glory to Hind. Parsis, known by their second name* ***Charities*** *(almost all of which are cosmopolitan), are indeed the miraculous results of* ***Mother India's*** *5000-year-old tradition of democracy, equality and liberty.*

18

Epilogue: Towards a Neo-era of Peace, Security and Enlightened Living

18.1 The lamentable tale of anti-democratic global orders

We now come to the end of our sentimental journey of the survey of how, even in recent times, human beings have generally lived in discontent and frustration, under subjugative (and even forced) cooperation, unable to develop their full (psycho-spiritual) potential let alone progress to their ultimate desideratum. So, let us again very briefly survey the governance systems that have prevailed, in the second half of the last century. For instance, in a monarchy system, all community functions are carried out as designated by the monarch, and all government appointments are made as personal favors. The most glaring aspect of monarchy is the enormity of the monarch's personal wealth, pomp and autocracy governance. Even in countries wherein democracy and monarchy function side-by-side, the personal wealth of the monarchy family can be mildly termed as a socio-economic aberration and conundrum. In the capitalist democratic system, it is the uni-polar capitalists* who support costly election campaigns, and hence indirectly influence government policy to provide them maximal economic and political advantage. In communism, the party officials become tyrants and institute state terrorism. Recent history is replete with purges meted out by communist party bosses in the name of people's cultural revolutions.

History has recorded that the self-proclaimed "civilized world nations" occupied, ruled and depleted the so-labeled uncivilized nations of Asia and Africa, to ("supposedly justifiably") enhance their economy and standard of living. The pioneer-navigators who landed there must have wondered at the naivity of the local rulers and the people of these lands for not only welcoming them as traders,

*The term uni-polar capitalists (as opposed to multi-polar capitalists of collective capitalism) refers to those capitalists who own big corporations, wherein the employees do not participate and/or have a share in business development and/or profits. In collective capitalism, it is recognized that all the employees have contributed to the generation of capital. Hence they (in the form of a cooperative) are joint owners of the capital.

but for showering them with elaborate gifts. After more than a century of colonial rule, the civilized nations could not "understandably" tolerate any protests (even non-violent protests) at their continuing occupation of the colonies. Thousands of these so-called terrorist protestors were imprisoned, while many of them laid down their lives in freedom struggles (i.e. separatist movements from the colonial countries). The colonial nations must have felt gratified that their homelands remained safe through all of these freedom-demanding terrorist acts in the colonies.

Another "supposedly justifiable" protectionist movement, supported by these self-professed civilized world nations, was the apartheid order, levied by the white rulers of African homelands on their black indigenous peoples. Throughout this "supposed era of civilization", the "so-called uncivilized" black people were not just kept segregated but also lynched, while all the civilized world peacefully traded in precious stones and other valuable natural resources of their lands with the white-ruling governments of these nations. Why did it not occur to these powerful nations (to these advocates and preachers of human rights and fair governance) to do something to end the horrible plight of the native people?

The beginning of the second half of the 20th century saw the curtain eventually come down on one of these "global" orders, namely colonization. However, it was many torturous years later that the disgraceful apartheid order also came to an end, after immense freedom struggles by the native people. After the colonies had got their independence, they were all brought together in the commonwealths of their former colonial nations, and even some trade privileges were graciously given to these commonwealth nations. When the capitalist colonization global order came to an end, the communist colonization came to the fore. In fact, following the dismantling of capitalist colonization, two other hegemonial orders emerged to fill the vacuum, namely the so-called "democratic multinational capitalism" (supposedly to enable smart and free-thinking but affluent people to be elected) and "dictatorial and colonial communism" (to supposedly free the working class).

In the newly independent but impoverished former colonies of capitalist countries (labeled as Third World nations), there was once more social, economic and political turmoil. The powerful nations proponents of democratic capitalism decided to confront and oppose the global spread of communism, but only on Asian soil. The Asian nations got caught in this crossfire between the civilized (capitalist and communist) superpowers. As a result, some Asian nations again suffered significant loss of lives, while the homelands of the superpowers again remained safe.

In the former colonies, many local politicians took charge of governance, some through (questionably fair) election campaigns, while others as local and regional political-party bosses. However, a very big letdown was the caliber of politicians bosses who emerged onto the political stage. Even fifty years after independence, some of the former colonies had the dubious distinction of being ranked among the most corrupt nations of the world, while others gained world attention as among the most hardline nations of the world with an atrocious human rights record. So, for all of these reasons, the developing countries, to this day, have continued to struggle to reduce (let alone eradicate) poverty. What a tragedy for the people of these countries!

However, irrespectively, instead of forming an economic alliance to alleviate poverty, most of the developing nations are even today still divided and more dependent than ever on the militarily and industrially powerful affluent nations for their economic survival. They hence continue to have a subservient relationship with these affluent countries, and thereby adopt attitudes and policies that are neither in their peoples' collective interests nor in their staying united to help their peoples' cause. Today, there is a crisis of political and social morality. The political heads of many countries (especially newly-developed countries) are ready to support the powerful nations' policies, in return for some benefits (such as free-trade pacts) against the conscience of their people. They have, in fact, sacrificed the interests of the people of still-developing nations to adopt policies solely serving their nations' interest, contrary to the collective wishes of their people. This is why, there is a dire need for a new system of people-based economic democracy, a new people-based electoral and governance system, and a neo-humanistic global order.

Hence, for all times, be it in monarchy or capitalist democracy and even more so in communism, the people have been governed and have had no say on policy-making. In all these systems, the government members and party heads of newly independent countries (that had been colonies of imperialistic countries) have become virtual rulers, while invariably lacking in competency and morality; the people have become bystanders. The media reporting is entirely concerned with the activities of the government and party politicians, and the public becomes the adoring fans of these so-called public leaders. When one ruling party is replaced by another, the public adulation also shifts.

In Third World nations (irrespective of the systems of governance), the so-called professional politicians and the government heads never retire, even after they suffer from dementia. It is they who control and dictate public policy, decide whether to wage war (while keeping themselves comfortable), and portray themselves as supremely patriotic. They remain impervious to overall intra-nation discontent, as well as by the suppressed communities. Their tactic, in the face of public disfavor, is often to divert attention from continual "abject non-governance" on their part, by inciting public emotions and stirring up threats from neighboring countries in the guise of super-patriotism. The public remains as followers and adulant bystanders. It is high time for the public of developing and under-developed nations to unequivocally express the need for sincere and competent governance (to hold the government officials and politicians accountable for mis-governance, apathetic governance, incompetent governance, corrupt immoral governance, and failure to invoke state-of-the-art know-how in governance) and for the implementation of true democracy in which the policy decisions are made at the grassroots level.

In the present day ubiquitous democratic system, within Third World nations unaccountable people's funds are wasted in mega election campaigns, while unjustifiable time is spent on inter-party political squabbles. It is indeed rare for ministers to care for and carry out their portfolio duties. Their civil service administrators take care of their department roles, while the ministers are full-time engaged in inter-party propaganda, political gamesmanship and more often in garnering personal wealth. In fact, a minister of average affluence is a rarity and an oddity. It is no wonder that in this mockery of democracy, the societal and people's problems and issues are totally neglected. Further, the ministers (and their clerks) have to be looked up to (and even at times worshipped and bribed) by the people, in order to have them attend to their problems. It is this deplorable state of affairs that makes the present day democratic system a curse for the average/common persons of developing countries, because ever so often they have to placate the government staff and grease their hands as well as those of the ministers with "goodwill money".

18.2 The partyless socio-economic democratic governance system

It is out of due recognition of the unfairness of all the previous and present day governance systems and injustice meted out to the people under these systems, that we are proposing the partyless socio-economic democratic system of governance. In this proposed partyless government, made up of elected representatives of the community's societal sectors (represented by the sectorial associations, such as teachers' association, lawyers' association, healthcare professionals' association, business cooperatives' association, agricultural cooperatives' association, etc.), the ministers would be able to concentrate on their portfolio's remits, without getting sidetracked into having to downsize the other parties to safeguard their portfolios.

Then, in order to involve local people in local development and governance as well as to give them a stake in bringing prosperity to their community, it is proposed to coalesce micro-communities or socio-economic units (having homogenous cultures and/or like-minded views) into functionally-sustainable communities (FSCs), to in turn constitute a self-reliant economic bloc (SEB). In terms of the current setup, a state or province of a nation could be regarded as an SEB. Two more SEBs decide to form a self-reliant economic zone (SEZ), corresponding to a nation. The FSCs would have decentralized governance (including economic planning and management), and partyless democratic system of governance, wherein the government members would be the elected representatives of associations representing all the sectors and categories of community operations and functions.

It is to be emphasized that we are certainly not advocating a one-party system of governance nor a dictatorial governance system. We are essentially replacing the roles of the various political parties by the societal roles of the various associations representing all the sectors of community function and operation. We are then replacing the present-day elected political parties by the communities' grassroots organizations: professional associations, community agencies, peoples' councils elected representatives, from which the general public will vote and elect governance officers. In this system of governance, each sector of the community will have a say in the most effective and beneficial governance of that particular portfolio. We will be assured of the governance portfolios being handled by the most competent people in the various sectors of community life. What is particularly significant is that these community sectors' representatives to the government will be competent to develop policies most appropriate and benefiting to the people, also because they would not need to tow the political parties' agendas. Further, these governing officials will have to function as peoples' representatives, and could not assume self-glorification. On the contrary, they would be held accountable for corruption, negligence and mis-governance. The benefits of this new democratic system of governance simply outweigh the colossal drawbacks of the present day mockery of democracy.

A particularly noteworthy feature of this proposed community functional reorganization (and the associated neo-democratic system of governance) is that all economic activities, production outfits, business enterprises will be conducted through cooperatives. Thus, agriculture and dairy produce would be carried out by farmers' and dairy cooperatives; production and manufacturing companies in different sectors (pharmaceutical, consumer-items, etc.) will be organized as cooperatives; even legal practices and medical practices would be organized as cooperatives. Thus, people will be involved in and have a stake in economic benefits in all sectors of community living; this collective system of capital development and management can be termed as collective capitalism. Further, the representatives of these cooperatives' associations would be involved in governance. Thus, this set-up would (for the first time in societal history) contribute to the institution of socio-economic democracy. Indeed, it is intended that (through this book), we provide a template of a truly democratic organization of society in the form of civilian democratic governance.

The FSCs would come about not only for localized human resource and economic development, but also for providing a safe home and security to marginalized people. The choice and boundaries for the FSCs would be decided by and/or based on public choice, to be carried out in an orderly and dignified manner. In other words, the people of and from different micro-communities would need to decide to come together, so as to constitute a FSC. These people from different micro-communities would need to feel confident that they could function in a spirit of enlightened and neo-humanistic cooperation, so that their new community could be "self-reliant". In other words, the revenue generated from the exports of the community resources would need to match and pay for the funds needed for their local community services (such as water supply and sanitation, electrical power, public transport, healthcare delivery, education, social/civil/physical security, etc.) as well as for the imports needed to maintain a decent quality of life in their new community.

A number of FSCs would then constitute an SEB. Likewise, a number of SEBs would make up a SEZ, while a number of SEZs of a region or continent would make up a self-reliant regional federation (RFD), such as the European Union (EU). All the RFDs of the world would come under the world government. Any new community, desiring to be recognized as an economic block or unit of an FSC (or even to constitute an SRC on its own), would be able to make a representation to its SEB parliament. In the context of the present political setup, the states of a nation would represent SEBs, and one or more states would constitute an SEZ. Hence, an SEZ could be a present day nation or even a group of nations cooperating to enhance their internal development and effectiveness. It could well happen that, in time and by people's choice, two or more nations could start functioning as an SEZ, for more effective socio-economic development as well as for global cooperation. The SEZs would in turn be organized into Regional Federations (or RFDs), to all come under the aegis of a world government.

In an FSC, the people's elected representatives would serve the people's interests, and be accountable to their constituencies for their governance management. This would represent true democracy and knowledgeable governance. The world government would provide to the people a hitherto unavailable and unprecedented security in all spheres of living. In such an environment, there would be ample scope for people to develop supra-mentally, to develop noble ideas, and to live ideologically in harmony with the cosmological order. Verily, this would constitute the framework of sustainable peace!

18.3 Relocating economy among the people generating economy

Socio-economic democracy is indeed a novel concept entailing all economic activities in the community being carried out by the local people. In this system, all companies would be set up and administered as cooperatives. As a result, the capital will be developed and shared collectively and cooperatively, giving rise to another neo-concept of collective capitalism. All production would hence be made as per consumers' demand. There would be no need for gluttonous over-production (on the part of companies' capitalists) and market-flooding, resulting in over-saturation of people's needs and fall in consumer demand, decrease in production and consequential traumatic layoffs.

The issue of controlling stocks, shares and the stock markets will not arise. The cooperatively organized companies will get financially reviewed (by the cooperative banking system) for their capacity to payback business development loans from cooperative banks and/or from international banks. Thus, they will not need to issue public shares. A corporation would operate as a cooperative; all the members of the cooperative would jointly generate capital, and would hence be joint (not equal) owners of the capital (by owning shares in terms of the equity of the corporation). This verily amounts to collective capitalism, in contrast to so-called uni-polar present day capitalism involving capitalist employers and subordinate employees.

The stock market would then have no role and need for existence, thereby eliminating "virtual earnings" (by stock players, capitalists and banks), and the possibility of economic collapse. Over the years, the stock market has been the venue of people becoming rich on non-tangible produces or services, and that too on the labor of those actually engaged in production and services. Conversely, the stock market has also been the graveyard of many common people, who have been naively led to believe in the stock market trail as the avenue for becoming rich. Without the need for existence of stock markets, these unfair and deceitful practices will also end.

In the framework of our new economic political order (of FSCs, SEBs, SEZs, RFDs and the world government), the government officials of FSCs, SEBs, SEZs and RFDs will be dutifully administering public governance services. They will not be in a position to play decisive (and often machivalent) roles in economic mismanagement through misguided and self-benefiting policies. Hence, the question of countries becoming irresponsible over-borrowers, and/or unrealistic over-developers, and ultimately becoming insolvents will not arise. There would still be a role for the International Monetary Fund and the World Bank. However, they would be re-constituted as truly international and global institutions, with branches within regional economic zones and blocs. These branch units would deal with and give loans to communities' cooperatives (to initiate and/or expand their business), and not to countries as a whole.

The neo-political setup of SRCs under SREZs and SRFs, in conjunction with the dysfunctioning of stock markets, will put an end to stock trading, currency betting and speculation. In fact, this new community functional and governance system of socio-economic democracy will bring about economic stability, and put an end to the periodic cycles of inflation, recession and depression. All activities and involvements in economic colonization and manipulation will cease, and stable economy will be maintained!

18.4 Human rights and democratic global order of parity among all nations

Today, many societies (especially of developing countries) are burdened with narrow sentimental psychological attitudes, which are impediments to progressive living for their inhabitants. Some of these attitudes include racism and castism, psycho-cultural suppression and psycho-linguistic subjugation of certain minority groups, racial-prejudicial inciting, and even self-assumed rights to eliminate persons (even from other nations) on the pretext of their being suspected of plotting future violence activities. Such anti-humanity acts will no longer be possible in the new political re-organization of regions, because each FSC will ultimately have to abide by the World Government's constitutional principles. A number of FSCs in a geographical region would be bought together to function as an SEB. A number of SEBs would then constitute an SEZ, while the SEZs in a continent would comprise a RFD. All the SRFs would come under a world government, with a constitution oriented to human rights, physical and social security, local (FSC) governance autonomy and economic democracy.

The formation and geographical boundary detection of FSCs, SEBs, SEZs and RFDs would be entirely carried out by the people, as per their choice and convenience. Generally, this would be more useful in the Third World regions of the world, where entire rural belts are under-developed, and the nations are struggling to cope with rural poverty and capital generation for financing community services. It can also be useful for certain communities of developing nations to be constituted as an FSC, based on an analysis that their economic development can be best addressed through their being organized as a FSC. In the industrialized developed regions of the world, the formation of FSCs may not be necessary, and the current political setup (of states or provinces within a nation) can continue.

While the European Union is an example of the first such regional federation, it is unfortunately dominated by a couple of nations; this is because of the intrinsic fallacy of the electoral and governance system. In these developed regions, people can continue with the current system or choose to adopt the proposed neo-electoral procedure for party-less political governance, which (as indicated before) is less costly and more transparent. This neo-electoral system would also help place, in the governance system, only the most competent representatives (in their respective fields) with a people service attitude, so as to help evolve a people-centered political order.

In the present day democratic system, all the governance members (belonging to the ruling party) are compelled to adopt a uniform policy, e.g. towards social security, healthcare, education, taxation, human rights and foreign policy. Every few years, this policy changes, depending on the party in power, this makes it difficult to pursue a stable course of overall progress. However, under the new political system of community associations, with grassroots involvement in governance of community functions, there will be no scope of a grand alliance among governance officials. Hence, it will be impossible for a FSC or SEB (state or province) of a developing nation (or SEZ) to have an eccentric governance, such as forming a uni-religious state, not allowing women in the workforce, death penalty for religious proselyting, and encouraging terrorism against racial minority groups, etc. This is because, in this new proposed system, all the governance officials (i.e. the ministers in charge of various portfolios) will be working independently, unlike in the party system of governance wherein all the governance officials (from one ruling party or an alliance of political parties) are obliged to follow the party ideology. Further, the constitutions of all the FSCs would be based on certain common cardinal principles, formulated by the world government.

In this new resulting socio-political order, it will also not be necessary or possible for a select group of five to eight (so-called industrially developed and responsible) nations to control global economy and trade policies, as well as to monitor and control the armamentarium development in other nations. The current attitude of competing to acquire multi-polar global hegemony may be said to be primitive, compared to the enlightened way of living by sharing the world resources and collectively advancing to the supreme desideratum. We are in dire need of such a people-centered enlightened global order.

18.5 Towards global security

Inter-nation border disputes and conflicts also constitute the order-of-the-day in Asia, Africa and Eastern Europe. Mediation is often hampered because the so-called elected heads-of-states have to represent the narrow sentimentality of their political parties. They do not want to be perceived as having given away concessions (which is looked upon as weakness on their part), and hence come under attack from the opposition parties (who are ever-anxious to win points with the public). However, under the proposed system of government make-up and governance, the defense minister and/or the foreign minister (supposedly to be persons of integrity as well as competent in their respective portfolios) could honestly discharge their roles in settling border disputes, in the best interests of peace and harmony, without feeling pressure from the opposition parties as having given away too many concessions.

Today, in so many developing regions of Europe, South America, Africa and Asia, intra-nation conflicts are based on so-called freedom struggles by people wanting to be free from unfair and subjugative governance. In our neo-political framework, these people would be able to come together to form an economic unit or a FSC, for self-governance and cultural preservation. The formation of FSCs would help to fulfill the needs of disgruntled communities of people, who feel that they have been deprived of social and economical development and are psychologically and politically suppressed — this will help to root out terrorism. Hence, is it not better for FSCs to live peacefully as neighbors, rather than have large groups of discontented people embroiled in continual conflict for independence (harboring violence and even terrorism out of desperation)! Likewise, is it not better, for the sake of peace and economic stability, for neighboring nations to cooperate in all realms of living, and constitute an SEZ!

The establishment of the world government would constitute the decisive step towards eliminating the present day inter-nation intelligence-gathering agencies and inter-nation hostilities, armaments race, and the need for nuclear stockpiles. It would be a prime role of the world government to prevent any and all hostilities stemming from some over-zealous and militarily powerful nations wanting to dominate weaker neighboring nations. At the same time, if a micro-community within a nation or FSC or even communities from two or three geographically neighboring countries wanted to be constituted as a new FSC, there would be a mechanism to bring their request to the attention of their respective SEZ and even to the corresponding regional federation and to the world government. For this purpose, a committee of a SEZ government would be constituted to entertain and review such requests. It would also be possible for the FSC-aspiring community representatives to directly take their proposal to the regional federation or even to the world government minister in charge of new FSC formation.

Some of the beneficial end results of the establishment of the world government would be assurance of human rights and fair governance, as well as social-civil-economic-political justice for all the people of the world. Further, no nation or SEZ would need to (or be allowed to) divert community funds (meant for quality of life enhancement) for armament build-up. Hence, community generated funds would be almost entirely employed for improving the living standards of the community people. However, in case a nation or an SEZ flouts this neo-charter of peaceful co-existence, then the world government would deploy its defense militia to suppress such a move, and protect the threatened community. For this purpose, every FSC, SEB, SEZ and RFD would provide personnel for the world government defense forces, and the world government would judiciously distribute and position these defense forces all over the world.

18.6 Summary of neo-concepts introduced in this book

Our proposed socio-economic democracy and world government system will bring together all the communities of the world into one big global cooperative, typifying a neo-humanistic global order. In all regions of the world, people with similar skills and know-how will be paid at the same rate for similar types of work, in the true spirit of globalization. This will lead to global parity in living standards. It is out of compassion for the Fourth World people (the grossly persecuted people, the poverty-stricken people, the depressed marginalized people, and the totally neglected destitute people of the world) and the poverty-stricken inhabitants of the Third World, that this book is written and dedicated to. It is also hoped that this book will inspire people to transcend their psychic urges for materialism and power as well as their narrow sentimentalities (of caste and religion, race and nationality) which have caused these painful socio-economic differentials and chasms, and start moving along effulgent skyways onto cosmic realms.

Let us enumerate the new insights and concepts introduced in this book:

- the political and economic colonization background, as the etiology of under-development of Third World countries;
- FSCs for local (de-centralized) development by the local people, along with an illustrative design of an FSC;
- optimal utilization of natural resources and manufactured products on the one hand and of physical/intellectual/spiritual human resources on the other, to develop not just a knowledge-based economy but also a neo-humanistic society;
- socio-economic democracy, involving people's participation in economic enterprises, as well as in planning and development;
- all business and economic enterprises to be organized as cooperatives (whose members will collectively generate and own capital), entailing a new collective capitalism system;

- elimination of stock markets and opportunities for stock market and currency players to do manipulation, thereby resulting in stable economies;
- neo-electorate systems for a partyless democratic system of governance, representing the collective voice of people in all walks of life;
- people-centered political order, instead of a politicians-centered political order;
- re-organization of global human habitats into FSCs, SEBs, SEZs and RFDs (in parallel with the present day setup of nations), operating under a world government;
- all grievances of communities (including application to form a separate FSC) to be represented to the governance council of SEB, and to also be brought to the attention of the world government parliament;
- world government establishment and charter;
- true globalization, catering to the welfare of indigenous people of developing countries by involving them in industrial partnerships between developed and under-developed countries, to eventually coverge to global parity in salaries and living standards;
- terrorist attacks on innocent people to be (i) ended (not by militarily wiping out the entire community but) by apprehending the terrorists, and (ii) prevented, by obviating the supposed causes (namely suppressive governance of communities, land occupation, denial of nationhood threat to religious fundamentalism) that create terrorists and fuel terrorism;
- both terrorist attacks on innocent people as well as military attacks on the civilian community to be constitutionally regarded as *crimes against humanity*;
- neo-concept of human rights and constitutional guarantees to the people (including the rights to education and employment, with minimal wage to be adequate for the basic necessities of living), the rights to progressive governance and criticism of public policy without governmental harassment and/or persecution, rights to social and physical security, and even the right to demand for autonomic governance by a community that feels neglected, discriminated and exploited;
- an evolved concept of human society, constituting people working and living cooperatively, and progressing in unison;
- psychic upliftment of the people above narrow sentimentality of racism and castism, religious bigotry and cultural elitism, regional and global hegemonism;
- constitutional offense for perpetrating discrimination and persecution of people, due to race and caste, religion and culture, gender and color, and socio-economic standing; people's courts to be set up, to provide quick resolution of such problems;

- all disputes between FSCs to be solved at the SEZ level by the SEZ Court of Justice; all problems between SEBs to be solved at the SRF level by the SRF Court of Justice; all disagreements between SEZs to be solved at the world government level by the World Court of Justice;
- any attempt by the government representatives of an SEZ (or SEB) to intimidate another SEZ (or SEB) would not be permitted; any military action ordered by an SEZ (or SEB) government head against another SEZ (or SEB or its FSC) would be regarded (as per the world government constitution) as a crime against humanity (to be brought to the attention of the World Criminal Court);
- redundancy of nuclear stockpiling, inter-nation intelligence services and militarism, due to the formation of the world government;
- Third and Fourth Worlds' liberation;
- neo-humanistic global order towards sustainable peace.

These concepts have been woven together into a new ideological system of human society, democracy and global order. In years to come, this new paradigm of society can help to provide guidelines for the emergence of a new era of human sharing and cooperation, rights and guarantees, and (above all) the concept of partnership between people and government for a true democratic governance. It is hoped that this new concept of society and governance can (over the years) undoubtedly inspire a myriad of dissertations and theses, which will all contribute to a more altruistic and dignified individual and collective living.

18.7 Living neo-humanistically

It is verily out of deep concern for the people, living without hope as well as for others living meaninglessly materialistically, that we have proposed this neo-humanistic global order to:

- formulate and usher a neo-humanistic and socio-economically democratic global society, and
- thereby induce an awakening in noble ideals, compassion and cooperation, and supra-aestheticism.

So, as we part company, we would indeed be echoing the benevolence of Shri Shri Prabhat Ranjan Sarkar (1921–1990), the propounder of Neo-humanism, that:

- everyone live in peace and harmony;

- everyone can have unbarred opportunities for all-round development and for contributing to mutual welfare;
- no one be neglected and threatened, be left starving and without shelter, be left ill and uncared for, be tormented and made dysfunctional; and
- all can move together in unison, to the pinnacle of human existence and cosmic desideratum.

This book is committed to the ushering of such a neo-humanistic global order and era!

Shambala, the ethereal city of light and universe-city of great spiritual learning, is generally linked with teachers from the ancient city of Tibet. It is from this land that many are supposed to have ascended to become great teachers of wisdom and sacred knowledge of the higher realms and the nature of our reality.

Index